HIGH PERFORMING COLLEGES

HIGH PERFORMING COLLEGES
Volume I: Theory and Concepts

Associates

John R. Barker
Valerie Broughton
Thomas E. Corts
Linda Deneen
Satinder K. Dhiman
Ronald F. Dow
John P. (Jack) Evans
John W. Harris
Mary Ann Heverly
Susan G. Hillenmeyer
Jon A. Hittman
Marian L. Houser
Reid Johnson
Elisabeth A. Luther
William McEachern
Kathleen A. O'Brien
James T. Rogers
Daniel Seymour
Gary Shulman
Eugene R. Smoley, Jr.
Gloriana St. Clair
Susanna B. Staas
Linda M. Thor

HIGH PERFORMING COLLEGES

The Malcolm Baldrige National Quality Award
as a Framework for
Improving Higher Education

Volume I: Theory and Concepts

Daniel Seymour and Associates

Prescott Publishing Company
Maryville, Missouri

High Performing Colleges: The Malcolm Baldrige National
Quality Award as a Framework for Improving Higher Education
Volume I–Theory and Concepts
Daniel Seymour and Associates

Copyright© 1996 by Prescott Publishing Company
106 South Main Street, Maryville, Missouri 64468 U.S.A.
1/800-528-5197

Printed in the United States of America
First Printing: 1996
10 9 8 7 6 5 4 3 2 1

Publisher's Cataloging in Publication
(Prepared by Quality Books Inc.)

High performing colleges / edited by Daniel Seymour.
    p.cm.
    CONTENTS: Vol. 1. Theory and concepts. -- Vol. 2. Case and practice.
    Includes bibliographical references and index.
    ISBN: 1-886626-04-9 (v. 1)
    ISBN: 1-886626-05-7 (v. 2)

    1. Education, Higher--United States--Administration. 2. Malcolm
Baldrige National Quality Award. 3. Total quality management   I.
Seymour, Daniel, 1947-

LB2341.H54 1996   378.73
                                                   QBI95-20546

CIP 95-71523

To Matilde, *una bellezza inquietante*

Contents
Volume I: Theory and Concepts

—PART THREE: QUALITY ASSURANCE—

Foreword

A group of eighteen colleges and universities joined together in 1993, calling themselves the Academic Quality Consortium (AQC). Two common threads pulled the eighteen together: the recognition that higher education is being challenged by the complexity and speed of change in its environment, and the belief that adaptations to this change will be required within the academic world if colleges and universities are to continue to serve the needs of the society that created them.

The original eighteen, later joined by three more institutions, share another important belief—that the tenets of continuous improvement (called "total quality management" in industry, and "continuous quality improvement" in health care and education) should be explored to determine whether they could provide a sound methodology for focusing the change and adaptation efforts in higher education.

They began the endeavor in a spirit of inquiry and activism: let's understand it, let's try it, let's see if it makes a difference, let's learn together.

The collaboration of these colleges, supported by the American Association for Higher Education (Washington, DC) and the William C. Norris Institute (Minneapolis), resulted in an unusually rich mix of institutions (public and private, two- and four-year colleges, regional and research universities) sharing their successes, their frustrations, their pursuit of a deeper understanding of what's needed to increase institutional effectiveness.

While initial attention was often directed to administrative processes, Consortium members from the beginning have seen learning as a core process in their institutions. They therefore have sought ways to understand how quality approaches could be applied to academic processes.

While Consortium members were naturally interested in advancing their own learning, they also saw a responsibility as well as an opportunity in sharing learning with the larger higher education community. As a consequence, the Continuous Quality Improvement Project (CQI Project) was created to serve as a networking hub and resources clearinghouse, seeking to advance knowledge about CQI by keeping close tabs on campus activities nationally and by creating outlets for the exchange of ideas, practices, and innovations.

Early on, the group recognized that there was growing interest in Congress to extend the Malcolm Baldrige National Quality Award (MBNQA) to education. Continuing in the spirit of inquiry, they invited Dr. Curt Reimann, director of the national award office, to join them in a day of thoughtful discussion. The hours spent in deliberation had many consequences, not least among them the assurance of Consortium members that Dr. Reimann's sole interest in the creation of an education award was the value it might contribute to improving the quality of higher education.

A second important consequence was the dawning realization of the power of the self-assessment process that award applicants pursued. The core values, the criteria, the framework, and the examination used in the Baldrige Award process suggested a comprehensive way to think about focusing improvement efforts in education.

At Dr. Reimann's invitation, participating colleges underwent training in the self-assessment process. They also sought the advice and guidance of experienced industry professionals as they struggled to adapt a set of industry criteria to education.

None of it came easily. While all institutions had completed self-evaluations for accreditation agencies, none had much experience in flow-charting processes, collecting process and outcome measurements, and showing the linkages across the institution that resulted in systemic understanding.

A number of AQC member institutions eventually participated in MBNQA's pilot study of education criteria. Several of the first education examiners for the pilot study came from the ranks of the AQC. The results of their work have been shared at national conferences, on the Internet, and on-site at a number of campuses. *High Performing Colleges* is the first comprehensive presentation of what they have learned in easily accessible form.

Is there life after Baldrige? For AQC, this work with the self-assessment criteria is recognized as just an early step on a quality journey. As one member noted, "By assessing our university as an organization against the Baldrige criteria, we believe we will learn to become continuously strategic in organizational behavior."

In *Dakota: A Spiritual Geography*, author Kathleen Norris observes, "Resisting change does not recapture the past; it loses the future." AQC members are committed to confronting the changes that come their way. They persist in exploring continuous improvement as a methodology that supports the kind of strategic leadership they will need to address those changes.

MONICA M. MANNING
Executive Director
Academic Quality Consortium

The Academic Quality Consortium (AQC) is a collaboration of AAHE and the William C. Norris Institute created to provide campuses committed to implementing continuous quality improvement the opportunity to learn and work collaboratively by exchanging information, building on one another's experiences, and expanding on the assessment practices already being utilized.

In January 1993, the AQC initiated the AAHE Continuous Quality Improvement (CQI) Project as a way to share with the wider higher education community the Consortium's experience and knowledge of quality practices. The CQI Project has since grown in size and scope.

The AQC and AAHE's CQI Project jointly seek: 1) to explore the intelligent application of CQI principles to higher education; and 2) to provide for the effective exchange of ideas and findings regarding continuous quality improvement among all higher education practitioners.

For more information about resources, publications, and or goals, please contact Monica Manning: 612/222-5838, fax: 612/222-2915, Internet: mmanning@maroon.tc.umn.edu.

Preface

A paradigm is a set of rules that establishes boundaries and tells us how to behave inside the boundaries in order to be successful. For most individuals in higher education, the concept of "performance" is interpreted within the context of such a paradigm—a resource/reputation paradigm. It states that higher levels of reputation is a function of selective admissions policies, large endowments, and highly-credentialed professors. The better the resources, the better the reputation. "Performance," a word that implies both subtantiality and achievement, loses much of its hard edge when viewed from within the boundaries of this belief system. Moreover, the rules of the paradigm mistakenly suggest that high levels of performance follow, *ipso facto*, from increased reputation.

This book describes a different set of rules, one in which performance is a function of what you add rather than what you get, by design rather than by default, and by reflective practice rather than by standard convention. It challenges the mind-set of accreditation, the rituals of disciplinary fragmentation, and the ideology of reputation. It defies the doctrine of resource maximization and denies a tradition that states that we as academy members, and only we, are the arbiters of excellence. This new set of rules, this altered perception of performance, is captured in the core values, framework, criteria, and examination items of the Malcolm Baldrige National Quality Award.

High Performing Colleges is divided into two volumes. The first, *Theory and Concepts*, takes a descriptive approach to the topic. The chapters in this volume describe a broad range of issues surrounding the Malcolm Baldrige National Quality Award, from a detailed discussion of its role as an institutional assessment tool to its relationship with current accreditation practices. The volume is scholarly in tone and substance. Individual authors explore the literature in their respective areas and build arguments to reinforce their views; often, institutional experiences are used to substantiate or build upon their conclusions.

Volume I consists of four parts: Baldrige Basics, Performance Criteria, Quality Assurance, and the Appendix. The chapters in the Baldrige Basics section explore many of the fundamental issues involved in extending the Baldrige to higher education. The emphasis is on synthesizing and analyzing the evidence that has accrued over the eight years that the Baldrige has been used as an organizational evaluation instrument. Moreover, authors provide a historical and organizational context for considering the efficacy of a Baldrige approach to college and university self-assessment.

The second part, Performance Criteria, focuses on the seven categories that form the substance of the Malcolm Baldrige National Quality Award evaluation process: (1) Leadership, (2) Information and Analysis, (3) Strategic and Operational Planning, (4) Human Resource Development and Management, (5) Educational and Business Process Management, (6) School Performance Results, (7) and Student Focus and Student and Stakeholder Satisfaction. The authors of these chapters have played key roles in piloting self-assessment projects at their institutions. In each case, they explore the concept of the category as it relates to both the education and management literatures, then reflect on their experiences in applying the category requirements to their institution's practices.

Quality Assurance is the title of the third part in this volume. These chapters offer the reader a different view of the Malcolm Baldrige National Quality Award and its application to the higher education community. While the previous section focuses on institution-based issues of an operational nature, these chapters reflect the perspectives of other constituencies. State legislators, trustees, and accrediting agency officers care about developing and maintaining policies and procedures that assure their various constituencies of proper and efficient use of scarce institutional resources. The authors of these chapters explore the Baldrige Award evaluation process as it relates to the current array of quality assurance approaches.

The Appendix of this volume contains an adaptation of the Malcolm Baldrige National Quality Award's 1995 Education Pilot Criteria; it provides background information about the Education Criteria as well as their purposes and goals. The core values and concepts are described in detail while key education themes are also enumerated. The Education Criteria Framework—a visual schema—

is presented. Finally, the Criteria themselves are enumerated along with their accompanying Items and Areas to Address. For those readers who have little knowledge of the Baldrige process, it is recommended that they read the Appendix first before beginning with the chapters in Part I.

The second volume, *Case and Practice*, is different in both substance and style. Prescriptive in orientation, it emphasizes the practical application of a Baldrige self-assessment to a college or university. There are no citations; there are many recommendations. In effect, this volume extends the discussion beyond the mere advocacy of a Baldrige approach to reflective practice. The question now becomes: *How do we do it?* The answer, I believe, can be found in this volume's three parts: Application and Evaluation, Implementation and Research, and the Appendix.

The first part, "Application and Evaluation," entails a full Malcolm Baldrige National Quality Award 1995 Education Pilot Study application. The application—from Northwest Missouri State University—is preceded by an introduction written by the University's leadership. Northwest's application was evaluated by a Baldrige examiner prior to their submitting it for formal review by Malcolm Baldrige National Quality Award office as part of the 1995 Education Pilot process. The examiner's feedback report and scoring summary is included in this section; specifically, portions of the feedback report that deal with "strengths" and "areas for improvement" for a particular category are placed directly following Northwest's response to the category requirements. To gain the most from this section, it is advised that each category—both application write-up and feedback—be read together. Further, it is recommended that the reader study the Scoring Guidelines in the Appendix and attempt to follow the examiner's reasoning as each Item is evaluated and scored.

A second part, "Implementation and Research," offers the reader a rigorous set of ideas and approaches to the use of the Baldrige Award Criteria as an institutional effectiveness instrument. These prescriptions move far beyond theory. The authors enumerate specific suggestions based upon their studies of actual implementation efforts in higher education. These chapters—in conjunction with the Northwest Missouri State University application and its accompanying feedback report—provide a strong resource for those who wish to consider using a Baldrige self-assessment effort to drive performance improvement at their own institutions.

Finally, there is the Appendix. Because of the nature of this volume, it follows that the material presented here is more practical and prescriptive than the material presented in the appendix to the first volume. Specifically, the MBNQA application Overview is explained along with guidelines for preparing it. There are also guidelines for responding to Criteria Items. Finally, the scoring system and scoring dimensions used in a Baldrige evaluation are described in detail.

I extend a sincere "thank you" to my associates—all twenty-eight of them—who made *High Performing Colleges* a gratifying reality. They endured unreasonable deadlines, frank critiques, and late-night faxes. They suffered through months of silence followed by urgent pleas for revisions. Such is the business of editing a two-volume book of this size and scope; still, they attended to their work with steadfastness and good cheer. I cherish their friendships and praise their professionalism.

Most of the institutions represented in this book are members of the American Association of Higher Education's Academic Quality Consortium. This small, intrepid band of schools—a handful of community colleges, some research universities, and several religiously-affiliated colleges—formed an alliance several years ago. Vastly different in mission and vision, they had one thing in common: an interest in investigating divergent operating models. Consequently, they have actively engaged themselves and each other in the pursuit of experiments in which they could try and fail, learn and grow. They are to be applauded for the simple reason that they have taken a few tentative steps down a less-traveled road.

A final acknowledgment is warranted. A Baldrige self-assessment can be an ego-shattering experience. The experience is not unlike that of a local high school football hero who finds himself up against 300-lb. linemen in his first collegiate game, or the aspiring repertory theater actor who, after traveling to New York, finds herself in an audition with veteran Broadway performers. Saying, as an institution, that you are committed to academic excellence makes for fine rhetoric; suggesting that quality is a function of admission decisions and endowment levels is standard thinking within the academy's resource-driven mind-set. The faculty, staff, and administration of Northwest Missouri State University have opted, in stark contrast, to test themselves against the Malcolm Baldrige National Quality Award's standards. As you will see in the pages to come, the Baldrige is a big-time reality check. It is the institutional effectiveness equivalent of a 300-pounder or an accomplished thespian. While none of my Missouri friends would tell you that they have figured all of this out yet, they have managed to create a culture of divine discontent that is unique in higher education—one in which fact is more important than opinion, in which complaints are valued as opportunities to improve, and in which the courage to create a new tomorrow has triumphed over the willingness to merely let yesterday replicate itself today.

As an institution and as individuals, I admire you.

DANIEL SEYMOUR

Part One: Baldrige Basics

The Malcolm Baldrige National Quality Award program was launched in 1987. Since that time, more than one million copies of the Criteria have been distributed, almost 300 companies have applied for the Award, and there have been twenty-eight winners. The national award has also spawned a series of state awards—nearly thirty in all. The chapters in this section scan the past near decade in order to synthesize and analyze both research and practice relating to the use of the Baldrige as an organizational evaluation instrument. Moreover, authors provide a historical and organizational context for discussing the issue of extending the Baldrige to education. Their insights extend deep into the critical issue that all of the higher education community faces: How to create more effective, more efficient colleges and universities.

1

Introduction: Another Paradigm, Another Plan

Daniel Seymour

There is an old story told by Hebrew rabbis, that before the Great Flood there was an enormous giant called Gog. After the flood had reached near full tide, and every man was drowned except those taken into the ark, Gog came striding along. The water was over the mountain-tops and still rising—raining hard night and day. The giant hailed Noah.

"Who is there?" Noah asked.

"It is I," said Gog. "Take me in; it is wet outside!"

"No," replied Noah, "you're too big. Besides, you're a bad character. You would be a very dangerous passenger, and would make trouble in the ark. I shall not take you in," Noah said, and clapped the window shut tight.

"Go to thunder," said Gog. "I will ride, after all." And, with that, he strode after the ark, wading through the waters, and climbed to the top; with one leg over the larboard and the other over the starboard side, Gog steered it just as he pleased.

Some of today's organizations know what it is like to have a Gog attempting to sit astride them. Take health care, for instance. Twenty years ago, most health insurance was delivered through traditional indemnity, or fee-for-service, plans. But because doctors were reimbursed for every service performed, traditional insurance provided a significant incentive to over-treat patients using sophisticated technology and expensive laboratory tests. Health care costs started spiraling upward at double-digit rates annually.

After almost two decades, the brakes have been applied to this run-away train. Today, managed care in the form of health maintenance organizations (HMOs) have radically transformed the practice of medicine and physicians' relationships with their patients in many states. Squeezed by employers to cut costs, these managed care organizations are effectively rationing health care by redefining—in their terms—what is or is not medically necessary; they contend that they are meeting the demands of employers and society to lower costs.

In contrast, many critics believe that in the rush to bring some sanity to a notoriously inefficient and expensive medical system, insurance plans have acquired too much authority. Some use diagnosis-related groups (DRGs) to reimburse doctors and hospitals according to a fixed price menu—an appendicitis operation is worth $3,000, a tonsillitis operation goes for $2,500. Scorecards are kept. Incidents of sickness, complications, and death are tied to a diagnosis code, then calculated for each hospital, compared, and published. Hospitals are being forced to restructure, and, in some cases, the quality of care is being compromised as externally-driven, simplistic metrics are used to force doctors and hospitals to change the way they practice medicine. Gog-like insurance companies, not health care professionals, are steering health care reform as it continues its inexorable march across the country.

This tidal wave of change has been a shock to many. Doctors see the events as unsettling and unwarranted. Their professional lives, their judgments and standards, are being challenged by others who may have only a sliver's understanding of the practice of medicine. Certainly the events are unsettling, and possibly unwarranted, but they really should not be characterized as shocking or in any way unforeseen. Indeed, the scenario just described was perfectly predictable. In *Structure in Fives: Designing Effective Organizations* (1983), Henry Mintzberg enumerates and discusses five different organizational structures, one of which is the "professional bureaucracy." These types of organizations are complex, but rather than being controlled by a hierarchy, they emphasize authority of a professional nature—the power of expertise. A hospital is such a professional bureaucracy. It relies for coordination on the standardization of skills and its associated design parameter, training, and indoctrination—or, in this case, medical school and residency programs. Duly trained and indoctrinated specialists are hired for the operating core, and then given considerable individual control over their own work.

Control over work, according to Mintzberg, means that the professional works to a large degree independent of colleagues, but closely with clients (e.g., patients). Most of the necessary coordination between the operating professionals is handled by the standardization of skills and knowledge; in effect, by what they have learned to expect from their colleagues. Other forms of standardization are troublesome to the professional. The work processes themselves are too complex to be standardized directly by analysts. Similarly, the outputs of professionals' work cannot be easily measured and so, they believe, do not lend themselves to standardization.

As long as the environment remains stable, the professional bureaucracy encounters few problems.

As long as the environment remains stable, the professional bureaucracy encounters few problems. The autonomous nature of the organizational structure allows the professionals to perfect their skills, free of interference. Problems arise, however, when conditions change—say, as health care costs begin to outstrip the capacity of individuals and corporations to pay. Because professional bureaucracies tend to be conservative bodies, they are usually both unwilling and unable to respond to the vagaries of a dynamic environment. Their unwillingness stems from the universal nature of inertia and perceived threats to closely-held beliefs and standard operating procedures; the inability to respond to new conditions results more directly from the organizational structure itself. Since there is virtually no control of the work aside from that exerted by the professionals themselves, there is no way to correct deficiencies that the professionals choose to ignore.

What action does this lack of responsiveness evoke? Most commonly, people outside the profession see the problems as resulting from a lack of external control. And so they do the obvious: they use direct supervision, standardization of work processes, or standardization of outputs to exert control. That is, for example, precisely what a DRG is—an output that has been standardized by decree. To the HMO, appendicitis is appendicitis. No special situations are recognized, no extenuating circumstances are considered, and no unanticipated variations are allowed. Gog is in charge.

Given this description of a professional bureaucracy, it should not be surprising to the reader that another type of organization that falls into the professional bureaucracy rubric is "the university." Institutions of higher education have most of the same characteristics as hospitals: highly specialized in the horizontal dimension, significant autonomy for professionals, protection of the professional's autonomy by administrators whose job it is to "buffer" them from external pressures, and coordination accomplished through standardized skills and knowledge. Moreover, higher education is also in the midst of a storm, a rising tide of discontent involving the cost of education versus the quality of instruction.

For more than a decade, a chorus of questions has been raised: *Why has a college education become so expensive? How do I know which college provides the best education for the money? Why is there so little attention given to teaching undergraduates? Why can't I get the classes I want?* These questions have largely been met with a stony silence. Occasionally an institution will announce that it is holding the line on tuition and fee increases; often there is the rhetoric of an institution rededicating itself to teaching, complete with the announcement of a newly-initiated teaching award. Still, few substantive innovations are evident across the higher education landscape. Colleges and universities have largely continued on a business-as-usual basis: great researchers still earn far more than great teachers, the lecture format endures as the education delivery vehicle of choice, quality and selectivity remain joined at the hip, and tuition rate increases predictably outpace inflation increases by a factor of two or more.

All across the country, organizations are getting leaner, sharpening their focus, serving their customers and trying to adjust to the dictum of doing more with less and doing it better. Enterprises of every kind are facing competitive challenges and having to pay much closer attention to the quality of everything they do. That is the revolution that is sweeping this country; the public naturally expects higher education to participate. And most colleges and universities are not.

The predictable response according to Mintzberg—and evidenced by our sister professional bureaucracy, hospitals—is more direct supervision and more standardization of processes and outputs. That is what is predicted and that is precisely what is happening. For example, twenty states now require public colleges and universities to set up programs to assess what students learn in college. In 1994-95 twenty-four states conducted faculty workload studies for public colleges. States have even begun to feel as though it is necessary to mandate the English language. Seventeen of them now require public colleges and universities to certify that their teaching assistants are competent in English. We have report cards now, too. Governing boards, education regulators, and state legislatures are latching onto simple-minded algorithms that can be used to compare and contrast institutions. From the general notion of "increased accountability" to the derivation of specific performance funding formulae, external regulators continue to scan the horizon in search of ever-more-perfect accountability weapons, ones that will force us to demonstrate the effectiveness and efficiency of the services we provide.

Like hospitals, we are allowing Gog to get astride our colleges and universities—and he is beginning to steer us just as he pleases.

The question that remains is this—*If these events are so predictable, why haven't we intervened?* Just because a series of events are predictable does not mean they are necessarily inevitable. Nothing has been sprung on us. We have not been blindsided by a cruel and unjust world. Indeed, we have the luxury of the health care crisis as a leading indicator. Still, we have not adjusted. We have dealt with our deficiencies in only the most superficial way. There has been no fundamental rethinking of the way we conduct the core business of the higher education enterprise. *Why?*

> *There has been no fundamental rethinking of the way we conduct the core business of the higher education enterprise. Why?*

The primary reason we have not responded, I believe, is because as a professional bureaucracy we are locked into a paradigm that focuses on resources, reputation, and a transcendent notion of quality. According to this model, we maintain the sole right to define our own professional responsibilities. Any incursions are interpreted as threats to academic freedom. We perceive accountability efforts as blatant attempts to usurp the exclusive authority of faculty members to determine how, when, and where they provide their services; such efforts should be identified, neutralized, and dispatched, because "we know quality when we see it and we are under no special obligation to explain our processes and outcomes to the unenlightened." Higher education professionals are, in effect, interpreting the world through the filter of Mintzberg's professional bureaucracy.

Moreover, we suffer from paradigm paralysis because we have no alternative models to pursue. The situation is not dissimilar to the one described by former Secretary of Defense Robert S. McNamara, in his brutally self-critical memoir, *In Retrospect: The Tragedy and Lessons of Vietnam* (1995). McNamara says that even when he and President Lyndon Johnson's other aides knew that their Vietnam strategy had little chance of success, they pressed ahead with it, ravaging a beautiful country and sending thousands of young Americans to their deaths year after year, because they had no other plan.

We, too, have had no other plan. Such is the power of the paradigm. We whine, we moan. We tell everyone who will listen that we are losing our best professors due to budget cuts. We politic. We argue *ad nauseam* about how we are special and that whatever we are asked to do, simply can't be done. When we are forced to act, our initial solutions come from within the paradigm. In response to data inquiries, we hire more institutional researchers; in response to budget crunches, we hire more fund-raisers. When board members or state legislators lecture us about productivity or efficiency, we dismiss the concepts because they involve "biz-speak." We argue that performance-based funding is fine, as long as it is on top of a fully-allocated budget. We engage in the organizational equivalent of the psychiatric condition known as the "delusion of reprieve." We hunker down and rationalize that the rising tide will soon ebb. We convince ourselves that all we need to do is ride out the budget crunch, and that everything will be fine when our funding is restored.

But we seem unwilling or unable to question—at a fundamental level—the way in which we conduct the business of our organizations. The nature of performance or institutional effectiveness is never debated. Alternative paradigms are not explored. We are locked into a thought pattern that precludes options. The power of our own expertise reigns supreme. Like Noah, our ark is our world. Problems are handled by dismissing the uninvited guest and shutting the window tight. We have no other plan.

This book explores a different way to both think about and operationalize organizational effectiveness. It is another plan. The Malcolm Baldrige National Quality Award (MBNQA) for education has been carefully constructed on a foundation of core values, then on criteria that manifest those values. A framework specifies the dynamic relationships among the criteria/categories, while examination items provide a set—twenty-eight in total—of results-oriented requirements.

These four elements—core values, criteria, framework, and examination items—constitute a comprehensive way to codify performance improvement principles. The Award is both a standard of excellence, as well as a diagnostic system that enables an organization—in this case a college or university—to assess itself against that standard. As such, the Baldrige process is about knowledge creation. It involves planning, the execution of those plans, an assessment of progress, and the revision of plans based upon assessment findings. In addition to such learning cycles, the Baldrige and its Criteria emphasize the alignment of mission with operational performance. The concept of "excellence" in such a system is not left to chance. The Baldrige requires that the organization be able to demonstrate a well-conceived and well-executed assessment strategy that results in value-added performance. The characteristics of such a strategy include: (1) clear ties between what is assessed and the institution's mission objectives, (2) a main focus on improvement, (3) assessment that is embedded in the institutional culture and ongoing, (4) clear guidelines regarding how assessment results will be used, and (5) an ongoing approach for evaluating the assessment system to improve the connection between assessment and student success.

Our willingness to engage ourselves in such reflective practices may well be the way that we regain control over our own future.

The Baldrige, then, is a performance paradigm, one in which such typically vaporous terms as "quality" and "excellence" have been transformed into a robust system that stands in sharp contrast to the "we-know-it-when-we-see-it" approach that dominates a professional bureaucracy (the reader is advised to study the section "Concept of Excellence" in *Volume I*'s appendix, as well as the section "Understand the Meaning of Performance" in *Volume II*'s appendix). The intent is to foster innovation and learning by providing a yardstick that yields insights and ideas for improving organizational practices. Our willingness to engage ourselves in such reflective practices may well be the way that we regain control over our own future. By implementing a diagnostic approach that yields tough-minded feedback, by pursuing a methodology that involves a diligent search for bad news, colleges and universities may be able to correct deficiencies that heretofore have been ignored or, at the very least, tolerated.

In some ways, the scenario that is captured in this book is mindful of the economic roller coaster this country has experienced in recent decades. In 1960, the United States' share of the World GNP was thirty-five percent, and Japan's was three percent. In 1980, our GNP share had shrunk to twenty-two percent while Japan's had spurted by over 300 percent to ten percent. Akio Morita, co-founder of Sony Corporation, made this frank observation: "American companies either shifted output to low-wage countries or came to buy parts and assembled products from countries like Japan that could make quality products at low prices. The result was a hollowing of American industry. The U.S. was abandoning its status as an industrial power." Then he added, "We weren't taking away your manufacturers' business—you gave it up."

Just as American manufacturers "gave it up" to Japan, just as hospitals and doctors "gave it up" to insurance companies, American higher education is in the process of "giving it up" to government regulators and educational bureaucrats. The Baldrige evaluation process is comprehensive and rigorous. It is unforgiving. It does not abide rhetoric or whimsy. It may also be one of the best chances that we have to prevent the hollowing of our own industry.

2
A Baldrige Scorecard: Aims Achieved and Lessons Learned

John R. Barker and Daniel Seymour

The statute that created the Malcolm Baldrige National Quality Award, Public Law 100-107, was grounded in frustration. Members of the U.S. Congress, encouraged by American corporate leaders who had seen the dramatic impact of quality management practices in Japan, developed a strategy to bolster sagging corporate America. The strategy—one that focused on improving corporate bottom lines—was the Baldrige Award program.

The Award has been earned by twenty-four American manufacturing, small business, and service companies in the eight years the award has been presented. Participation in the Baldrige process, however, has not been limited to the few winners. Hundreds of thousands of companies have used the Criteria for self-assessment and improvement efforts (Hiam 1993). In addition, Baldrige program officials have estimated that more than one million copies of the Award Criteria are in circulation. Twenty-eight states have developed award processes, many patterning their efforts after the Baldrige program.

When Curt Reimann, the first Director of the Malcolm Baldrige National Quality Award, speaks about the Baldrige, his comments tend to be broad-sweeping in scale. In one article he states, "In creating the award criteria, our intention was to get people in all types of organizations involved in focusing on key quality requirements and in assessing themselves against tough standards. We feel that to succeed, the award must be much more than a contest" (Reimann 1993, 15). In an interview that appeared in *Quality Digest*, Reimann again emphasizes the "more-than-a-contest" theme:

> To me, the contest "pays the rent" for everything and gets the
> attention. . . . But, more importantly, what we're trying to do is
> develop quality as a body of knowledge that stimulates improve-
> ment in the products and services of all organizations, not just
> businesses. That means schools, hospitals, government agencies,
> and so on. (Paton 1991, 4)

In effect, Reimann sees the Baldrige Award as an educational
program in which the contest and all of its attendant hoopla is a great
opening for the real show—promoting change by way of a body of
knowledge about quality that connects process and results.

Not all voices, however, have praised the intent or impact of the
Baldrige on American business. Criticisms suggest that the Baldrige
application and review process is cumbersome and has turned into a
consulting boondoggle (Zemke 1991), that the judging is incompe-
tent (Smith and Oliver 1992), and that the criteria are old-fashioned
(Crosby 1992). One management writer has even concluded that the
Baldrige is a "dubious achievement" given that, in his mind, it has
quickly become "a frivolous exercise in corporate vanity" (Houston
1990, 44). Harvard's David Garvin (1991) has identified three principal criticisms of the Baldrige award: it requires large expenditures
on the application and preparation for site visits, fails to predict a
company's financial success, and does not honor superior product or
service quality. Although Garvin provides evidence to dispel these
myths, many Baldrige critics are resolute in doubting its benefits.

As the Baldrige Award office pursues the establishment of an
Education category and higher education institutions experiment with
the newly-minted pilot Criteria, it is critical that we attempt to resolve disparate impressions of the Baldrige: boondoggle or body of
knowledge, legitimate criticism or reactive cynicism, driver of reform or silly pretentiousness. Perhaps the best way to respond to
these issues is to analyze the award-cum-educational program in a
more systematic way. Public Law 100-107 provides a structure for
analysis by detailing the following aims of the Baldrige program.

> (1) . . . helping to stimulate American companies to improve
> quality and productivity for the pride of recognition while ob-
> taining a competitive edge through increased profits;

(2) recognizing the achievements of those companies that improve the quality of their goods and services and provide an example to others;

(3) establishing guidelines and criteria that can be used by business, industrial, governmental, and other organizations in evaluating their own quality improvement efforts;

(4) providing specific guidance for other American organizations that wish to learn how to manage for high quality by making available detailed information on how winning organizations were able to change their cultures and achieve eminence.

The following sections, then, take a critical look at each aim and briefly discusses the implications for higher education.

IMPROVING PERFORMANCE

The Baldrige Award Criteria offer a performance framework that connects process with results, cause with effect. If the Baldrige achieves the first aim as described in Public Law 100-107, evidence should indicate that adopting and practicing quality management principles, as manifested and evaluated in the Criteria, leads to improved organizational performance—that is, greater efficiency and effectiveness, and, perhaps, greater profitability. Does it?

Critics of the Baldrige Award have made Wallace Company, the 1990 small business category winner, their poster child.

Critics of the Baldrige Award have made Wallace Company, the 1990 small business category winner, their poster child. The Houston-based pipe and valve manufacturer started handing out pink slips within a year of receiving the Award. By 1992, banks had cut off Wallace's credit and forced the company into Chapter 11 bankruptcy. While Wallace may be the most prominent non-performer, there have been others that have stumbled after winning the Award. Design problems occurred at Motorola, international difficulties at Federal Express, and depressed demand at Cadillac. The conclusion among some, therefore, has been that the Baldrige is flawed because it fails to predict a company's success, especially its financial success.

The most forceful response to this criticism has come from David Garvin (1991):

> Here the critics are right—but wrong. The Baldrige Award and
> short-term financial results are like oil and water: they don't mix
> and were never intended to. . . . Indeed, winning is neither a
> necessary nor sufficient condition for financial success. It is not
> *necessary* because there are routes to profitability other than
> superior quality management. A long-standing patent, for ex-
> ample, or a one-of-a-kind production process can ensure finan-
> cial success even if a company falls woefully short on the
> Baldrige criteria. Nor are the criteria *sufficient* for financial suc-
> cess, since they leave out such vital tasks of management as
> effective marketing, innovative R & D, and sound financial plan-
> ning. (83)

It follows from what Garvin suggests, that if the goal is merely to
achieve financial results, it would be easier to just collapse all the
categories into a profit-and-loss statement instead of focusing on
generic quality-system requirements that connect to a body of knowledge. Such a narrow interpretation would be useless to those organizations that are interested in understanding the drivers of performance
improvement. John Wallace, the Wallace Company's CEO, put much
of this debate into context when he accepted responsibility for his
company's financial problems, but added that the Baldrige was the
best thing that had happened to the company. Without Wallace's quality initiative, he said, "We wouldn't have made it this far" (Smith
and Oliver 1992, 59).

While an emphasis on financial results would seem to be a narrow, self-defeating interpretation of the Baldrige's intent, there is still
a very real need to avoid the other extreme—getting caught up in the
hype of a beauty contest. Arden Sims, the President and CEO of
Globe Metallurgical Inc., suggests that his company's Baldrige Award
in 1988 was a by-product of broad and fundamental changes that
Globe had made: "Quality for Globe was a matter of economic survival, not part of a calculated effort to win an award. To compete in a
global market, we had to provide our customers with the highest quality products at the lowest possible cost" (Sims 1992, 126). Economic
survival is a legitimate concern. Although quarterly profits are not
an appropriate focus of the Baldrige, long-term performance results
should be. Too many organizations pursuing a quality initiative and
invest heavily in tool training, visioning, and other activities without
developing an accompanying results orientation. However, as cases

---

like Globe Metallurgical indicate, Baldrige winners see improved performance outcomes as a return on quality investment.

The Malcolm Baldrige National Quality Award office agrees. While the award is reviewed and undergoes annual modifications, the 1994-1995 cycle produced significant changes, particularly in the results area in particular. In the 1994 Criteria, category 6.0, "Quality and Operational Results," examined "the company's achievement levels and improvement trends in quality, company operational performance, and supplier quality. Also examined are current quality and operational levels relative to those of competitors." The point value was 180 out of 1,000. In the 1995 Criteria, category 6.0 was retitled "Business Results" and examines "the company's performance and improvement in key business areas—product and service quality, productivity and operational effectiveness, supplier quality, and financial performance indicators linked to these areas. Also examined are performance levels relative to competitors." The point value jumped to 250. As explained in the guidelines, the changes reflect a greater emphasis on the importance of operational and financial performance results and the use of these results in guiding performance improvement.

In addition to these general impressions and reactions to the question of whether or not the Baldrige has achieved its aim of recognizing performance improvement, there are three more specific sets of findings: (1) self reports, (2) effectiveness studies, and (3) hypothetical investment reports. We will look at each in more detail.

Self Reports

Since 1988, when the first Baldrige Awards were given several, many winners have commented on how much the process has meant to their business. In newspaper articles and television interviews senior executives have overwhelmingly supported the aims of the Award and the influence it has had on their efforts to improve performance. Some winners, like Xerox's vice president Norman Rickard, have an even broader perspective—"Any company that assesses itself against the Baldrige criteria and uses the assessment as a road map for continuous improvement is a winner in my book" (Rickard 1992, 146). Although not everyone agrees with Rickard, Kymberly Hockman of E.I. du Pont, has reacted to those individuals who have been the award's strongest critics by saying, "It is interesting that these criticisms never come from companies that have won the award or have scored well against its criteria, but from those that may feel threatened in some way" (Hockman 1992, 137).

Baldrige Award winners have been analyzed and scrutinized. The Malcolm Baldrige National Quality Award office publishes a "Profile of Winners" on a regular basis. Business journals such as *Fortune*, *Harvard Business Review*, *Business America*, and others regularly run detailed stories about Baldrige-winning companies. In many cases there is also a swell of interest within a winner's industry. When the Ritz-Carlton won the Award in 1992, the hospitality and hotel industry publications ran stories and interviews that described Ritz-Carlton's success; when Eastman Chemical won in 1993, the chemical industry was equally eager to document its success strategies. And there have been books. Marion Mills Steeples, for example, does a business overview, highlights, strategies, and results for all the Baldrige winners in her book, *The Corporate Guide to the Malcolm Baldrige National Quality Award* (1993).

Figure 1, "Return on Quality Investment," is a very brief synopsis taken from winner profiles compiled by the Baldrige office—that highlights some of the reported performance-related results that recent winners have achieved.

Effectiveness Studies

Empirical studies of organizational effectiveness provide another way to evaluate the performance improvement aim of the Malcolm Baldrige National Quality Award. There have been several. At the request of Congressman Donald Ritter (R-Pa), the General Accounting Office (GAO) reviewed twenty companies that were among the highest-scoring MBNQA applicants (seven of which were winners) in 1988 and 1989. Using a combination of questionnaire and interview method, the companies were asked to provide information on various performance measures, including employee-related indicators, operating indicators, customer satisfaction indicators, and business performance indicators. The study's summary findings are:

• Companies that adopted quality management practices experienced an overall improvement in corporate performance. In nearly

Fig. 1. Return on Quality Investment

1994 Winners

Over the past 5 years, AT&T Consumer Communication Services has saved approximately $26 billion in local carrier connection costs as a result of reengineering, process, and quality management improvement.

GTE Directories Corporation reduced publishing errors by 9% from 1991 through 1993, lowered billing and collection errors by 71%, and improved on-time directory delivery performance by 24% over the same period.

Process reengineering and simplification have enabled Wainwright Industries, Inc., to cut the lead time for making one of its principal products to 15 minutes as compared with 8.75 days 3 years ago, and to reduce defect rates tenfold.

1993 Winners

Twenty percent of Eastman Chemical Company's sales come from new products developed in the last 5 years—much greater than the industry average. For the past four years, over 70% of its worldwide customers have ranked Eastman as their number one supplier.

Ames Rubber Corporation reports that "through sharing quality techniques with our suppliers, they have achieved a 99.9% quality and on-time delivery status." For Ames largest customer, Xerox, the defect rate has been reduced from 30,000 parts per million in 1989 to just 11.

1992 Winners

From 1988 to 1993, Granite Rock Company's number of customer accounts has increased 48% while recession decreased construction industry spending in its market area by nearly 50%. Revenue earned per employee has risen to 30 percent about the national industry average.

Since winning the Baldrige, The Ritz -Carlton Hotel Company has eliminated $75 million in costs through improvement projects. Moreover, according to independent surveys, 92% to 97% of hotel guests leave with a "memorable visit" impression.

Since 1989, AT&T Network Systems Group, Transmission Systems Business has cut new product-development time in half and realized cost savings totaling $300 million. Warranty costs have been reduced to one percent of revenues in spite of introducing a five-year warranty.

Texas Instruments Inc., Defense Systems & Electronics Group, has trimmed organizational layers from eight to five while increasing on-time deliver rate by 24%. The reliability of TI-DSEG systems exceeds the specifications of the Defense Dept. by a factor of four or five.

all cases, companies that used total quality management practices achieved better employee relations, higher productivity, greater customer satisfaction, increased market share, and improved profitability.

• Each of the companies studied developed its practices in a unique environment with its own opportunities and problems. However, there were common features in their quality management systems that were major contributing factors to improved performance.

• Many different kinds of companies benefited from putting specific total quality management practices in place. However, none of these companies reaped those benefits immediately. Allowing sufficient time for results to be achieved was as important as initiating a quality management program. (General Accounting Office 1991, 2-3).

An internal IBM study also sheds light on the relationship between quality and performance as operationalized in the Baldrige Criteria. It contrasted the performance of IBM business units in general with a group of fifty-seven business units that scored 500 or better on the Baldrige Criteria (as applied within IBM's formal application and review process for the company's internal quality award). The results are described in detail by Laszlo Papay, director of Market-Driven Quality Strategy, Assessment, and Consulting Service at IBM, in testimony to a U. S. House of Representatives Subcommittee:

> We conducted a study comparing those IBM organizations that had scored 500 or better to the overall performance of the IBM corporation. Those organizations improved significantly more in the categories we compared, namely: customer satisfaction, employee morale, market share, gross revenue, and operating profit . . . [They] had five percent higher customer satisfaction, nine percent higher employee morale, and significantly higher revenue and operating profit. (Hiam 1993, 23)

A very different type of study was conducted by Knotts, Parrish, and Evans (1993). They sent surveys to CEOs in a variety of organizations: Fortune 500 industrial corporations, Fortune 500 service firms, small manufacturing firms, and small service firms. The survey's purpose was to assess management attitudes toward the Baldrige Award. While the survey authors asked numerous questions across a broad range of topic areas, one question relates specifically to the Baldrige aim of improving performance and competitiveness: *Do the Baldrige Criteria measure excellent performance that improves competitive position?* The results (reported in figure 2) suggest widespread agreement with the linkage between the Baldrige Criteria and business performance.

Do the Baldrige Criteria measure excellent performance that improves competitive position?

Another empirical study that explores the Baldrige quality-performance relationship, is reported in the *International Journal of Quality & Reliability Management.* Wisner and Eakins (1994) performed a competitive analysis of Baldrige Award winners, paying particular attention to the financial characteristics of four publicly-held firms: Motorola, Xerox, Federal Express, and Solectron. Profitability and stock market-based ratios were used to assess the financial performance of these winners by comparing them with industry averages. Wisner and Eakins find that the financial performance of the firms analyzed is mixed. During a period of economic recession, all four firms experienced significant sales growth; however, two of the four firms were not immune to market conditions and experienced declining profitability over the period of investigation. From the analyses—warranty costs, defect rates, employee productivity, and so on—of the broader group, the authors conclude: "It is apparent that the quality improvement efforts of these 17 companies . . . have had a positive effect on the operating characteristics of the firms" (21).

Hypothetical Investment Reports

A final approach to the performance question involves a matter of game playing. Several authors have asked the financial question what would happen if you invested a hypothetical $1,000 in Baldrige Award winning companies? The Commerce Department's National Institute of Standards and Technology (NIST), the executive agency responsible for administering the Baldrige program, put their "play money" to the test. NIST "invested" $1,000 in each of five publicly-traded, whole company winners of the Baldrige Award and the par-

HIGH PERFORMING COLLEGES

Fig. 2. Do the Baldrige Criteria Measure Excellent Performance
that Improves Competitive Position?

| | Percent of Respondents | |
	Agree	Disagree
Fortune 100 Industrials	77%	2%
Rest of Fortune 500 Industrials	75	8
Small Industrials	63	0
Fortune Service 500	51	9
Small Service	46	0
Overall	64	6

(Combines Agree/Strongly Agree and Disagree/Strongly Disagree)

Knotts, U. et al. 1993. What Does the U.S. Business Community Really Think About the Baldrige Award? *Quality Progress* (May).

ent companies of seven subsidiary winners. The investments were tracked, from the first business day in April of the year they won the award to October 3, 1994. Another $1,000 was invested in the *Standard & Poor's 500* at the same time. NIST found that the five whole company winners—Eastman Chemical Co., Federal Express Corp., Motorola Inc., Solectron Corp., and Zytec Corp.—outperformed the *S&P 500* by a ratio of 6.5 to 1, a 188 percent return on investment compared to a twenty-eight percent return for the *S&P 500*. The second group—the parent companies of seven subsidiary winners—generated a ninety-two percent return, compared to a thirty-three percent return for the *S&P 500*. Taken together, the companies outperformed the *S&P 500* by almost 3 to 1.

Another investigator has been tracking the returns of Baldrige winners since 1991. B. Ray Helton (1995) uses a methodology similar to the one employed by NIST. According to his calculations (see figure 3), an investment of $1,000 in each of the publicly-owned award winners has yielded a ninety-nine percent return through September 1, 1994. His corresponding investment in the Dow Jones Industrials yielded a 41.9 percent gain, or a 34.1 percent gain if invested in the *S&P 500*.

Summing Up the Evidence

Across a broad range of evaluation methods—self reports, effectiveness studies, and hypothetical investment reports—the Malcolm Baldrige National Quality Award programs appears to be fulfilling its aim of helping to stimulate quality and productivity among American companies. Is there a lesson in this aim for higher education? In the previous chapter it was argued that higher education was in the process of abdicating control of its own institutions because of an inability to respond to legitimate societal and stakeholder concerns. Many of those concerns involve performance issues, the same issues that were driving the corporate world in the mid-1980s when the Baldrige was initially being discussed and developed, and the same issues that are captured in the first aim detailed in Public Law 100-107.

Fig. 3. The Malcolm Baldrige Award "Fictitious" Fund

Winner or parent company	Date of Baldrige Award	Amount	Value	Change
Eastman Chemical	12/93	$1,000	$1,163	+16.3%
Texas Instruments (Def. & Elec.)	12/92	1,000	1,632	+63.2%
AT&T (Universal Card)	12/92	1,000	1,124	+12.4%
Solectron	10/91	1,000	4,538	+353.8%
Federal Express	12/90	1,000	2,140	+114.0%
General Motors (Cadillac)	12/90	1,000	1,471	+14.1%
IBM (Rochester)	12/90	1,000	601	(39.9%)
Xerox (Business Products)	11/89	1,000	1,864	+86.4%
Motorola	11/88	1,000	5,664	+466.4%
Westinghouse (Nuclear Fuel)	11/88	1,000	566	(43.4%)
TOTALS		**$11,000**	**$21,887**	**+99.0%**

A Comparison	**Baldrige Return on principal**	**+99.0%**
	Major indexes:	
	• Dow Jones Industrials	+41.9%
	• Standard & Poor's 500	+34.1%

Helton, B. R. 1995. The Baldie Play. *Quality Progress* (February): 44.

The 1995 Education Pilot Criteria have a significant focus on performance. For example, one of the core values enumerated in the Criteria (see appendix) is "results orientation." It states that an institution's performance system should center on results, with an emphasis on performance indicators that offer a means to communicate requirements, monitor actual performance, and concentrate resources on improvement efforts—"From the point of view of overall school effectiveness and improvement, two areas of performance are particularly important: student performance, and the effectiveness and efficiency of the school's use of resources." The concept of educational excellence is also defined in the Education Pilot Criteria. Excellence is demonstrated through "value-added" performance and evaluated by year-to-year improvement in key measures. In addition, the Criteria stipulate that organizational mission objectives must be articulated, assessment strategies must be embedded and ongoing, and improvement efforts need to show a connection between assessment and student success. All of this is reflected in the language and scoring guidelines for category 6.0–Institution Performance Results, which commands nearly one-fourth of the total possible points. In particular, Item 6.1–Student Performance Results asks the applicant to "Summarize results of improvement in student performance using key measures and/or indicators of such performance" and has the highest point value (100) of any of the twenty-eight Items in the Baldrige Education Criteria.

All of this fits with the performance paradigm for higher education described in the first chapter, "Another Paradigm, Another Plan." The new emphasis is on building a quality system rather than relying on self-indulgent rankings to generate a favorable reputation compared to other institutions. The emphasis has shifted toward developing and demonstrating methodologies for adding value rather than narrowly focusing on fine-tuning fund-raising and student selection strategies. By shifting our attention from inputs to studying the relationship between process and outputs, as the Baldrige does, we may be in a better position to articulate our worth and resist the type of external controls discussed earlier. In effect, the Baldrige process has, apparently, been successful at "stimulating American companies to improve quality and productivity." Perhaps Baldrige can help higher education focus more of its attention on performance as well.

In effect, the Baldrige process has, apparently, been successful at "stimulating American companies to improve quality and productivity."

RECOGNIZING ACHIEVEMENTS

On December 5, 1994, at a ceremony in Washington, D.C., Vice President Al Gore stated:

> There are those who are predicting that the 21st century will be called the century of quality. It will probably be called a lot of other things, too, but there's no doubt that, in order to stay competitive, U.S. businesses will have to understand how quality management can help them. Of course, they have to focus on customers. They have to create partnerships with employees and suppliers. They have to be creative, responsive, and focus on continuous improvement.

The Vice President then shifted his emphasis from the general to the specific—"That's what AT&T Consumer Communications Services, GTE Directories Corporation, and Wainwright Industries, Inc. have done. And that's why we honor these three winners here today."

The second aim identified in Public Law 100-107 focuses on recognizing the achievements of those organizations that excel at developing quality systems that yield high performing results. Although the aim seems simple and reasonable, there are critics who believe the Baldrige—and the Baldrige process—is more about prizes than performance. In the same way that Wallace Company is used as an illustration of how poor bottom-line performers can win the Award, Cadillac is pointed to as an award-winner that appeared to be more interested in collecting trophies than improving quality and productivity (see the chapter by Johnson and Seymour in this section for a more detailed discussion of this topic in higher education). Management writer D. Keith Denton (1993), who attended a presentation in which Cadillac and Federal Express talked about winning the 1990 Award, summed up the feelings of some critics when he commented in an issue of *Business Horizons*:

> Cadillac has obviously made tremendous strides, but doubt about its ability to compete in the world marketplace lingers. I realized that my doubt began almost immediately when the Cadillac representative noted the improvements and compared the corporation to its number one competitor—Lincoln! . . . In the end, I was left with an overriding feeling that Cadillac had been after the prize and had won, whereas Federal Express was after world competition and was winning. (1)

This criticism—that too many companies are intent on winning headlines rather than on winning market share—is not supported by the facts. Noted earlier, more than one million copies of the Award Criteria have been distributed in its eight years, yet approximately 500 companies have submitted an application. The overwhelming majority of companies that have been exposed to the Baldrige know that winning an award is not a valid reason for pursuing a quality initiative. They understand that the value of the Baldrige lies in the discipline it inspires, not the prize itself.

Still, the Award—the twenty-five pound, fourteen inch high, Steuben crystal obelisk—is a critical aspect of the Baldrige Award process because it symbolizes excellence. As such, the Award has two meanings: (1) it means that winning organizations deserve to be honored for their efforts, and (2) it means that they should be looked to as role models of organizational performance. When management submits a Baldrige application, that sends a powerful message to employees that their company is a world-class competitor. When an applicant wins, as Texas Instruments (TI) Defense Systems and Electronics Group did in 1992, the Award is the embodiment of an exhaustive effort on the part of organizational members. The process and the prize become one. TI's president, Jerry Junkins (1994), notes "The Baldrige was the culmination of years of organizational and cultural changes, and the process leading up to the award gave focus and coherence to business activities that TI had been engaged in for decades" (58).

When management submits a Baldrige application, that sends a powerful message to employees that their company is a world-class competitor.

Baldrige Award winners also serve as examples to others. Companies, just like people, are helped along by having role models to follow. In the business arena, those companies that compete successfully for the Baldrige award truly symbolize quality. The major reason for this is that the Baldrige has strict requirements that few organizations can meet. You can't win by just writing a good report. You can't buy one. The selection process is punishing. As director Reimann asserts, "maybe the Nobel Prize is more rigorous"—but not much else. So it should not be surprising that of the more than a million Criteria in circulation, there have only been twenty-four companies to walk away with one of the Steuben obelisks.

So, is the Baldrige achieving its aim of recognizing the efforts of those companies that have developed world-class quality systems and does the Baldrige highlight them as role models? In their 1992 book, *The Race Without a Finish Line*, Schmidt and Finnigan quote Jerry Jazinowski, the president of the National Association of Manufacturers, as saying that whereas ten years ago CEOs talked about their strategic goals of cutting costs and becoming "leaner and meaner," they are now talking more about the pursuit of quality as the key to achieving success in world markets. Schmidt and Finnigan (1992) concur with Jazinowski and offer an explanation: "The executives we have talked to have given the Baldrige Award credit for contributing to this significant change of priorities" (297). Moreover, Ron Brown, U. S. Secretary of Commerce, has told Baldrige Award winners, "You are part of an elite group of companies that are leading the way to America's competitive rebirth through extraordinary attention to quality, responsiveness, and innovation. As the pace of competitiveness quickens, I encourage American companies to follow your wonderful example."

The conclusion must be that the Baldrige does indeed recognize the achievements of those companies that improve the quality of their goods and services. The question might be asked, then, whether such an aim has equal relevance in the higher education community. Does it make sense to envision the President or Vice President of the United States beginning a speech on December 5, 1997 as follows:

> There are those who are predicting that the 21st century will be called the century of quality. It will probably be called a lot of other things, too, but there's no doubt that, in order to stay competitive, U.S. colleges and universities will have to understand how quality management can help them. Of course, they have to focus on students. They have to create partnerships with schools and industry. They have to be creative, responsive, and focus on continuous improvement. That's what Riverside University, Palm Desert Community College, and Rose College have done. And that's why we honor these three winners here today.

Many people in higher education disavow such crass competition. Our elite institutions would probably not apply. They have nothing to gain—they are already held in high regard. Other institutions would simply dismiss it as a fad. They would dredge up every idea or initiative that didn't work or didn't last and use it to buttress their indulgence of the status quo. Still, the fact is that colleges and universities vie for recognition everyday. Accreditation practices certainly aren't faddish, but institutions regularly enter the competition to see if they can win the prize. We count our books and Ph.D.s; we describe our facilities and equipment. If we meet the minimum standard, we get to market our appellations and pedigrees—ABET, WASC, ALA, NASM.

There are numerous other recognition paths to follow. While most educators are repulsed by the idea of being ranked by the *U.S. News and World Report*, they still complete the forms, fret about the order of finish, and use their standing in promotional literature. The National Research Council (NRC) ranks graduate programs according to their "scholarly quality." Again, the competitors worry that a low ranking will affect their ability to compete for the very best doctoral candidates. Nobel Prizes provide another source of recognition. A Nobel Prize-winning professor can fully expect that the president of the institution will use a press conference opportunity to argue that the Prize is indicative of the prestige and stature of the entire campus community.

The issue, then, is not the quest for recognition; that quest is ubiquitous. The issue centers around what we, as institutions, choose to recognize. In the case of accreditation, we choose competence in acquiring and administering a minimum threshold of resources. The *U.S. News and World Report* focuses on inputs as well—student selectivity, spending per student, faculty resources. The NRC methodology is based solely on reputation; the University of New Mexico's doctoral program in geosciences is ranked forty-seventh because other geoscientists perceive it as such. Conversely, the Baldrige Award recognized organizational operations management requiring good stewardship of resources, outcomes as a function of input and processes, excellence as measured by achievement, and teamwork as the sum of individual contributions.

The lesson is this: We don't have any means—like a Baldrige Award—to recognize high performance in colleges and universities. We don't currently have any means to provide an example of excellence that shines a bright light on an institution that, for example, knows how to maximize student learning. We celebrate a lot of things, but we don't celebrate the things that really matter. Perhaps the Baldrige will help us do that.

EVALUATING IMPROVEMENT EFFORTS

The third aim of the Malcolm Baldrige National Quality Award program is to establish guidelines and criteria that can be used by organizations in assessing their own quality improvement efforts. The idea is to aid in the process of organizational learning. By looking at themselves, then comparing themselves to the Criteria, organizations can identify areas for improvement that can guide a change strategy. Is this aim—for Criteria to become a nationally recognized and widely used self-assessment instrument—being achieved? The quick answer is, "yes."

Given the number of copies in distribution, Karen Bemowksi and Brad Stratton (1995), editors of *Quality Progress*, recently asked themselves an obvious set of questions: *"What happened to the other 999,000 or so copies? Have companies or individuals used them? Were they pitched into the 'circular file,' never to be seen again?"* (42). To find out how the MBNQA Criteria are being used, they surveyed 3,000 people worldwide who requested copies between 1992 and 1995. While approximately eighteen percent of the respondents indicated that neither they nor their companies used the Baldrige Criteria (the aforementioned circular file), the vast majority used them at least once.

What did they use them for? Fifteen different response categories were provided in the survey (with multiple responses allowed), including "source of information on business excellence" (the highest ranking response category with seventy percent) and "to improve existing processes department wide" (the next largest response with forty-nine percent). Four categories used self-assessment language: (1) "for written self-assessment company wide," (2) "for written self-assessment department wide," (3) "for informal self-assessment company wide," and (4) "for informal self-assessment department wide." These categories garnered a range of responses from forty-four percent to thirty-five percent. Only one conclusion is possible: The Baldrige is being used, and it is being widely used, often by organizations who want to assess their own quality improvement efforts.

Survey numbers, however, don't tell the full story. Many individuals have expressed their personal opinions about the Baldrige's special niche or its unique strengths. Globe's Arden Sims (1992) has stated:

For companies not competing for the award, the application provides a framework for implementing a quality program and establishes the necessary benchmark from which all future progress can be measured. . . . Similarly, for those who have already implemented quality programs, the Baldrige Award is incomparable as a tool for measuring their progress. (126)

A former member of the Baldrige Board of Overseers says, "The best way to understand the Baldrige Criteria is as an audit framework, an encompassing set of categories that tells companies where, and in what ways, they must demonstrate proficiency" (Smith and Oliver 1992, 27). Organizational consultant and Baldrige examiner, Maureen Heaphy (1992) offers her opinion on the nature of such internal improvement efforts as enumerated in figure 4.

Fig. 4. Using the Award Criteria for Internal Improvement

Provides framework for company's total quality management system:

• Helps achieve consensus on what needs to be done
• Helps maintain direction over time
• Saves internal development of definition of total quality

Defines self-assessment and self-evaluation:

• Provides objective, nationally accepted, written criteria
• Provides actionable feedback
• Provides measure of progress over time

Identifies improvement opportunities:

• Focuses improvement where it is most needed.

Heaphy, M. 1992. Inside the Baldrige Award Guidelines.
Quality Progress (October): 43.

This evidence points to the Baldrige being used as a mechanism to engage institutions—and its individuals—in reflective practice. The Baldrige is an audit tool that enables companies to assess their efforts and determine what steps to take next. It is a benchmark of what a world-class organization should be. The comments of Norma Rossi (1993), a Metropolitan Life executive, are illustrative:

> Our motivation was not to win the Baldrige Award but to use its criteria to help us define the types of actions that we should be taking and to provide an objective yardstick by which to measure our efforts. . . . We view this self-assessment as a tool for developing and implementing needed action plans. (18)

This same type of thinking is embedded in the words of Patrick Mene (1994), a Ritz-Carlton hotel general manager, as he recently discussed the hotel's experience with the Baldrige:

> After taking one look at the Baldrige criteria, we decided they were written by engineers for engineers. We were hoteliers. All we knew was relationship management. None of us had one science course in our whole life. We thought this stuff was irrelevant and burdensome. And we rejected it.
>
> Then we started looking at the questions more carefully. We determined to our own satisfaction that we were being asked, "How do leaders drive values? What kind of data do you have for your system? How do you make quality goals as important as your marketing and financial goals? How do you realize the full potential of your people? How do you manage processes? (We didn't even understand what processes meant.) What kind of results are you getting on quality? How satisfied are your customers?" Those were good questions. So we started using the criteria. And we applied for the Baldrige. We got creamed the first year—they drove a truck through us. But it was a learning experience, and we used what we learned to formulate a new strategic plan. We got better . . . (11)

In effect, the single best reason for an organization to commit to a Baldrige evaluation (whether through self-assessment or submitting an application) is to learn about itself. From its feedback report, L.L. Bean learned that it needed more bottom-up involvement in the company. Employees are now being asked to solve problems instead of asking their supervisors to do it. When IBM Rochester's leaders read their Baldrige feedback report, they learned the company was weak in six areas: consistent and committed leadership, cross-functional teams, focused teams, focused training, benchmarking, and customer connection. The feedback, according to company officials, acted as a wake-up call that demanded attention.

The results of a Baldrige assessment lend themselves to such action. Phrases like "process is not evident," "limited deployment," and "trends not shown," are common in a Baldrige feedback report and direct the organization's attention to specific areas for improvement. Granite Rock, a 1992 winner, organized the 110 areas for improvement in its first two Baldrige feedback reports into ten categories, and formed "corporate quality teams" to work on each category. Each team had a senior executive facilitator and five or six employees, including one middle manager and people from all levels of the company. Xerox's Baldrige self-assessment was merciless. In 1989, at the completion of its evaluation, Xerox identified 513 "warts" (or, areas for improvement). These "warts" were later categorized, prioritized, and folded into the company's five-year planning process. Similar approaches have been used by Eastman Kodak, AT&T, Intel, Carrier, Corning, Honeywell, Baxter Healthcare, and others that have either applied for a Baldrige Award or created internal systems assessments using the Baldrige Criteria as an audit tool.

As an evaluation instrument, then, the Baldrige has specific benefits: facilitating stronger alignment of the organization around processes, customers, and results; strengthened common language of quality, change management, and organizational improvement; significant management education, and encouragement of personal growth and development of those involved in the process. In effect, if you win the award, great. But that's not the primary purpose. The key point is to make the organization better.

In effect, if you win the award, great. But that's not the primary purpose. The key point is to make the organization better.

Higher education, of course, has a rich tradition of self-assessment in the form of accreditation (with its self-study component) and program review. So, while the Baldrige Award is apparently being used as an effective self-assessment mechanism in industry, there is a real question as to whether it would help colleges and universities in the same way. A corporation focuses most of its attention on quarterly reports, income statements, and balance sheets. It must generate profits to stay in business. It is easy to lose or minimize one's reflective capacity in a headlong rush to maximize market share. Higher education, in contrast, is contemplative by its very nature. It is not obsessed with the short run or the bottom line.

Still, as other chapters detail (see, for example, Johnson and Seymour or Corts et al. in this volume), our traditional evaluation efforts are severely limited in both their nature and scope. Limitations of accreditation and program review include:

- What is being assessed—Most accreditation and program review efforts focus on inputs, with spotty attention given to outcomes. Little or no attention is given to linking processes to outcomes.

- How assessment is conducted—Often there is a small group of people involved. Rather than reporting trends of key performance measures, anecdotal evidence is often relied upon.

- The aim of assessment—Institutions generally approach traditional evaluation efforts as a series of questions that need to be answered. The primary emphasis is on accountability and meeting minimum thresholds.

- The cycle time of assessment—Accreditation cycles average between five and ten years, while program reviews can go well beyond once every decade.

These limitations are severe. Traditional approaches to measuring institutional effectiveness in higher education are simplistic, non-systemic, narrow, reactive, subjective, and untimely. They are characterized by a flurry of activities followed by long stretches of indifference and neglect. What gets reported is whatever is handy and will satisfy the examiners. This approach to evaluation should be familiar to every college professor—cramming, data dumping, getting by. Forgetting. It has everything to do with passing and little to do with learning. Indeed, when was the last time you heard a university president talk about accreditation the way Globe's CEO talked about a Baldrige self-assessment—"[It] establishes the necessary benchmark from which all future progress can be measured." Do the words of the Ritz-Carlton hotel general manager reflect the sentiments of any department chairperson you know?—"We got creamed the first year—they drove a truck through us. But it was a learning experience, and we used what we learned to formulate a new strategic plan. We got better . . . ." Is that the typical reaction to a faultfinding program review? Do our traditional evaluation efforts generate an analog to Xerox's "wart report" that is used to categorize, prioritize, and incorporate the results into our institution's five-year planning process?

Until our approaches to self assessment can do a far better job of answering a few basic questions—*What is our aim? How do we know if we are successful? What is our plan for improvement?*—it would appear that we have much to learn from the Baldrige process.

SHARING INFORMATION

On the inside cover of the 1995 Malcolm Baldrige National Quality Award Criteria booklet is a picture of the Award and a quote from of Ron Brown U. S. Secretary Commerce,—"The criteria for the Baldrige Award are now widely accepted as the definition of what constitutes world-class quality." Toward the bottom of the page is this statement: "The recipients are expected to share information about their successful performance strategies with other U.S. organizations." This is the fourth aim of Public Law 100-107.

So, have Baldrige winners achieved the vision of Congress by serving as role models for organizations wanting to learn from then? It would appear that recipients have responded to this expectation with enthusiasm. The actual requirements of the award program are minimal. Winners are asked to participate in the award's annual Quest for Excellence conference. The conference is described by the Baldrige Award office as "the principal forum for Award winners to present their overall strategies in detail." They are also asked to provide materials on their company's quality strategies and methods to those who request it, and to answer news media inquiries.

But for many winners information sharing becomes a substantial organization activity. In the year following its winning of the Baldrige, Motorola people made 352 speeches to conventions and corporations, answered queries from 1,162 companies, and held monthly five-hour briefings for 150 executives of other companies. Westinghouse published and distributed 6,000 copies of a report that chronicled its Baldrige-winning strategies. Since winning, Xerox has had visits from representatives of most of America's largest companies to see what has worked well and what hasn't worked at all. Xerox leadership and staff have given more than 2,500 presentations to more than 125,000 customers. According to the Baldrige office, there have been more than 50,000 sharing presentations by Award winners and volunteer participants (that is, Baldrige examiners) since its inception in 1987.

Numerous other sharing venues have spontaneously evolved. In 1991, three Baldrige winners—Xerox, Motorola, IBM—joined with American Express, Ford, and Proctor & Gamble to sponsor the Total Quality Forum, a collaborative effort with colleges and universities to advance the practice of continuous improvement principles in higher education. The Baldrige has also spawned twenty-eight state quality awards—often referred to as "mini-Baldriges" since many are based on the Baldrige Criteria. Another mechanism for sharing best practice information is the development of internal programs. At Westinghouse, for example, all ninety corporate divisions compete for the George Westinghouse Total Quality Awards, modeled on the Baldrige. And there is the emergence of supplier certification programs based on the Baldrige Criteria and quality management principles. Motorola initiated this practice when they told their 3,600 suppliers that they should be prepared to conduct a Baldrige self-assessment, and then offered them training to do so.

There are two spin-off questions that come to mind. The first is, *Is there anything in this for the winners?* After Norman Rickard (1992) of Xerox described all the presentations that Xerox had made, he added: "That's good for them, and we know it's been good for us." His conclusion has been confirmed by others. For example, Schmidt and Finnigan (1992) report that the major gain to Baldrige winners is access to top executives in a new array of organizations. In addition, there is the satisfaction generated among employees that comes from sharing useful ideas. Schmidt and Finnigan conclude that, "One result of this sharing has been the discovery that the advantage of holding proprietary secrets is not nearly as valuable as the goodwill that comes from sharing them" (298).

The second question is, *Does all this sharing matter?* The answer to this question is found in the Knotts et al. study reported earlier. In the entire sample of CEOs, sixty-seven percent agree that "feedback from previous winners is valuable," while only twelve percent disagree with the statement. Apparently, respondents aren't just quietly listening to the stories; they are using Baldrige winners as benchmarks against which to improve their own management methods.

By any measure, from any perspective, it is clear that Baldrige recipients have chosen, on their own, to exceed the award program's expectation. David Garvin (1991) concludes his *Harvard Business Review* article by speaking about "The Baldrige Legacy." The Baldrige is a demanding competition, according to Garvin, with every company subject to the same stringent requirements and only six possible winners a year. One would expect these rules to exacerbate the secrecy and paranoia that has dominated industry in the past. In fact, Garvin states that "the results have been the opposite: an outpouring of cooperative behavior and a level of corporate sharing seldom seen in this country." He goes on to add:

> Business audiences have shifted from politely listening to speeches about quality to absorbing them. Xerox talks to over 100,000 people a year, many of them customers and suppliers. All come seeking information and advice. "We absolutely don't believe this would have happened without the Baldrige Award," said one Baldrige examiner. (93)

Garvin's conclusion has been echoed by others. Curt Reimann has stated: "We had no idea how much the winners would do. They have done more, by a factor of ten, than anyone ever anticipated" (Zemke 1991, 30). Marion Mills Steeples (1993) is equally forceful in her book. Again, while noting that Baldrige recipients are obligated to share their quality strategies as a means of fostering quality management improvement throughout the country, she asserts that "no one ever imagined that the Baldrige winners would 'open the kimono' as far as has been the case. The transfer of information from Award recipients to others has been phenomenal" (31).

We had no idea how much the winners would do. They have done more, by a factor of ten, than anyone ever anticipated.

This aim—providing guidance on how winning organizations are able to change their cultures and develop their award-winning quality systems—is something that could have a tremendous impact in higher education. If colleges and universities were widgets, they would be 3,600 customer-made, one-of-a-kind widgets. Every campus views itself as special. Its inhabitants see the institution's situation as unique from every other institution's situation. While all colleges and universities have, for example, academic programs, the English department at Rutgers University and the English department at Arizona State University would undoubtedly see their programs in vastly different ways. The advisers at Whittier College and Simmons College would also have dissimilar perspectives on their mission, vision, and approach. An individual's perception of grant accounting depends on whether the person works in that office at USC or UCLA. In other words, colleges and universities operate by exception.

Much of this makes sense; many circumstances are unique. However, there is some amount of common learning taking place. Within state systems there are both formal and loosely-knit groups of campus officials who share data. There are various consortia. The Fund for the Improvement of Postsecondary Education (FIPSE) has pressed ahead with efforts to disseminate proven reforms. Largely, though, higher education is an exercise in continuous and costly reinvention of the wheel.

The Baldrige is basically an education program built around sharing information about best practices. Motorola learned, then shared. Xerox tried, failed, improved, perfected and then shared. It is hard to believe that there are not best practices in the design and delivery of academic programs, such as English, that can't be shared. There are no aspects of advising processes and grant accounting that would not lend themselves to a similar identification of best practices and world-class standards. A Baldrige Award winner in education may be colleges and universities' best bet to shift the emphasis from "why we are different" to "what we have in common." It may help us reduce the cycle time of learning by identifying institutional practices that are profoundly effective and efficient. Such sharing may spur individuals and institutions to internalize stretch goals that act as incentives for learning and continuous improvement.

CONCLUSION

Given the evidence presented, there should be little doubt that the Malcolm Baldrige National Quality Award has achieved stated aims. In 1991, David Garvin stated: "In just four years, the Malcolm

Baldrige National Quality Award has become *the* most important catalyst for transforming American business" (80). The evidence we have reported and analyzed suggests that the ensuing four years have brought continued success in stimulating quality efforts, recognizing achievements, establishing guidelines for evaluation, and sharing best practices. In a country in which we tend to view things in the extreme—winners and losers, hits and misses—the Baldrige is a big-time winner. It is a hit blockbuster.

Can the Baldrige have a similar impact on higher education? The answer is, unfortunately, probably not. The reputation-resource paradigm is too much ingrained in our campus cultures. Our institutional structures and norms, designed to resist change, have proven to be formidable opponents of many an innovative initiative. We don't have a Japan to inspire us the way American industry did in the 1980s. Certainly it would be different if a major university declared bankruptcy or if students began staging massive protests against tuition increases. It would also be a powerful message if major corporations began to interact with colleges and universities the way they do with their other suppliers—consciously reducing the number of suppliers, and developing and enforcing supplier certification programs. In the short run, however, such changes are not likely to happen.

Still, the continuing erosion of control—slow, incremental, piecemeal—by those external forces described in the previous chapter, will provide our institutions with sufficient reason to explore, if not embrace, this new paradigm. As Ted Marchese (1994), vice president of the American Association for Higher Education, says: "What the public truly needs from higher education is not more accountability but better results. A system that brings just half the talent it enrolls through to the degree, and just half of whose graduates achieve literacy levels four and five on the National Assessment of Educational Progress, has plenty of room for improvement" (4). The Baldrige Award is not just another plan, it is an improvement plan. It is a plan whose aims are compatible with the kind of performance-driven future our colleges and universities need to begin to create.

REFERENCES

Bemowski, K. and B. S. Stratton. 1995. How Do People Use the Baldrige Award Criteria? *Quality Progress* (May): 42-47.

Crosby, P. 1992. Does the Baldrige Award Really Work? *Harvard Business Review* (January/February): 126-47.

Denton, D. K. 1993. Behind the Curve. *Business Horizons* (July/August): 1-4.

Garvin, D. A. 1991. How the Baldrige Award Really Works. *Harvard Business Review* (November/December): 80-93.

Hart, C. 1993. What's Wrong—and Right—with the Baldrige Awards. *Chief Executive* (November/December): 36-47.

Heaphy, M. 1992. Inside the Baldrige Award Guidelines. *Quality Progress* (October): 74-79.

Helton, B. R. The Baldie Play. *Quality Progress* (February): 43-45.

Hiam, A. 1993. *Does Quality Work?: A Review of Relevant Studies.* New York: The Conference Board.

Hockman, K. K. 1992. Does the Baldrige Really Work? *Harvard Business Review* (January/February): 126-47.

Houston, P. 1990. Dubious Achievement. *Business Month* (July): 40-44.

Junkins, J.R. 1994. Confessions of a Baldrige Winner. *Management Review* (July): 58.

Knotts, U., L. G. Parrish, and C. R. Evans. 1993. What Does the U.S. Business Community Think about the Baldrige? *Quality Progress* (May): 49-53.

Marchese, T. 1994. Getting the Baldrige Right. *Change* (January/February): 4.

Mene, P. 1994. The Winning Practices of Baldrige Award Winner Ritz-Carlton Hotel Company. *Tapping the Network Journal* (spring): 10-14.

Paton, S. M. 1991. An Interview with Curt W. Reimann, Director, Malcolm Baldrige National Quality Award. *Quality Digest.*

Reimann, C. 1993. Establishing Quality Initiatives. In *Sustaining Total Quality,* edited by T. Brothers and E. Miranda, 15-16. New York: The Conference Board.

Rickard, N. 1992. Does the Baldrige Award Really Work? *Harvard Business Review* (January/February): 126-47.

Rossi, N. 1993. Creating a Common Language. In *Sustaining Total Quality,* edited by T. Brothers and E. Miranda, 18-19. New York: The Conference Board.

Schmidt, W. H. and J. Finnigan. 1992. *The Race Without a Finish Line.* San Francisco: Jossey-Bass.

Sims, A. C. 1992. Does the Baldrige Award Really Work? *Harvard Business Review* (January/February): 126-47.

Smith, J. and M. Oliver. 1992. The Baldrige Boondoggle. *Machine Design,* 6 August, 25-29.

Steeples, M. M. 1993. *The Corporate Guide to the Malcolm Baldrige National Quality Award.* Homewood, IL: Irwin.

United States General Accounting Office. 1991. *U.S. Companies Improve Performance Through Quality Efforts.* Washington, D.C.: National Security and International Affairs Division.

Wisner, J. D. and S. G. Eakins. 1994. A Performance Assessment of the U.S. Baldrige Quality Award Winners. *International Journal of Quality and Reliability Management* 11(2): 8-25.

Zemke, R. 1991. Bashing the Baldrige. *Training* (February): 29-39.

3
The Baldrige as an Award and Assessment Instrument for Higher Education

Reid Johnson and Daniel Seymour

The purpose of this chapter is to extend the discussion of the Baldrige in two of its primary higher education functions: as an award—a mechanism for identifying and recognizing colleges and universities whose performance indicates truly outstanding levels of quality, and as an assessment instrument—a means of defining each institution's unique goals, measuring their degree of attainment, and indicating needed improvements.

The award function suggests a particular perspective best defined by three terms: recognition, outcome, and high profile. The Baldrige award honors excellence by recognizing the results, or outcomes, of an organization's commitment to a methodology for renewal. It does so with a high profile award ceremony that seeks—unapologetically—to shine a light on the winners. By showcasing award winners, the Baldrige is, in effect, a national education program that fosters the sharing of best practices information throughout the country.

In contrast, the assessment function can best be defined by the terms reflection, process, and low profile. As an assessment tool, the Baldrige challenges an organization to use the Criteria as a way to reflect on its own work processes. To the same extent that the award function is high profile, the assessment function is low profile. It is a backstage exercise in which the organization evaluates itself against a set of requirements, then uses gap analysis and feedback mechanisms to drive continuous improvement. The award function and the assessment function are, therefore, two sides of the same coin—a coin labeled "high performance."

Our nation's colleges and universities are currently facing a crisis in confidence, largely focused on performance-related issues—students, parents, legislators, and citizens are seriously questioning whether the quality of education is keeping pace with the cost of education. Our stakeholders want answers; they want changes. Whether the Baldrige's extension into the higher education arena eventually proves to be a catalyst for untying the Gordian knot of performance reform issues, or is merely another confounding variable in the puzzle, will more than likely hinge on its efficacy as an award and as an assessment instrument.

AN AWARD: RECOGNIZING EXCELLENCE

Again, (MBNQA) Public Law 100-107 states that a national quality award program would help improve quality and productivity by—among other things—"recognizing the achievements of those companies that improve the quality of their goods and services and providing an example to others." The Award is, therefore—in a very real sense—an award. The ceremony is held in Washington, DC each year. Engraved invitations are sent out by the Secretary of Commerce. The press is invited; speeches are made. The award presentation involves plenty of hoopla and handshaking as the award is presented to the few, select winners. It is quite a show.

The award presentation involves plenty of hoopla and handshaking as the award is presented to the few, select winners.

As described in the previous chapter, however, the pomp and circumstance surrounding the "show," has lead some to criticize the Baldrige as being superficial; they argue that companies have become too intent on winning the award rather than on fundamentally improving their performance. One of the most cynical perspectives is offered by Patrick Houston (1990) in an article entitled "Dubious Achievement?" He begins by describing the Baldrige as a trophy, one that takes time and money to get. Lots of money. "Ah, Baldie," he writes. "Are you a symbol of corporate America's best intentions or an icon of wretched excess?" (41). Houston goes on to quote others such as George Labovich, president of the consulting firm ODI, who states that before there was a prize it was hard to get some CEOs excited about quality, despite the benefits of the process—"As soon as you put a prize out there, it became a game. There's still a lot of good-ol'-boy football mentality in America" (41). The following year, *Fortune* ran an article by Jeremy Main (1991) entitled "Is the Baldrige

Overblown?" It showed a picture of the Baldrige Award with the caption "The trophy that makes CEOs' mouths water." The conclusion was that the award wasn't perfect, took time and money to apply for, and didn't solve all of a company's problems. More importantly, the recurring fear expressed by one industry consultant was that, "The goal of winning may displace the goal of achieving real quality" (63).

This is the most frequent misrepresentation of the Baldrige: that the objective is to win it outright, have a great party, cart the trophy back to headquarters, and then use the prize as a kind of hood ornament for a revamped marketing campaign.

Still, if the idea of "going for a prize" generates criticism in the competitive world of modern commerce, it should not be surprising that the same sentiment has emerged from within the academy. In Seymour's (1995) study of colleges and universities that worked with the MBNQA office in generating the Education Pilot Criteria (see Seymour, "Piloting the Baldrige: Observations and Impressions from Nine Institutions," in *Volume II—Case and Practice*), one of the key challenges that surfaced involved the "award." He quotes campus administrators:

> "Where I am concerned is the competitiveness of it—the prize," is how one individual stated it. Another response was: "It could be a dysfunctional kind of tool if people are running around trying to get the award." Still another individual said that he kept running into an anti-prize sentiment on his campus. The attitude, as he described it, was—"What are you trying to get some kind of prize?" They didn't understand, or didn't want to understand, what the real value was. So we got quite a bit of flak.

While there is always a danger that the Baldrige Award will take on some of the characteristics of an expensive beauty contest, there are several strong representations that reinforce its value as an award in higher education: it is a reward for hard effort, it focuses an organization on improvement, and it provides an example to others.

A Reward for Hard Effort

In an interview in *Harvard Business Review* (Rayner 1992), Globe Metallurgical's CEO, Arden Sims, described the Award as a reward for quality improvement efforts that they had been pursuing since

1985. Robert Bruno (1992), an executive with GTE Corporation and a 1993 winner, emphasized the same point by saying that the Award put a spotlight on a host of employees who had turned a company around and allowed those employees to enjoy the recognition they earned. Again, like Globe Metallurgical, GTE had been pursuing an improvement strategy for awhile. GTE's initial focus on quality was introduced company-wide in early 1982 with a strategy that included competitive benchmarking, employee involvement, and market sensitivity. To these people and others, the award is not perceived as the finish line of a 100-yard dash which is then followed by a lazy jog around the track while fans throw flowers and the winner blows kisses. A better analogy might be to view the Award as a marathoner's cup of cold water. The race is long, and the end isn't in sight. The water—the Award—is the well-deserved pause that refreshes.

Higher education doesn't have a bottom line like industry. It can't measure how well it is doing by a profit-and-loss statement or other conventional metrics. It should not be surprising, then, that such rankings as the *U.S. News and World Report* and *Money Guide* are so popular with the general population. Still, such rankings reflect an institution's reputation and the amount of resources it has available, not its performance. They reflect selective admissions standards and fundraising capabilities, not the hard work of developing and implementing a methodology for renewal and performance improvement. It follows that a college or university that spends a decade refining its vision, developing critical success factors, designing processes, and scrutinizing its measures to the point that it wins a Baldrige Award, would necessarily deserve recognition.

A Focus on Improvement

Bruno (1992) goes on to suggest, in his article, a second benefit the Award earned for GTE: "It focused us on 'winning' versus merely being this year's winner. It focused us—permanently, we hope—on continuous and aggressive quality improvement" (8). The case-in-point is made in a recent story about AT&T's Universal Card division. On October 14, 1994, the Department of Commerce announced that the division had won the Baldrige Award. Much of that day was spent exchanging enthusiastic high-fives. On October 15, Paul Kahn, Universal Card's chief, told his troops it was time to get serious—

General Motors and General Electric were elbowing into the marketplace. He issued a stern warning: The organization must continue improving its operations. In this view, the Award represents a moving goal. By showing everyone the gap between where the organization is now and where it needs to be, the idea of continuous improvement gets embedded in the culture.

Our culture operates with long stretches of passivity, punctuated by brief periods of frenzied activities such as program review and accreditation.

This aspect of the Award—a focus on continuous improvement—would seem to be particularly important to higher education. Our culture operates with long stretches of passivity, punctuated by brief periods of frenzied activities such as program review and accreditation. These activities separate the winners from the losers. There is a sense of finality to it all. Then, five or ten years later, the game is played again. Our culture lacks what the Baldrige Award values—not winners, but the constant self-scrutiny of systems and processes that enable an institution to reflect and grow. As a culture, we don't yet value this type of winning.

An Example to Others

As we have noted, the Award is intended to help improve quality and productivity by "recognizing the achievements of those companies that improve the quality of their goods and services and providing an example to others." It is this latter notion of "providing an example" that has unique importance to higher education and deserves an extended discussion.

Most of higher education's perceptions about quality are self-determined. We largely follow the dictum "We know it when we see it" based upon a craftsmen-like belief that excellence is a personal and professional responsibility. Much like a heart surgeon or other highly-skilled professional, a college professor is understood to be driven by an internal standard of excellence that is self-evident. Indeed, the intellectual basis for academic freedom is that scholars should be allowed to explore a broad range of ideas in their personal attempts to generate and disseminate knowledge. Such individuals—disciplinary specialists who have undergone years of education in their fields—need to exert total control over their own work to do this. Hence, professors decide the content of their courses and the faculty as a whole enjoys near-total authority over the curriculum.

As discussed in "Another Paradigm, Another Plan," such a self-indulgent perspective on excellence has a predictable outcome over the long haul (Mintzberg 1983). In Mintzberg's powerful analysis of professional bureaucracies—organizations like universities and hospitals that are highly specialized in the horizontal dimension—he suggests that it should come as no surprise that such organizations tend to be conservative bodies. With autonomy, individuals within these organizations continue to perfect their skills. As Mintzberg states, "Thus, the professional has the best of both worlds: he is attached to an organization, yet free to serve his clients in his own way, constrained only by the established standards of his profession" (646). This is fine as long as the environment remains stable. Unfortunately, those same characteristics of autonomy—self-determination and discretion—also contain the basis for major problems when change is required. Given that there is no control of the work aside from that by the profession itself, there is also no way to correct deficiencies that the professionals themselves choose to overlook. So, when such deficiencies do occur and nothing is done, those outside the profession see the problems as resulting from lack of control. And then, they do the obvious: they try to gain control by decree, direct supervision, standardization of work processes, and so on.

If we apply the algorithm described by Mintzberg to the scenario we find ourselves in—institutions and individuals that have historically been allowed to reach their own definitions about excellence, combined with runaway tuition, demographic shifts, and a loss in public confidence—the result is easily predicted: more control. External agencies and interests will attempt to exert greater and greater influence on internal affairs. Beginning in the 1980s with such publications as "To Strengthen Quality in Higher Education . . ." (National Commission on Higher Education Issues 1982) and continuing largely unabated through the 1992 amendments to the federal Higher Education Act and the National Policy Board's 1994 draft eligibility requirements and criteria for national accreditation standards, there has been increasingly strident calls for more accountability and external quality controls for American colleges and universities, especially public institutions. To paraphrase Peter Ewell's (1992) cogent observation, in the eyes of government officials, state-supported colleges have gone from being perceived as natural resources to be supported and nurtured, to public utilities to be regulated and exploited. The halcyon days of routine support—or perhaps benign neglect—by the governors, legislators, and bureaucrats who have always held the regulatory and financial purse strings of public institutions are over, and a new age marked by stricter and even punitive government oversight has begun.

Does the Baldrige Award provide a partial answer to this puzzle? Let's return to Mintzberg's hypothesis for a moment. He suggests that higher education and other professional bureaucracies are destined to encounter autonomy problems because of their inability or unwillingness to deal adequately with issues that are critical to external forces. It appears that part of our problem, as described in the previous section, is that we don't think about quality in a way that lends itself to being responsive to legitimate inquiries. We see quality as a function of our own self-regard—or, we know it when we see it. The Baldrige Award, however, is presented to organizations that have developed world-class systems that are capable of exceeding the requirements of the users of their products or services. This concept of excellence focuses on value-added contributions. Resources and reputation are not critical factors. What is critical to the Baldrige Award is a set of well-defined and well-designed processes that are capable of improving the performance of an organization along a set of measures that reflect the aims of the organization.

The Baldrige Award, then, appears to be a legitimate way to think about quality in the academy and a way that we can be more responsive to external concerns.

The Baldrige Award, then, appears to be a legitimate way to think about quality in the academy and a way that we can be more responsive to external concerns. Indeed, the Baldrige may represent a unique opportunity by which we can, according to Mintzberg, "correct deficiencies that the professionals themselves choose to overlook." The participants in Seymour's (1995) study mentioned earlier expressed a similar belief. In one section in which Baldrige-related opportunities were discussed, Seymour began by noting that offices of institutional research have been the greatest growth area in the last decade. He says:

> Some of the growth is called for; most of it is not. A significant portion of the new resources, unfortunately, has been devoted to answering questions that someone else is asking. It has been devoted to collecting data to satisfy external agencies' perceived

HIGH PERFORMING COLLEGES

need to force colleges and universities to be more responsive. This drive to make institutions of higher education more accountable is a simple reaction—if they won't do it themselves, we will do it for them. The result is "report cards," state mandated assessments, and numerous studies that seek to identify statistical outliers via methodologies that compare peer institutions.

In an earlier article that summarizes the major problems and opportunities that a Baldrige Award presents to the higher education community, Seymour (1994) states that most measures of "quality" used in higher education are worse than useless—they are misleading:

> The Baldrige could change all that. One only has to study the Baldrige Award Criteria Framework to see a different way to think about quality. Abstract and wispy words are replaced by a focus on developing discrete measures to track critical processes. Process outcomes are, in turn, expected to meet specific customer requirements. A Baldrige-type assessment in education would transform "quality" from a swirl of rhetoric devoid of meaning or the minimal expectations of accreditation to precise operational indices that link processes with outcomes. (26)

Considering, then, the environment within which higher education currently finds itself, and the characteristics of the Baldrige as a set of requirements that establishes the degree to which quality-producing systems are in place, how might the Baldrige Award best serve higher education? We believe the Award—as an award—will serve colleges and universities well by providing powerful examples of high performance. In a broader sense, the Baldrige Award will also address a series of needs:

1. The need for a fair, academically relevant definition—with appropriate criteria—for educational quality.
2. The need for agencies and constituencies outside the higher education community to establish credible and understandable external standards for higher education quality and quality improvement.
3. The need to involve all of higher education in internal constituencies—faculty, students, staff, administrators, trustees, and so on—in a cooperative quality-definition-and-improvement endeavor.

4. The need to circumvent, break through, redefine, or otherwise overcome the vested interests and internecine political conflicts that have prevented such internal and external cooperation in the past.

AN ASSESSMENT INSTRUMENT:
PURSUING IMPROVEMENT

Curt Reimann (1993), the Director of the Malcolm Baldrige National Quality Award Office, has said, "In creating the award criteria, our intention was to get people in all types of organizations involved in focusing on key quality requirements and in assessing themselves against tough standards. We feel that to succeed, the award must be much more than a contest" (15). Again, while Public Law 100-107 states that a national quality award would help improve quality and productivity by recognizing the achievements of exceptional organizations, it also goes on to state that another way that the Award can improve performance is by "establishing guidelines and criteria that can be used by business, industrial, governmental, and other organizations in evaluating their own quality improvement efforts."

This suggests that the notion of "winning" has two interpretations when it comes to the Baldrige: there is "winning the Baldrige" and there is "winning through the Baldrige." The former interpretation involves the conventional idea of reward and recognition; the latter interpretation suggests that the Baldrige self-assessment process is its own reward. The application guidelines provide an objective, externally-directed blueprint while the Criteria set high standards and are useful for generating actionable areas for improvement.

Many industry types—both Baldrige winners and non-applicants—have described the importance and nature of their Baldrige self-assessment efforts:

> Early on, there was a tendency to see this as a lay-on—something you do in addition to the important job you have—rather than a way to measure and improve. We've addressed that by focusing more on the units' plans to improve rather than their score on the assessment.
> —George Vorhauer, AT&T
> (George and Weimerskirsch 1994, 244)

We didn't win the award in 1988 but we did decide at that point to use the Baldrige Criteria on an annual basis to assess how well our company is pulling through its quality journey.
—Al Robbins, Eastman Chemical

(Kennan 1994, 68)

At the hundreds of speeches I have given on quality since 1988, the most common question asked by smaller business is, "Where do we begin?" The answer is clear: adopt the Baldrige Criteria. Assess your business against the criteria, determine where you need to improve, and set a plan into action to get you to where you want to be.
—Kenneth Leach, consultant and senior examiner MBNQA

("Does the Baldrige" 1992, 139)

To improve a system, you must first know what condition it is in and where improvements need to be made. The Baldrige provides a detailed snapshot of an organizational system. It enables companies like AT&T to and Eastman Chemical understand the condition of their system. Further, a feedback report delineates the gaps between the snapshot and the requirement—it identifies areas for improvement. It provides a road map to higher levels of performance.

The extension of the Baldrige Award into higher education comes at an interesting time. The "higher education assessment (HEA) movement"—that large but amorphous and slow trend toward defining or redefining educational goals, measuring how well colleges and universities attain those goals, and using assessment results to spur quality improvement—is more than twenty years old in this country. Yet, while a few pioneering institutions are into their second or third decade of HEA, the large majority of U.S. colleges and universities have only been making serious attempts at comprehensive quality assessment for four to eight years, and some still haven't begun to this day.

Still, the quantity of HEA efforts thus far is impressive. Based on results reported by the American Council on Education (ACE) and others over the past five years (El- Khawas 1990-95; Johnson et al. 1991), more than ninety percent of U.S. post secondary institutions are presently involved in HEA, which translates into over 3,000 colleges and universities, tens of thousands of higher educators, and millions of students. Not coincidentally, over the same period higher education assessment mandates have been promulgated by government agencies in more than eighty percent of the states, and all six regional accreditation associations now require that comprehensive assessment standards be met for institutional accreditation or reaffirmation. Clearly, a significant amount of higher education administrators' time and effort is being devoted to conducting and reporting assessment activities.

Clearly, a significant amount of higher education administrators' time and effort is being devoted to conducting and reporting assessment activities.

But what do we know about the effectiveness of these assessment efforts? How many institutions are devoting sufficient time, resources, and expertise to mount first-rate assessment programs? How valid are the sampling, measurement, and analysis techniques in use on most campuses? And most importantly, what evidence do we have that these major investments in assessment are producing significant and lasting improvements in the quality of education being received by our country's college students?

Based on our collective experiences in regional accreditation, assessment workshop/conference presentations, and institutional assessment consulting, as well as extended interaction with a broad range of colleagues, it is certainly safe to conclude that the quantity of HEA efforts far exceeds their quality. Across all types of institutions, regardless of size, location, mission, or resources, progress on implementing high quality, comprehensive assessment efforts that produce clear and substantial improvements in educational quality has been slow and sporadic, at best.

Some of higher education's greatest current assessment needs can be summarized as follows:

1. HEA efforts are too often fragmented and inconsistent. To increase both their quality and efficiency, colleges need a parsimonious and consensual organizational framework to help educators better conceptualize, design, implement and evaluate their assessment programs.

2. HEA efforts often suffer from uneven participation by faculty, staff, administrators, and/or students. To increase meaningful involvement by internal constituencies, HEA needs a more team-oriented approach that can provide a relevant common denominator to attract contributors from all quarters.

3. Thus far, the most successful HEA measures compare institutional performance to the institution's own standards of goal attainment, an "internal validity" paradigm which is a necessary but not sufficient condition for overall integrity and credibility. What's needed is a fair and relevant means of also determining "external validity"— i.e., some external standard of institutional quality other than the quick-and-dirty "apples to oranges" comparisons based on norm-referenced test scores which are so popular with some naive external mandators and educators today.

4. Similarly, most current HEA measures—whether intended for internal or external validity purposes—feature outcomes assessment, i.e., summative scores indicating the level of students' competencies at or near the end of their programs of study, as the educational product of that program. Again, this is good assessment practice as far as it goes, but it should go farther. What's needed is a package of process measures to complement the product results and provide a more diagnostic profile of educational program strengths and weaknesses that need attention.

5. Another related need is for assessment tools that lend themselves more clearly and directly to successful intervention efforts. Too often, educators get caught up—even lost—in the assessment process, and lose sight of the fact that assessment is not an end in itself, but merely a means to the all-important end of educational quality improvement.

6. Lastly, accountability—i.e., to inform and reassure external constituencies such as governmental agencies, the media, and the public that higher education is an efficient and conscientious steward of its funds and resources—is one of assessment's main purposes. Yet despite the aforementioned quantity of the HEA extant, there is little evidence to suggest a perception among external constituencies that we have become more responsive. In fact, many states have produced increasingly prescriptive and proscriptive mandates in recent years, particularly regarding "purse string" issues. Higher education, it would seem, requires assessment tools that not only work for internal quality improvement, but which have enough credibility among external business and governmental leaders to restore their trust.

Although we would be among the first to argue that educators already have available numerous methodologies and resources to do assessment well, there can be little doubt that the HEA movement could use an intellectual and strategic infusion. Perhaps the Baldrige with its continuous quality improvement (CQI) emphasis could serve that important purpose, not as an either/or choice to replace current assessment efforts, but rather as a complementary framework to make good current assessment practices work better, to help involve recalcitrant higher education constituents, and to increase the external credibility of HEA efforts.

More specifically, the Baldrige's success as an assessment tool in higher education may well rise or fall on its track record in the following key areas:

Its ability to involve key constituents, both internal and external, in the HEA/CQI process. If the Baldrige can appeal to—and increase the participation of—higher education administrators, non-academic program staff, faculty in business and professional disciplines, nontraditional students, employers, trustees, and regulators, in a synergistic team approach, this would substantially increase HEA/CQI's resources, and its ability to fulfill its purpose(s).

Its ability to complement HEA's student outcome/product orientation with a means of assessing curricular strategies/processes and administrative policies/procedures, as well. The best current student assessment measures can diagnose curricular strengths and weaknesses, and some can even suggest improvement strategies. But many educators have been slow to develop logical extensions of outcomes assessment (i.e., pre-enrollment and interim assessments, longitudinal studies, multiple-baseline designs, etc.), and thus too often end up with a mass of student assessment results that give no clear direction for curricular reform. Further, current outcomes-based assessment models have obvious applications to academic programs; but what about academic support, institutional support, administrative offices, and other auxiliary services that play important roles in a college or university's overall quality? Again, current outcomes-assessment models and methods can be extended to evaluate non-academic roles and functions, but for reasons both strategic and political, often aren't. The Baldrige, with its heavy process and organizational emphases, should be of benefit in both these important areas.

Its ability to "close the loops" begun by HEA, and to produce significant, measurable improvements in the quality of instructional and non-instructional programs, institutional planning and budgeting, and internal and external accountability. Even among the better assessment programs and institutions, "closing the loops"—i.e., following the assessment process through to its ends of quality improvement—has been a nagging problem in HEA. Many educators have gotten lost in the complexities of the phase of the HEA sequence, while others have found it difficult to apply their assessment results to meaningful curricular reform. The Baldrige as an assessment tool must be, above all else, a change agent. It must stimulate educators to experiment continually with innovative educational policies, procedures, and techniques, in the best dynamic spirit of CQI, and foster both internal and external incentives for increased educational effectiveness. This would appear to be the Baldrige's greatest potential strength, its natural complementary role with higher education assessment.

The Baldrige as an assessment tool must be, above all else, a change agent.

Its ability to provide meaningful, practical standards of "external validity" for HEA measures and enhance HEA's credibility and accountability to external constituencies. As was noted earlier, one of HEA's most vexing dilemmas has been the fact that while many assessment programs can find measures that provide satisfactory internal validity (i.e., relevant comparisons of educational strengths and weaknesses to institutional standards of quality), no similarly appropriate indicators of external validity (i.e., comparisons of educational strengths and weaknesses to peer institutions, or programs at the regional or national level, or other consensual objective standards) are in widespread use. Currently, institutions sensitive to the need for external validation of their assessment programs face a conundrum: a choice between two different but equally inappropriate alternatives. They can either try to ignore or fight external comparisons, which merely worsens their credibility with external regulators and critics and invites more prescriptive assessment mandates; or they can devote significant assessment efforts and resources to standardized norm-referenced tests and surveys which promise such regional and national standards, but which in fact only (a) exacerbate the "apples to oranges" invalidity problems of directly comparing institutions with dissimilar programs, goals, resources, and students and (b) provide results that are virtually useless for educational quality diagnosis and improvement. Thus, the present choice is to antagonize external constituents by not giving them what they want, or conversely, to waste scarce resources and give them what they think they want, knowing that the data serves accountability purposes to the detriment of improvement efforts.

Here, again, the Baldrige appears to offer great promise in its benchmarking methodologies, which have apparently solved similar external validity and accountability problems in business and industry. Once translated into higher educational standards and criteria (e.g., program-level comparisons to peer programs, leaders in the field, or discipline-established "model programs"), the Baldrige could go a long way toward resolving this major dilemma.

CONCLUSIONS

The extension of the Baldrige Quality Award to higher education is a bold enterprise with an uncertain future. This chapter has engaged in an even riskier endeavor in trying to evaluate the Baldrige's potential as an award and an assessment instrument while it is still in the pilot stage. From this admittedly limited and speculative perspective, we have tried to raise some of the more important issues on the subject, appraise their significance to the Baldrige's eventual success or failure in higher education, and make some recommendations for enhancing its impact in this most important arena.

Every potential advantage the Baldrige offers higher education comes with a barrier or impediment. Perhaps the biggest concern that we see with the Award function is not with its ability to recognize performance improvement systems in higher education; we believe that the Criteria and scoring system are fully capable of capturing "world class" educational work systems. Our reluctance involves the follow-up purpose—"to foster sharing of best practices information among U.S. organizations." We have a history of awards in higher education. One in particular comes to mind. For several years now, colleges and universities have been pushed and prodded to increase the quality of undergraduate education. The feeling is that too much time, energy, and resources are being devoted to research endeavors and graduate work. One of the ways that many institutions have responded to this well-intentioned critique is to establish teaching awards. The idea, we suppose, is that by recognizing and rewarding good teachers, institutions demonstrate their commitment to teaching.

Unfortunately, the process of developing improved teaching and learning usually begins and ends right there, with the awards presentation. There is no evidence we know of that shows that institutions with teaching awards have any better teaching (much less learning) than institutions without them. The reason for this is twofold: first, there is no reason to believe that an award, by itself, will inspire not-so-good teachers to become great teachers; and second, there is usually no methodology in place by which non-award-winning teachers can learn about best practices from award-winning teachers.

This same phenomenon may play out with the Baldrige Award in higher education. An institution may use the Baldrige Criteria as a self-assessment tool and go through a series of learning cycles. Its primary goal is to get better, much like a good teacher who is always looking for ways to improve. The institution wins the Award not because the Award was the goal, but because it reflects and recognizes the hard work of all members of the institution. The real promise of the Baldrige will be tested in the next step; that is, will there be a broad push by other institutions to understand the best practices of the Award winner, or will the winner's practices be dismissed as being unrelated to their own institutional practices?

The greatest concern involving the Baldrige as an assessment instrument involves its "sponsorship" by business and government. As was previously noted, American higher education has a strong tradition of independence, in both policy governance and curricular methods. Many American higher educators—rightly or wrongly—believe their institutions are already the envy of the world. Further, they see the past thirty years of governmental intervention in K-12 education as having been needless and naive external meddling which has clearly come to no good. They also see business and education as being essentially incongruous enterprises, with fundamentally different and sometimes conflicting goals, methods, and performance criteria. Thus, the mere suggestion that business and government can come in and tell higher education how to use TQM or CQI to improve its quality—regardless of its track record outside the academy—strikes many in the academy as not only sinisterly threatening, but absurd on its face. This anti-anything-from-business-and-government

The greatest concern involving the Baldrige as an assessment instrument involves its "sponsorship" by business and government.

attitude runs so deep and strong, it cannot be successfully combated by manipulating how quality principles and practices are "introduced" or "packaged," but only by demonstrating empirically that the highest ideals of higher education can be better achieved through a more systematic approach to continuous improvement.

Whether as an award or an assessment instrument, the Baldrige application process is a win-win situation. If an institution wins, the Award will confirm the wisdom of its efforts. It will also shed a much-needed spotlight on a set of best practices that other institutions can study. If an institution loses or just uses the Baldrige as an internal self-assessment tool, it still wins. The feedback report and the "areas for improvement" represent unique opportunities to reflect, to learn, and to recreate. In either case, as an award or assessment instrument, the Baldrige can be a powerful catalyst for positive change in higher education.

REFERENCES

Bennett, W. 1983. *A Nation at Risk: The Imperative for Educational Reform.* Washington, DC: GPO.

Bruno, R. J. 1992. The Evolution to Market-Driven Quality. *Journal of Business Strategy* (October): 15-20.

Does the Baldrige Award Really Work? 1992. *Harvard Business Review* (January/February): 126-46.

El-Khawas, E. 1990. *Campus Trends, 1990.* Washington, DC: American Council on Education.

———. 1995. *Campus Trends, 1995.* Washington, DC: American Council on Education.

Ewell, P. 1993. Pocketbooks, Politics, and Promises: Rethinking Assessment for the 1990s. In *South Carolina Higher Education Assessment (SCHEA) Network Xchange.* Rock Hill, SC: Winthrop University.

George, S. and A. Weimerskirsch. 1994. *Total Quality Management: Strategies and Techniques Proven at Today's Most Successful Companies.* New York: John Wiley & Sons.

Houston, P. 1990. Dubious Achievement? *Business Month* (July): 40-44.

Johnson, P., J. Prus, C. Andersen, and E. El-Khawas. 1991. *Assessing Assessment: An In-Depth Status Report on the Higher Education Assessment Movement in 1990.* Washington, DC: American Council on Education.

Keenan, W. 1994. What's Sales Got to Do With It? *Sales & Marketing Management* (March): 66-73.

Main, J. 1991. Is the Baldrige Overblown? *Fortune,* 1 July, 62-65.

Mintzberg, H. 1983. *Structure in Fives: Designing Effective Organizations.* Englewood Cliffs, NJ: Prentice-Hall.

Rayner, B. 1992. Trial-By-Fire Transformation: An Interview with Globe Metallurgical's Arden C. Sims. *Harvard Business Review* (May/June): 117-22.

Reimann, C. 1993. Establishing Quality Initiatives. In *Sustaining Total Quality,* edited by T. Brothers and E. Miranda, 15-16. New York: Conference Board.

Seymour, D. 1994. The Baldrige Cometh. *Change* (January/February): 16-27.

——. 1995. Piloting the Baldrige: Observations and Impressions from Nine Institutions. In *High Performing Colleges: Volume II—Case and Practice*, edited by D. Seymour, 282-320. Maryville, MO: Prescott Publishing.

Steeples, M. M. 1993. *The Corporate Guide to the Malcolm Baldrige National Quality Award.* Homewood, IL: Richard D. Irwin.

4
Baldrige Barriers

Daniel Seymour
and Satinder K. Dhiman

The Malcolm Baldrige National Quality Award (MBNQA) Education Pilot Criteria is clear concerning the program's strategy. It states that the Baldrige Award Program strategy consists of two parts: (1) conceptual and (2) institutional (US Dept of Commerce 1995). The conceptual part involves the creation of consensus criteria (discussed in detail in Part II of this volume—Performance Criteria) that project clear values, set high standards, focus on key requirements for organizational excellence, and create means for assessing progress relative to these requirements. The institutional part of the strategy involves the use of the Criteria as a basis for consistent communications within and among organizations.

This is not a modest strategy. Indeed, the strategy is both deep (clear values, key requirements) and broad (consensus criteria, communication within and among organizations). It represents a significant shift from higher education's disjointed approaches to institutional effectiveness, a shift that suggests a comprehensive framework that educational institutions of all types can look to for guidance and thoughtful reflection as they seek to improve their performance. Such a framework—with its two-part conceptual and institutional strategy—could be a tremendous opportunity for colleges and universities as they struggle to meet the expectations of an ever-more demanding set of consumers and a maelstrom of social, demographic, and economic forces. The situation is not unlike the one described by Peter Drucker in his classic book, *Managing in Turbulent Times* (1980)—"The one certainty about the times ahead, is that they will be turbulent times. And in turbulent times, the first task of management is to make sure of the institution's capacity for survival, to make sure of its structural strength and soundness, adaptability to sudden change, and the ability to avail itself of new opportunities" (1).

The Baldrige Criteria are just the type of new opportunity that, according to Drucker, could enhance colleges' and universities' capacity for survival in turbulent times. Unfortunately, while its conceptual and institutional strategy represents a bold departure from the current melange of improvement efforts, that very digression from the status quo is interpreted by many parts of the organizational corpus as an intrusion—something to be identified, neutralized, and dispatched. The reaction is predictable. After all, the Baldrige Criteria are not the product of a campus-based task force or foundation-funded joint commission. Its heritage is industrial; its framework suggests a standardized approach. And so begins a natural effort to reject what doesn't seem to fit quite right.

This chapter is concerned with those forces within institutions that push back against efforts to introduce a planned change—specifically, a Baldrige self-assessment. By enumerating and describing these forces it is hoped that advocates and skeptics will have a better understanding of the likely "flashpoints" and be better prepared to engage in a meaningful dialogue. In the first section we will review some of the general issues regarding the process of change in higher education institutions. The second section takes a specific look at a series of barriers that we refer to as "theoretical/cultural." These barriers represent powerful forces that, while mostly unstated in the day-to-day activities of a college or university, can, nonetheless, cause debilitating reactions that prove fatal to change efforts. Another set of barriers is the focus of the third section. These barriers are referred to as "operational/empirical" because they are made manifest in the daily work of an institution as it attempts to introduce an innovation.

Knowing the general disposition that higher education has to change, as well as specific barriers—both theoretical/cultural and operational/empirical—that could be anticipated in the process of introducing a Baldrige approach to self assessment, can only improve the chances that such an opportunity will succeed.

CHANGE IN HIGHER EDUCATION

Change is the altering of tradition and the modifying of patterned ways.

Change is the altering of tradition and the modifying of patterned ways. There are two basic types of change: one is referred to as "organizational adaptation," while the second is referred to as "organizational development," or "planned change." Organization adaptation involves modifications and alterations in the organization or its components in order to adjust to changes in the external environment. Its purpose is to restore equilibrium to an imbalanced situation. As Cameron (1984) points out in his work on organizational adaptation in higher education, while such a definition may imply an emphasis on reactivity, adaptation refers to a process, not an event, whereby changes are instituted in organizations. Such a process may well be proactive—or, in a sense, anticipatory adaptation. Nonetheless, according to Cameron (1984), "the emphasis is definitely on responding to some discontinuity or lack of fit that arises between the organization and its environment" (123). Cameron goes on to describe four different categories of approaches to organizational adaptation: population ecology, life cycle, strategic choice, and symbolic action.

While the organizational adaptation literature is devoted to theorizing about change processes, organizational development focuses on the process of actually creating change and is devoted to methods and techniques. Winstead (1982) suggests that planned change in higher education is built on a series of underlying propositions: (1) there is a need to create planning mechanisms for renewal and redirection, (2) there is a need for leadership within an institution to encourage such mechanisms, (3) renewal mechanisms should be based on valid knowledge and objective research, (4) renewal mechanisms should include an internal planning specialist to facilitate the change process, and (5) there should be a consciousness of the desired direction throughout the system, rather than isolated interventions.

Whether or not the focus is on changes motivated by the external environment as described by Cameron, or on changes motivated from within the environment as detailed in Winstead's work, complex organizations have a built-in bias to counteract any form of change. This resistance to change is nearly universal and has been the focus of many studies, articles, and books. In one review, Nordvall (1982) offers the following list of organizational features (distilled from four other authors) that make change difficult:

- Inertia—reliance on patterns of known behavior.
- Conformity to organizational norms.
- Desire to maintain coherence—avoidance of changes in one area that necessitate unwanted changes elsewhere in the system.
- Vested interests—resistance to ideas that threaten the prestige or economic livelihood of individuals.
- The sacrosanct—development beyond organizational norms of taboos and rituals that cannot be violated.
- Rejection of outsiders—avoidance of change that comes from external pressures or ideas.
- Recruitment of similar members—attraction by organizations of persons who agree with the organization's activities.
- Clinging to existing satisfaction—finding these satisfactions especially comfortable when compared with the fear of the unknown (6).

Many researchers and writers in higher education have discussed certain features of academic institutions that exacerbate this general tendency of organizations to resist change. For example, in the area of organizational structure, most studies (Blau and McKinley 1979; Hage and Aiken 1970) suggest that structural complexity (defined as the number of occupational specialties in an organization) impedes innovation. The basic organizational unit of most modern colleges and universities is the department—a collection of faculty members conducting research and teaching in a specialized discipline. In a review of structural impediments to innovation in higher education, Seymour (1988) notes that while increasing fragmentation of the disciplines may increase innovation within those disciplines, it is a formidable barrier to change when it comes to cross-disciplinary issues that relate to the basic mission of the institution. Some observers of higher education (Hefferlin 1969, 16; Nordvall 1982, 7) go so far as to state the case in explicit terms: academic institutions deliberately structure themselves in this way to resist change, especially precipitant change.

The values of an organization is another area that has been studied extensively. According to Duncan (1972) there are three different value dimensions that relate to an organization's change-making ability: 1) the perceived need for change, 2) the perceived openness to change, and 3) the perceived ability of the organization to implement change. Sikes, Schlesinger, and Seashore (1974) state that since the results of education are difficult to measure, it is hard to demonstrate the value of change. Further, Nordvall (1982) lists a series of research studies and articles to support his contention that the traditional academic reward system places little, if any, emphasis on innovation. In effect, in the same way that institutions of higher education are uniquely structured to discourage change efforts, our institutions also embrace a set of values that serve to validate the wisdom of the status quo.

Finally, Hage and Aiken (1967) state, "It could be argued that change occurs in organizations because the organization has a high proportion of individuals who are favorably oriented to social change" (513). This area—resistance to change by individuals—has a rich tradition in numerous disciplines. One of the most often-cited articles on this topic is by Watson (1972) in which he lists sources that contribute to stability in personality, including habit (responding in the accustomed way), homeostasis (reverting to complacency as a basic psychological characteristic), selective perception, and insecurity.

Again, higher education institutions may well involve an extreme illustration. In a large sample study of college and university administrators and business executives, Seymour (1987) confirmed the results of previous work on the risk-taking propensity among academic administrators. He found that experienced administrators (ten years or more) were significantly more adverse to risks than a matched sample of senior business executives. Further, in an article entitled "Institutional Resistance to Renewal," Jon Fuller (1985) restates a reality that we all know but oftentimes seem to forget, that "we must never underestimate the resistance and suspicion with which any appeal to a large cause will be greeted within the academy." He goes on to add, "Skepticism about large causes is at the very heart of the educational process" (88). This is not an indictment; it is a statement of reality. Since the time of Socrates, teachers have made a habit of forcing students to question the fundamental assumptions of what appears to be an appealing idea. As institutions, therefore, we attract and nurture individuals—both administrators and professors—who are skeptical by nature and risk-averse by practice.

While there is a great deal of evidence to suggest that colleges and universities are more resistant to change than other types of organizations, that does not mean that organizational adaptation and organizational development is absent from the campus scene. A trio of ASHE-ERIC volumes—*Instituting Enduring Innovations: Achieving Continuity of Change in Higher Education* (Curry 1992), *Meeting the Mandate: Renewing the College and Departmental Curriculum* (Toombs and Tierney 1991), and *Developing Academic Programs: The Climate for Innovation* (Seymour 1988)—have documented certain aspects of successful change initiatives.

Curry's volume looks at the University of Massachusetts/Amherst's and the University of Massachusetts/Boston's attempts to restructure their cultures—to become, in the true meaning of the word, multicultural. Her focus is on "institutionalization," the final part of a change process in which an innovation loses its specialness and becomes part of a routine behavior. According to Curry, institutionalization has several features: changes must show results so as to establish a causal relationship, and members of the organization must embrace the norms and values associated with the changes. She believes that this can happen in educational communities that are also learning organizations where self-study, reflection, and creative activity are valued. Toombs and Tierney are interested in curricular change. After acknowledging and exploring a series of organizational barriers to implementing curricular change, they detail a set of components—incentives, idea champions, and structure—that are linked to lasting innovation. Seymour also enumerates a set of impediments to change in his analysis of new program development processes in higher education. Like the others, however, he also recognizes and describes successful change strategies. His "practical prescriptions" include:

- Bring innovative people into the institution,
- Move innovative people around in the institution,
- Develop the means to look outward, . . . and so on.

Since the time of Socrates, teachers have made a habit of forcing students to question the fundamental assumptions of what appears to be an appealing idea.

If there is a bottom line to this initial discussion of change in higher education, it might be found in a single line in Nordvall's monograph. After a careful review of the forces that work against any reform efforts in higher education, he states—"these institutions must make special efforts to become open to new approaches" (Nordvall 1982, 7). In effect, one should never underestimate the amount of energy that goes into maintaining the steady state of colleges and universities. Their structures are designed to resist change, their values have evolved to work against perceived incursions by non-members, and their people are largely risk-averse. Colleges and universities are content with the idea that whatever change needs to take place should be driven by organizational development considerations, not by reactions to shifting environmental conditions. That is a reality that has served academe well for five centuries. And for those who think there is "a better way," whether it is developing multiculturalism, seeking curriculum reform, or advocating a new approach to improving performance, that simply means—as Nordvall suggests—that they will need to make "special efforts" to overcome the powerful forces of institutional inertia.

THEORETICAL/CULTURAL BARRIERS

As we saw in Chapter Two, the Malcolm Baldrige National Quality Award has been successful in industry. The new Education version poses similar opportunities for higher education: it can help improve institutional performance by providing an integrated, results-oriented set of key performance requirements; it can help facilitate the sharing of best practices within and among institutions; and, it can help foster the development of partnerships between higher education and schools, businesses, and other organizations. On the other hand, it requires only a cursory review of the 1995 MBNQA Education Pilot Criteria booklet to conclude that many individuals on a college campus would see the Criteria not as an opportunity, but as a threat. Others, while not directly threatened, may simply not be able to grasp the complexity of the Baldrige. The framework, the Criteria, the Items, and the scoring system could be overwhelming to the average campus administrator who has spent a decade operating within the narrow confines of a small box on the organizational chart. Still others may react, not with fear or with reticence, but with incredulity—*What does this have to do with me?*" In all of these situations, the responses are not necessarily those of the individuals. More than likely, it is the culture that is speaking.

Perhaps the most succinct way to think about culture is that of the social or normative glue that enables an organization to solve its problems. The shared meanings of a group allow it to develop commonly understood ways of conducting daily work. For better or worse, every organization has a culture—"how we do things around here"— and because culture is context-bound, every organization's culture is different (Seymour 1992, 144). It follows, then, that the ease or difficulty with which a new idea or innovation is adopted by an organization is a function of how well that idea fits into that organization's life. In his book *Why Innovation Fails*, Levine (1980) looks to the boundaries of organizations to determine how and when an innovation is ultimately adopted:

> Boundary expansion is the adoption of the innovation's . . . traits by the host, or more simply an acceptance by the host of some or all of the innovation's differences . . . . In boundary expansion, the convergence of organization innovation boundaries and conflict resolution [takes place] when the organization legitimizes some or all of the innovation's differences and agrees to live with or absorb those differences. Acceptance or absorption can involve establishing the innovation as an enclave or diffusing it throughout the organization. (14)

According to Levine, another mechanism is used by an organization's culture to reject an innovation:

> [Boundary contraction occurs] in such a manner as to exclude innovation differences. The innovation, which is then outside organizational boundaries, is viewed as illegitimate and labeled "deviant." The deviant label serves to define and highlight the organization's boundaries by singling out previously not accepted norms, values, and goals as now clearly inappropriate for the organization. Having identified the presence of a deviant subpart, the organization has two available sanctions . . . . The two sanctions of boundary contraction are resocialization or termination of the innovation. (15)

Perhaps the most succinct way to think about culture is that of the social or normative glue that enables an organization to solve its problems.

In effect, the separate boundaries of an innovation and an organization converge during institutionalization resulting in one of a series of possible organizational responses: diffusion, in which the innovation's characteristics are allowed to spread throughout the host institution; enclaving, in which the innovation assumes an isolated position within the organization; resocialization, in which the innovative unit is made to renounce its past deviance and institute the acceptable norms and practices; and termination, in which the innovation is eliminated.

Given what we know about change in higher education, as well the nature of cultures and their abilities to expand or contract in response to an innovation, the question to be asked is: What aspects of the social or normative glue are most likely to cause a contraction when the boundaries of the Baldrige Criteria and a college campus converge? A review of various literatures—higher education administration, organizational behavior, quality management, and Baldrige studies—yields three areas that are likely to incite boundary contraction: organizational identity, defining quality, and unit of analysis.

Organizational Identity

A person's construction of reality provides the filter or frame through which he or she interprets new information.

A person's construction of reality provides the filter or frame through which he or she interprets new information. One particularly powerful schematic filter is the set of beliefs members hold about his or her organization's identity. According to Albert and Whetten (1985), organizational identity is the set of constructs individuals use to describe what is central, distinctive, and enduring about their organization. As such, it has been shown to limit organizational actions, especially efforts to introduce change. Reger et al. (1994) state: "Because organizational identity is composed of beliefs about that which is enduring and is based on deeply ingrained and tacit assumptions, organizational identity is likely to provide an inertial barrier hindering planned organizational change" (569).

A college or university has an identity. Those people who work within its boundaries develop a set of shared meanings that define— in their own words and thoughts—the nature of the institution. That identity is made manifest in the stories people tell, the rituals they adhere to, the heroes they create and admire, and the decisions they make in their daily work lives. Some educators suggest that understanding organizational identity and consciously developing it is the key to renewal. Fuller (1985), for example, suggests that "academics should reclaim their heritage of ritual and ceremony, for it can contribute to the renewal of our institutions more powerfully than practices and terminology borrowed from sectors of society that for the moment seem more vigorous" (87). Others such as Tierney (1988) advocate improved methods for assessing organizational culture and beliefs so that administrators will be in a better position to change elements in the institutions that are at variance with the culture.

How does organizational identity influence the acceptance or rejection of the Baldrige Criteria in higher education? We believe the issue is made manifest at two levels: one is with the Baldrige as a whole, the other with specific values associated with the Baldrige. At the aggregate level, the greatest problem involves a sense of uniqueness that is associated with any organization that has a strong identity. As Reger et al. (1994) explain:

> One result of a strong organizational identity schema is that members believe their organization presents a unique domain. Members are likely to believe that a new program will not work in their organization because organizational identity provides an idiosyncratic cognitive frame. (971)

From the perspective of any particular college or university, individual members would view the Baldrige as a common framework involving a driver, a system, goals, and measures of progress. Indeed, at the macro level, the framework is identical for all educational institutions—Yale University, Clackamas Community College, Palm Desert Middle School, or Occidental College. While the Baldrige states that "a major practical benefit from using a common framework for all sectors of the economy is that it fosters cross-sector cooperation and sharing of best practices information" (US Dept of Commerce1995, 5), individual practitioners on individual campuses may not be so liberal with their boundaries. Lewis and Smith (1994), for example, are cautious on this point in their discussion of conditions that may hinder the use of "total quality" and continuous improvement efforts on a college campus. These authors opine that colleges and universities think of themselves as different from other social institutions and consider that they are (or should be) exempt from the assessment and evaluation criteria applied to other institutions. According to Lewis and Smith, "This makes it difficult to initiate self-analysis and to appreciate and respond to the views of individuals and groups outside the academy" (13).

This phenomenon is reflected in the results of Carpino's (1995) depth study of three institutions that used the Baldrige Criteria to further their quality improvement initiatives. Using a survey instrument and follow-up interviews he attempted to assess ten different aspects of quality, one of which involved "quality assurance procedures." The question was: "Does the college have a systematic approach for assuring the quality of its services and for continuously improving its offerings?" Only twenty-two percent of the overall respondents (seventeen percent of faculty members) felt that their college or university had a systematic approach for assuring the quality of services. More importantly, the interviews suggested that the idea of a systematic approach did not fare well with too many faculty members; for example—"I think there would be (resistance). If it involves university measurement of improvement in my classes . . . if it involves university involvement in the processes in my classes, that would be considered an intrusion" (93).

At a second, more reduced level, the Baldrige has been carefully constructed on a foundation of core values (enumerated in the appendix), ranging from "leadership-centered education" to "results orientation." To what degree do these core values parallel the organizational identity of any particular college or university? Seymour (1995a) conducted a study of nine institutions that provided pre-pilot case materials for the Malcolm Baldrige National Quality Award Office (this study is presented in full in *Volume II: Case and Practice*). Each of the institutions conducted a self-assessment using one or more Baldrige Criteria. Using a series of depth interviews, he explored a measure of "cultural congruence" by asking "How well do the core values fit with the culture of your institution?" The following values were deemed to have the greatest fit problems:

 • **Faculty staff participation and development**—The real difficulty seems to be that while we think we value employee participation and development, the fact is that much of what is entailed in this value does not fit the culture of our colleges and universities. As an example, several respondents pointed specifically to the reaction among faculty members to organized efforts to improve the practice of teaching. The mind-set was stated as: "Who are you to tell me what to do?" On the staff side, education and training is not seen to be part of an expectation: to grow and develop in your professional life. Consequently, most professional development is perceived as extra—something that you do in addition to your normal work. Interpreted as such, development is not perceived by the individual as an investment in them by the institution but as an added chore to be endured.

• **Fast response**—According to this Baldrige value, response time improvements often drive simultaneous improvements in organization, quality, and productivity. While the logic of this statement is undoubtedly true, the idea that doing things faster is something to be valued is foreign to higher education. Indeed, one interviewee began by saying, "Fast response is an alien concept." He then explained that "People here like to discuss things for a long time. And they honestly believe that a slower process will yield a higher quality outcome."

• **Continuous improvement**—This value states that the notion of continuous improvement must be embedded in the way the organization functions; in effect, there must be a culture that thrives on discontent and that operationalizes that discontent with regular cycles of planning, execution, and evaluation. This value represents a real "fit" problem for higher education because we have historically viewed quality in terms of events—program review, accreditation. One respondent said it well: "We go through the North Central accreditation process and say how great we are. That is not a reflective process; it is not going to help us get better, but that is how people think."

The notion of organizational identity, therefore, may represent a significant impediment for those who are interested in using the Baldrige approach for performance improvement. At a macro level, the Baldrige may invoke a general response, such as "What does this have to do with us?" Each member, believing that his or her institution is somehow unique from others, may simply dismiss the Baldrige as an extra-institutional oddity. At the micro level, values that are manifested in the Criteria and Items may not fit with campus-specific values. In either case, the response of an institution's members may well be that the Baldrige is an innovation that does not adequately fit their own identity.

The Baldrige may invoke a general response, such as "What does this have to do with us?"

Quality Defined

The nature of quality and excellence has been discussed, debated, and dissected by philosophers, artists, educators, writers, scientists, and business people. Hesiod, the Greek poet wrote that "Badness you can get easily, in quantity; the road is smooth, and it lies close by. But in front of excellence the immortal gods have put sweat, and long and steep is the way to it, and rough at first." The twentieth-century statistician, W. Edwards Deming (1993), had a much more utilitarian view: "What is quality? A product or service possesses quality if it helps somebody and enjoys a good sustainable market" (2). In between the immortal gods and the ephemeral marketplace there are dozens of definitions and interpretations of "quality."

Higher education comes at the issue of quality or excellence from several perspectives. One might be called "quality is excellence." This is, according to Garvin (1988), a transcendent notion of quality in which excellence is equated with superior craftsmanship. This definition closely parallels the historical or traditional notion of quality as described by Tuchman (1980)—"Quality is achieving or reaching for the highest standard as against being satisfied with the sloppy or fraudulent" (38). Such innate excellence—derived from the close association between producer and the product—is still sacred to many of today's professionals, including doctors and professors. The quest for quality is a personal, intimate struggle against compromise with the second-rate. While such a perspective cannot be reduced to measurement or external validation, colleges and universities do use an unstated proxy measure—average class size. In effect, an institution that hires great professors (who have an innate desire to pursue the highest form of their craft), and then puts them in close proximity to a small group of students, is sure to produce excellent results.

Colleges and universities use other definitions of quality, too. Accreditation and program reviews (and other traditional peer review evaluations) reflect a quality of conformance perspective that measures the degree to which a specific school or program conforms to a design or specification. Indeed, Young (1983) define accreditation as "a status granted to an institution or a program within an institution that has been evaluated and found to meet or exceed stated criteria of educational quality" (443). While the criticisms against accreditation are many, it still has a long and rich tradition as a quality assurance instrument. As Bogue and Sanders (1992) point out in *The Evidence for Quality*, "Despite its imperfections, it remains the best known signal and perhaps the most effective instrument for nurturing and guaranteeing collegiate quality" (64).

Another generally accepted way in which colleges and universities define quality involves the use of various quality characteristics. Most of these characteristics involve input features (selectivity, endowment size), some are internal characteristics (number of Ph.D. programs, percentage of the faculty with Ph.D. degrees), and a few— such as starting salaries of graduates and percentage listed in *Who's Who*—focus on outcomes. While these measures of quality are readily used in the day-to-day interactions of faculty members and administrators, the codified, comprehensive versions of "quality by characteristic"— *U.S. News and World Report's America's Best Colleges* and *Money Guide's America's Best College Buys*—are viewed with disdain by most academics. For instance, after a thorough review of colleges' rankings and ratings, Bogue and Sanders (1992) state— "We find no significant evidence that reputational studies furnish a very meaningful tool for enhancing student choice. Nor do we find that reputational studies make a demonstrable contribution to the most fundamental goal of evaluation and quality assurance—improvement" (92-93).

While the criticisms against accreditation are many, it still has a long and rich tradition as a quality assurance instrument.

Still, the view persists that academics tend to fall back on this reputational model of excellence. A report by the Association of Governing Boards of Universities and Colleges (1992) is uncomplimentary in expressing this opinion: "Quality is measured more by the kinds of students excluded and turned down than by the kinds of students included and turned out . . . . Quality, in short, has become something to stoke academic egos instead of students' 'dreams'" (22).

Quality, then, is largely defined in higher education in three ways: "we know it when we see it," "we are accredited," and protestations to the contrary, "we have resources and we are selective."

What is the Baldrige's perspective on the pursuit of excellence? At its most fundamental level, the Baldrige is a set of requirements. Its seven Criteria and twenty-eight Items represent standards against which an institution can assess itself. As such, the Baldrige evaluates the degree to which an institution conforms to a set of specifications. This use of quality is similar to accreditation in principle, while be-

---

ing largely different in practice (see Corts chapter for an extended discussion of this issue). By this we mean that most accreditation guidelines are looking to enforce or meet minimum standards, while the Baldrige is intent on inspiring organizations to reach for world class performance. Another departure is that the Criteria used in accreditation guidelines often involve a static numeric (e.g., "The total number of full-time equivalent faculty who are either academically qualified or professionally qualified must constitute at least 90 percent of the minimum required full-time equivalent faculty") whereas the Baldrige is interested in the applicant's ability to detail an underlying process (e.g., "Describe how new and/or modified educational offerings are designed and introduced") and a corresponding set of results (e.g., "Summarize results of improvement in student performance using key measures and/or indicators of such performance").

It should be noted that at least one accrediting body, the American Assembly of Collegiate Schools of Business (AACSB) has made a move to incorporate both approaches to excellence. In the preamble to its recently revised accreditation standards, AACSB states that its "standards set demanding but realistic thresholds, challenge schools to pursue continuous improvement, and provide guidance for improvement in educational programs."

A second—and potentially more problematic—way in which the Baldrige diverges from the academy's perspective on excellence involves the issue of transcendent quality mentioned earlier. The question, "Who defines educational quality at this institution?" would be answered "The faculty" at most colleges or universities in this country. Much of what faculty members do and how they learned to do it supports this transcendent notion of quality on a college campus. For example, we are highly specialized having spent years in training and indoctrination; we rely on credentialing and the notion of a "terminal degree" as a membership requirement; and, we are allowed exclusive control over our work through traditions known as "tenure" and "academic freedom." Everything in the socialization of a professor and most things in the operational aspects of a college or university reinforce the belief that excellence is an innate disposition, born in a graduate school and bred through years of intellectual inquiry.

The Baldrige takes a much more egalitarian point of view. It suggests that the quality of a service is best judged by the user of that service, not by the producer. The user of the service, the customer, may be the student or it may be one or more of many other stakeholders such as employers, other schools, or even another professor. The pilot Criteria states: "The concept of quality used in the Education Pilot Criteria is student- and stakeholder-driven quality. It refers to all program and service characteristics that contribute value to students and stakeholders and that influence satisfaction and preference" (US Dept of Commerce 1995, 36). The strength of this conviction is evident in the fact that Criterion 7.0–Student Focus and Student and Stakeholder Satisfaction is allocated 230 points out of 1,000 total points (Shulman and Houser's chapter explores the nature of this criterion in detail). While this perspective has some de facto sympathy in the academy—especially among those who believe in the principles of student and program assessment as articulated by Astin (1991) and his "talent development" concept of educational quality—there is, nonetheless, a strong disquietude among many in higher education with the notion that someone other than themselves should be making quality judgments and setting quality standards.

Both Carpino (1995) and Seymour (1995) support the contention that academics struggle with customer focus. Carpino asked, "To what extent are the needs and perceptions of constituent groups assessed and used as critical information in planning and developing administrative services and academic offerings?" Only 39 percent of the faculty members in the survey felt that the needs and perceptions of constituent groups were assessed and used. "A lot of us feel the idea of talking about students as customers is a big turn-off," is how one assistant professor responded in the interviews (80). A full professor, speaking for his colleagues, said—"They (the faculty) don't see students as customers." He goes on to explain, "They feel they already are doing a quality job, delivering a quality product, and they are constantly improving themselves, changing their courses, introducing new books, testing methods and different visual aids, and they feel they don't have to prove that to anyone" (73).

The same attitude emerged from the interviews that Seymour (1995a) conducted. For example:

A lot of us feel the idea of talking about students as customers is a big turn-off.

"It [a customer-driven approach] certainly was a problem with professors," is how one respondent put it. She went on to add: "It was a terrible battle. The connotation of 'those we serve' is what's important and what is so difficult. Our faculty did not see themselves that way. They were dispensers of wisdom." A similar sentiment was expressed by another respondent when he was asked to explain why there was resistance . . . and the idea behind it. He said, "The notion is that these young people don't really know what they want, can't know what they want, so how can they tell us? By saying they are 'customers' puts them in charge" (See Seymour, "Piloting the Baldrige: Observations and Impressions from Nine Institutions" in *Vol. II—Case and Practice.*)

The concept of customer-driven quality has proven to be a remarkably powerful device in industry for focusing the attention and efforts of disparate parts of a firm on a common aim. The Baldrige Criteria for Education assumes that the same approach holds true for colleges and universities; indeed, Student Focus and Student and Stakeholder Satisfaction (7.0) is the goal of the system. Such a perspective—one that suggests that the user of a service rather than the provider defines quality—will probably cause the boundaries of most colleges and universities to contract initially. It is an innovative idea that many may find to be illegitimate and deviant.

Unit of Analysis

Mintzberg's (1983) concept of a professional bureaucracy has been described in several earlier chapters. He suggests that some organizations—universities, hospitals, school systems, public accounting firms, and craft production firms—can be bureaucratic without being centralized. Their operating work is stable, leading to predetermined or predictable—in effect, standardized—behavior. But it is also complex, and so must be controlled directly by the operators who perform the work. Control over the work means that the professional works relatively independently from his or her colleagues, but closely with those whom they serve: doctors with patients, professors with students. In effect, the work is highly specialized in the horizontal dimension. Mintzberg goes on to describe a pigeonholing process that enables the "professional bureaucracy" to decouple its various operating tasks and assign them to individual, relatively autonomous professionals. It follows that these professionals can then focus on perfecting their skills rather than giving a great deal of attention to coordinating their work with peers.

A parallel line of inquiry has been pursued in higher education. Weick (1976), Cameron (1984), and others have used the term "loosely-coupled" systems to extend the discussion of how colleges and universities build and maintain categories or pigeonholes. According to Cameron (1984), "A loosely coupled system is one where connections among elements are weak, indirect, occasional, negligible, or discontinuous. Diffusion from one part of the organization to another occurs unevenly, sporadically, and unpredictably, if it occurs at all" (137).

While there are a number of positive benefits associated with professional bureaucracies or loosely coupled systems—the most important of which is the autonomy that allows professionals to perfect their skills, free of interference—there is evidence to suggest that significant costs are generated as well. For example, Massy, Wilger, and Colbeck (1994) conducted some 300 interviews, primarily with faculty members, at twenty colleges and universities. Their initial results indicate that three key features of academic departments constrain faculty in their ability to work together on teaching. According to the researchers, the most important pattern identified is a strong element of atomization and isolation among faculty. Moreover, they identified five major factors behind this pattern: autonomy, specialization, civility, generational splits, and personal politics.

Seymour (1992) noted the same problem when he discussed the results of a study by the Carnegie Foundation for the Advancement of Teaching. In the study—*The Condition of the Professoriate: Attitudes and Trends* (1989)—nearly two out of three professors felt their field of study was more important to them than their institution, only one in five felt they had significant opportunities to influence the policies of their institutions, and while almost ninety percent often participated in departmental meetings, only one-third exercised the same level of participation in campus-wide meetings. Seymour's conclusion: "These numbers should be downright frightening. A culture of quality? Shared meanings? Improving processes? A distinc-

---

tive vision? All of these things become virtually impossible goals to achieve in such a fragmented, isolated environment" (162).

All of these characterizations—"pigeonholes," "loosely coupled systems," "atomization," and "fragmentation"—that reflect institutions of higher education, stand in stark contrast to the approach being taken by many in organizational development. Colleges and universities have largely maintained their devotion to the primacy of the disciplines and to the department or division as the primary unit of analysis. It is a culture that is balkanized, sliced and diced into separate functions with rigid boundaries.

An opposing perspective, one that focuses on the whole rather than the parts, has been advocated by Ackoff, Forrester, Senge, and others. This "systems approach" suggests that there are structures that underlie the interrelationships among key components of an organization. These structures are often invisible; nonetheless, the manner in which the individual parts interact with each other determine how the system—the collection of parts—functions. Senge (1990) says that such systems thinking is a "discipline for seeing wholes." He goes on to add: "It is a framework for seeing interrelationships rather than things, for seeing patterns of change rather than static 'snapshots'" (68).

This "systems approach" suggests that there are structures that underlie the interrelationships among key components of an organization.

This same systems perspective is deeply embedded in the Baldrige philosophy and evaluation methodology. For example, the Education Criteria Framework (see appendix) has four basic elements: driver, system, measures of progress, and goal. The driver provides system leadership (1.0). The system comprises a set of well-defined and well-designed processes (2.0, 3.0, 4.0, 5.0) for improving institutional performance, while the goal (7.0) is the basic aim of the system, and the measures of progress (6.0) provide a results-oriented basis for establishing how well the system is doing relative to its goal.

The Framework, therefore, constitutes the structure, and the arrows that criss-cross the Framework show the interrelationships between components (Criteria). At the Item level, interdependencies are evident as well. For example, there is necessarily a strong relationship between Item 2.1 (Management of Information and Data) and 7.5 (Student and Stakeholder Satisfaction and Results). In order to be able to show current levels and trends in key indicators of stakeholder satisfaction, the institution would need to demonstrate how it evaluates and improves the selection, analysis, and integration of information and data. One would also expect, for example, that 3.1 (Strategy Development) and 3.2 (Strategy Deployment) would link with 5.1 (Education Design); that is, the planning process that developed a set of critical success factors would be deployed throughout the institution in such a way that they would necessarily reveal themselves in educational program design. Beyond these illustrations, many other inter-Item linkages exist as well. In effect, it is the network of these subprocesses that must work together for the aim of the institution.

The final way in which a systems perspective is made manifest in the Baldrige Criteria is in the scoring. There are three evaluation dimensions used: (1) approach; (2) deployment; and (3) results. (The three are described in detail in the appendix to *Volume II: Case and Practice*). "Deployment" addresses how broadly or narrowly the approach—or how the institution addresses the Item requirements—is applied. Major gaps in deployment act to inhibit progress in achieving the primary purposes of Items and, consequently, result in low scores. In contrast, when an approach is fully deployed without significant gaps in any areas or units, the system is seen to be well integrated and generally receives a higher score.

Colleges and universities, then, tend to pay attention to the actions of parts; the Baldrige and a systems approach pay attention to the interactions of those parts. It is a puzzle that has provoked both comments and inquiries. For example, Fuller (1985) states in "Institutional Resistance to Renewal" that the artificial aspects of disciplinary divisions is one of the causes of the troubles that now afflict academic institutions, yet the disciplines in their current form are also a primary source of strength and stability for institutions and for the academic profession. So, while a focus on the "parts" has proved to be a powerful organizational concept in higher education, according to Fuller, "Calls for institutional renewal, for a new start, for an exciting approach, for moving people out of old routines, will almost certainly involve an attack on the primacy of the disciplines" (88).

Lewis and Smith (1994) zero in on "intensive divisionalization" as a significant impediment to institutional renewal through total quality management. Divisionalization, say Lewis and Smith, encourages identification with subdivisions rather than the total institution, whereas total quality emphasizes interdepartmental, interdisciplinary, and even system-wide collaboration on problems and projects.

Finally, the issue of decentralization and loosely-coupled systems emerged from Seymour's (1995a) interviews of individuals who were directly involved in Baldrige pilot efforts on their campuses. After discussing the problems of exercising transformational leadership skills in a decentralized environment and developing partnerships in a barrier-rich culture, he quotes one of the study participants:

> We don't think in cross-linkages. We can think collegially when working on a task force. But in an on-going way, in the cross-over and sharing of information, that's tough. A variable or function that cuts across units is a problem. There are few rewards in an academic culture devoted to collectively improving those processes. (See Seymour, *Vol. II—Case and Practice.*)

Everything about the Baldrige speaks to the whole, to the forest, to the interconnectedness that gives living systems their unique character.

The unit of analysis, therefore, represents a significant barrier—both organizational and cultural—to the implementation of a Baldrige self-assessment in higher education. Everything about the Baldrige speaks to the whole, to the forest, to the interconnectedness that gives living systems their unique character. College inhabitants are largely tree people. They tend to narrow their vision and operate as if the parts are unrelated. The analog of a forest's eco-system, with largely invisible yet complex and powerful linkages, describes well the philosophy of quality management, systems thinking, and the Baldrige approach to performance improvement. It does not describe a college campus.

Together, organizational identity, quality definition, and unit of analysis are strong, broad-sweeping issues. Their ability to generate boundary contraction, as described by Levine earlier, will be a function of the weight that they carry at any particular institution and the disparity between the specific cultures of individual colleges and universities and the philosophy and approach of a Baldrige assessment. In general, however, figure 1 suggests that all institutions of higher education necessarily face some barrier problems with the Baldrige because of the perspective or focus that each takes when it comes to organizational identity, quality definition, and unit of analysis.

Fig. 1. Theoretical/Cultural Barriers

	Higher Education	*Baldrige Assessment*
Organizational identity	Specialness	Commonness
Quality definition	Self-judged	Other-judged
Unit of analysis	Parts	Wholes

The Baldrige provides a common set of requirements by which an entire institution or whole unit can be assessed against a definition of quality that is driven by the user of the service, not the provider. It is a robust system. While it does not prescribe any specific tools, techniques, or technologies, it is, nonetheless, a road map to assist institutions on a journey of continuous improvement. The conundrum is that while the Baldrige emphasizes common requirements, colleges and universities see themselves as unique domains; while the Baldrige emphasizes a system of connections, colleges and universities see themselves as a collection of independently owned and operated disconnections; and, while the Baldrige is passionate about the primacy of the customer (students and stakeholders are the final arbiters of quality), colleges and university are equally passionate about the primacy of its professionals to create their own innate excellence.

OPERATIONAL/EMPIRICAL BARRIERS

The theoretical/cultural barriers tend to be those that emerge from the question, "Why should we consider doing this?" If barriers such as organizational identity, quality definition, and unit of analysis can be overcome, there is still a second barricade protecting the institution from external incursions and the difficulties associated with boundary expansion. This second ring is a natural reaction to a second question, "How do we go about doing this?" In effect, even if an institution provides its members with a satisfactory answer to the "Why?" question, it still faces the very practical, and very daunting, "How?" question.

How do you assess yourself with a management-by-fact system when you historically operate in a management-by-opinion system?

The mind, behavioral scientists know, searches for evidence to confirm its beliefs and deny the validity or existence of contrary evidence. The best antidote to these distortions is management-by-fact. Indeed, few things do more to keep an organization on track than measuring the right variables and providing people regular feedback on those variables (Brown, Hitchcock, and Willard 1994, 84). The Baldrige Pilot Criteria embrace this notion by making "management-by-fact" one of its core values: "A strong focus on student learning requires a comprehensive and integrated fact-based system—one that includes input data, environmental data, and performance data" (4). Moreover, one of the seven Criteria (2.0: Information and Analysis) examines the management and effective use of data and information to support overall mission-related performance excellence. (See chapter six for an extended discussion of this Criterion.)

There is a general, well-established perception that much of what we do in higher education is not really measurable.

The operational barrier to overcome in higher education is not a lack of data, it is rather a lack of the right data and the actual use of that data to reduce uncertainty in decision making. In *Academic Strategy*, Keller (1983) describes colleges and universities as "backward" in their ability to gather useful information about themselves. In some areas, according to Keller, schools have plenty of information: space utilization, facility and equipment use and needs, patronage of the library, the book store, the student center, and the like. Information about costs and the flows of dollars are also readily available. But, "As for information about students, it is both superb and astonishingly meager," says Keller. "What is superb are the data on characteristics, abilities at entry, rates of dropout, financial help, and the like. What is meager is the information in two areas. One is market research and analysis of students . . . the other area is that of student outcomes" (132). A dozen years later, the situation may well be even more extreme. External agencies have increased their demand for accountability data and offices of institutional research have responded to the never-ending demand for reports and studies. Still, there is a general, well-established perception that much of what we do in higher education is not really measurable. Such a perception, especially as

HIGH PERFORMING COLLEGES

it relates to students, collides with various aspects of the Baldrige; for example, 6.1: Student Performance Results—"Summarize results of improvement in student performance using key measures and/or indicators of such performance" (26).

Then there is the actual use of information. Chris Argyris, Harvard psychologist, has spent a lifetime studying how we learn. He contends that people engage in defensive reasoning in order to screen out criticism. Highly-skilled professionals, according to Argyris (1991), become especially good at avoiding information that could lead to learning, something he refers to as "skilled incompetence." In their seminal study of Baldrige Criteria, Seymour and Collett (1991) confirmed this information avoidance phenomenon: "The person who has been a dean for a decade thinks that he or she does not need data because they have been practicing the art and science of 'deaning.' One respondent described the problem at her institution as follows: 'Our institution has quite a few high ranking individuals whose experience, intuition, and appeals to traditional values sometimes outweigh or obscure existing data'" (18).

Again, colleges and universities have plenty of data. What they don't have—and what the Baldrige requires them to have—is a thirst for data that can be used to assess how well the institution is doing on a set of critical success factors, especially how much learning is taking place.

How are people supposed to endure the discomfort of planned change when there is no sense of urgency in their academic community?

The crucial driver of change is the organization's receptivity to it. An organization that is populated by a critical mass of individuals who are willing to change, faced with a situation that requires change, will be able to respond accordingly. The key to successful change is felt need. The logic is straightforward: change is stressful, so if there is no pressing need to alter the status quo, individuals and institutions will avoid doing so.

The Baldrige, as a self-assessment instrument, is a major innovation. It requires a paradigm shift in thinking across a number of different dimensions already discussed—for example, How do we define quality? How do we measure success? Many of the practices such as application writing and using feedback (covered in *Volume II—Case and Practice*) are time intensive. The situation is akin to that reported by Marchese (1991). After visiting his first quality-related conference, he wrote: "I wondered out loud . . . why all firms hadn't given themselves over totally to the concept. 'They haven't,' an executive from McDonnell Douglas told me, 'because many companies haven't felt as hard-pressed as Ford and Motorola did ten years ago. Firms claim to be into TQM, but their implementation is spotty. It's too great a change to make without a big need at your backside'" (4).

We find no sympathy among leaders or the public for higher education's problems.

Is there a "big need" at the backside of most colleges and universities? Well, the crisis rhetoric is not lacking. Article after article, report after report, have trumpeted the need to begin anew, to look toward new and different ways of conducting the business of education. The Wingspread Report, *An American Imperative: Higher Expectations for Higher Education* (1993), is indicative. It begins: "A disturbing and dangerous mismatch exists between what American society needs of higher education and what it's receiving" (1). More recently, a national poll that studied the attitudes of the general public and opinion leaders on higher education issues concluded—"We find no sympathy among leaders or the public for higher education's problems" and that "Higher education appears to be standing on increasingly shaky ground" (Wadsworth 1995, 16-17).

But what about the average administrator or faculty member on the average campus? Do they feel this "big need" at their backside? A cursory review of the *Chronicle of Higher Education* suggests that administrators are concerned with money (budget cuts, tuition increases, and fund-raising), enrollment (keeping the classrooms full—but not too full), and facilities and technology (the problems of deferred maintenance and keeping up with the costs associated with computer technology). Indeed, scratching below the surface of the crisis rhetoric and the various calls for restructuring, one can find few actual examples of true innovation. Most efforts are reactive; most underlying assumptions are not being challenged. Indeed, the unstated belief is that if we can hunker down long enough—at least until the budget picture improves—things will likely get back to normal.

How do we keep the leadership of the institution repeatedly and consistently focused on quality issues, and not let them get distracted?

This question is taken directly from a study (Seymour 1993) of the hurdles that inhibit the implementation of quality management practices in higher education. The "leadership" issue ranked high on a "top ten" list, based upon the fact that three out of four respondents believed that leaders were easily distracted. Many people blamed the problem on budgetary issues. Others just saw it as the state of affairs: the leadership operates in a reactive mode. Other higher education observers have reached the same conclusion. Winter (1991), in his discussion of barriers to total quality management in colleges and universities, points a finger directly at presidents: "Many presidents devote their time and energies not to their campuses but to image-building efforts that will help obtain legislative, community, and funding support. They often leave leadership and policy-making authority to other administrators, who may view the organization more narrowly" (59). Lewis and Smith (1994) conclude that one of the impediments to implementing quality management is "fragmented leadership" with the president focusing on extra-institutional issues and abdicating a leadership role within the institution.

Even if the leadership is actively involved, there is a second issue—the degree to which the leaderships' rhetoric matches their actions. Seymour and Collett (1991) noted it under a heading, "More Than Lip Service," when studying the major frustrations involved in implementing quality. They suggest that practitioners are very tuned-in to signals from above and grow cynical quickly when what leaders "say" does not match what they "do."

Carpino (1995) notes the same phenomenon in his study when he quotes a faculty member—"It becomes an absolute necessity for senior administrators to be consistent. Every time there is an inconsistency (when senior administration violates one of the principles of quality), it gets filtered down (to faculty) and blown out of proportion." Another faculty member said: "You must always walk the talk because people are looking for examples of where the senior administrators are going to slip up" (78-79).

Finally, one of the lessons that Seymour (1995b) describes for improving quality and productivity in higher education is—"Followers, not leaders, are the best judges of hypocrisy." (89) He suggests that the changes that leaders expect from the individuals in an institution must be reflected in their own actions. Without such a personal commitment, leaders have no real ability to influence the direction in which their institution is headed.

There are two reasons why all of this is key to the Baldrige: commitment and performance. Conducting a Baldrige self-assessment is not easy. It requires a significant commitment of time, energy, and resources in order to detail an institution's strengths and areas for improvement. Implementing a learning cycle in which such strengths are integrated and fully deployed, and in which areas for improvement are analyzed and acted upon, requires institution-wide commitment. Why would anyone bother if the president and other senior leaders are not walking the talk? Second, the Baldrige framework is unequivocal in its view that leadership is the driver of the system. A quick look through the Leadership criterion (1.0) (see appendix) as well as the personal testimony of a college president (see chapter 5), strongly support the idea that high-scoring institutions have highly-involved leaders.

How is an institution supposed to conduct a Baldrige self-assessment when it has barely enough time to respond to current concerns?

It follows that a rigorous self-assessment will generate a lengthy list of needed improvements.

Organizations that use the Baldrige Criteria for self-assessment and improvement look at themselves, compare themselves to the Criteria, and then identify areas that need improvement. This learning cycle necessarily suggests that some initial training or knowledge development regarding the Baldrige must take place—administrators, faculty members, and staff must understand the framework, the core values and concepts, the Criteria, the Items, the areas to address, and the scoring system. Further, because the Baldrige is comprehensive and data-driven, the self-assessment stage can involve a significant number of people over a considerable period of time. And finally, institutions that score in the more moderate ranges (200—400) are just beginning to develop systematic approaches to improvement that are both well-integrated and well-deployed. It follows that a rigorous self-assessment will generate a lengthy list of needed improvements.

The point, of course, is that a self-assessment and improvement methodology is time consuming. Seymour and Collett (1991) noted this in their initial study of colleges and universities that were implementing quality management principles. Some of the survey respondents were quite articulate in speaking to their frustrations:

> The amount of time required to bring about transformation is enormous! We continue to fight fires as we struggle to recognize, let alone standardize, let alone improve our systems.
> The key frustration . . . is that for the process to be effective, it must be fairly comprehensive, touching many levels of the college. But to do so requires an expenditure of time and energy that places great demands on the employees. (26)

Several years later in a follow-up study with many of the same pioneering institutions, Seymour (1993) found that "time constraint" was the greatest hurdle the colleges and universities faced. Indeed, eighty-three percent of study participants said that "time" was either a major or primary hurdle they faced when attempting to introduce quality principles into their institutions.

While there are ways to reduce the amount of time required to conduct a Baldrige self-assessment, the unfortunate reality is that the Baldrige is competing against a broad and growing range of assessment efforts. As described by Seymour (1995a) in his study of institutions that conducted pilot Baldrige assessments:

> Our plate is full of assessment-type exercises, accountability reports, and learning opportunities. There is regional accreditation and specialized accreditation. There are state and local requests for data ranging from crime statistics to graduation rates. There are 'report cards' and ad hoc studies on such issues as faculty productivity and program duplication. (See Seymour, *Vol. II—Case and Practice.*)

Or as one respondent painfully noted—"People feel as though they are assessing themselves to death." The simple matter of time, therefore, is seen by many practitioners as a significant operational barrier, especially if you add a Baldrige self-assessment without taking anything else away.

How is it possible to engage in an institution-wide assessment effort when only a portion of the institution is actively engaged in a rigorous improvement methodology?

In 1992, the Health Care Advisory Board conducted a synthesis and analysis of the major research and case studies involving total quality management initiatives in the health care industry. One part of the report states that the biggest resistors are MDs and middle managers. Two reasons for MD resistance are given: (1) doctors believe TQM is just another hospital program that will take up their time and have little impact, and (2) they resent hospitals' intrusion on their turf and they believe they already offer high quality care, that there is no way to improve the "art" of patient care. Later on the report notes that hospitals are shying away from using TQM on issues that really matter (cost, MD retention, clinical quality), and are focusing instead on easier areas such as service quality and patient satisfaction. For much of higher education, it would be possible to take the Health Care Advisory Board report, substitute "college" for "hospital," "professor" for "doctor," and reach an identical conclusion—we are shying away from using quality principles on issues that really matter (time to degree, value-added learning), and are focusing instead on the easier areas of service quality and student satisfaction.

Substantial evidence to support this contention can be found in Seymour (1993) and Carpino (1995). Only thirty-seven percent of the faculty members Carpino surveyed expressed a favorable attitude toward the application of quality concepts in their institutions, compared to sixty-three percent of the administrators who had a favorable attitude. As one faculty member stated: "Overall on our campus, the staff and administration have bought into the quality concept much more easily than the teaching faculty" (77). Only four percent of the respondents in Seymour's survey felt the implementation of quality management on the academic side of the institution was "slight or no hurdle." As one respondent says, "This whole approach continues to be seen by many as something that may work for the janitorial and housing staffs, but the academic applications are limited—professors just don't buy it" (7). It should not be surprising, then, that most of the reported improvement efforts involve simplifying ad-

HIGH PERFORMING COLLEGES

ministrative processes, reducing the length of lines, or increasing various "customer" satisfaction measures.

The problem is that while the Baldrige does not dismiss the "easier areas," it also does not ignore the difficult areas. Beginning with the core values, the Baldrige focuses on key questions: What are the critical success factors for the institution? How do you measure your performance? How do you use performance measures to build in deep learning cycles? How do you continually improve your processes? At the heart of the Baldrige is educational program design (5.1) and delivery (5.2). These criteria require an institution to use specific design principles, to ensure appropriate delivery of that design, to have an evaluation system that enables the institution to assess learning, to be able to track performance over time and compare performance with other institutions, and to ensure that the systems and processes that are in place to deliver teaching and learning are studied and improved.

How do you use performance measures to build in deep learning cycles?

Thinking back to the work cited by Levine earlier in the chapter, the culture of a given college or university undoubtedly sees the use of quality management principles as an innovations that challenges its boundaries. Some institutions and their members see the innovation as deviant and contracted accordingly. Others have expanded their boundaries, but as the health care scenario and the higher education research indicate, they also tend to establish the innovation as a business-related enclave—away from clinical care and academic programs—rather than diffuse it throughout the organization. The Baldrige knows no such separation. It is looking for systemic, integrated, and consistently applied approaches.

SUMMARY

One of the many continuous improvement tools used by practitioners is the force field diagram. It is a tool that can be used when trying to identify obstacles to reaching a goal, possible causes and solutions to a problem, or important opportunities. The typical exercise involves agreeing on a definition of the current situation, then identifying the goal. For example, a college or university might decide that its graduation rate is too low. After some thought, the administrators could set a goal—say, to achieve an eighty percent graduation rate within the next five years. The next step involves asking the question—"What things are driving us toward our goal?" Driving forces are things such as actions, skills, equipment, procedures, culture, people, and so on. The next question is—"What is restraining us from achieving our goal?" Restraining forces, like driving forces, come in all shapes, sizes, and colors. A force field diagram is a useful tool because it requires people to enumerate all the various restraining forces, then think through what needs to be done to eliminate them. After that, energies can be shifted to the driving forces.

This chapter has been, in effect, a type of force field analysis. The current situation is a given level of performance at a college or university—say, "x." The desired situation or goal is to improve performance—say, "2x"—by using the Baldrige Criteria to identify areas for improvement. We have identified two broad types of restraining forces that push back hard against us: theoretical/cultural and operational/empirical. The task of readers interested in pursuing a Baldrige self-assessment on their own campuses is to understand that their well-intentioned intervention is likely to call forth responses from the system (barriers) that will work to offset the benefits of the innovation—even such a well-intentioned and viable innovation as the Malcolm Baldrige National Quality Award for Education.

REFERENCES

Albert, S. and D. Whetten. 1985. Organizational Identity. In *Research in Organizational Behavior*, no. 14, edited by L. L. Cummings and B. M. Staw, 179-229. Greenwich, CT: JAI Press.

Argyris, C. 1991. Teaching Smart People How to Learn. *Harvard Business Review* 69 (May/June): 99-109.

Association of Governing Boards of Universities and Colleges. 1993. *Trustees and Troubled Times in Higher Education.* Washington, D.C.: Association of Governing Boards of Universities and Colleges.

Astin, A. W. 1991. *Assessment for Excellence.* Macmillan Series on Higher Education. New York: American Council on Education.

Blau, J. R. and W. McKinley. 1979. Ideas, Complexity, and Innovation. *Administrative Science Quarterly* 24 (June): 200-19.

Bogue, E. G. and R. L. Sanders. 1992. *The Evidence for Quality.* San Francisco: Jossey-Bass.

Brown, M. G., D. E. Hitchcock, and M. L. Willard. 1994. *Why TQM Fails: And What to Do About It.* New York: Richard D. Irwin.

Cameron, K. S. 1984. Organizational Adaptation and Higher Education. *Journal of Higher Education* 55(2): 122-44.

Carpino, P. 1995. Faculty Perceptions of Continuous Quality Improvement: A Study of Three Post-Secondary Institutions. Dissertation. The Union Institute, Cincinnati, OH.

Curry, B. K. 1992. *Instituting Enduring Innovation: Achieving Continuity of Change in Higher Education.* ASHE-ERIC Higher Education Report No. 7. Washington, D.C.: The George Washington University School of Education and Human Development.

Deming, W. E. 1993. *The New Economics.* Cambridge, MA: MIT Center for Advanced Engineering Study.

Drucker, P. F. 1980. *Managing in Turbulent Times.* New York: Harper and Row.

Duncan, Robert. 1972. Organizational Climate and Climate for Change in Three Police Departments: Some Preliminary Findings. *Urban Affairs Quarterly* 8(2): 205-45.

Fuller, J. Institutional Resistance to Renewal. In *Leadership and Institutional Renewal,* edited by Ralph M. Davis, 83-89. New Directions for Higher Education, no. 49. San Francisco: Jossey-Bass.

Garvin, D. A. 1988. *Managing Quality.* New York: The Free Press.

Hage, J. and M. Aiken. 1970. *Social Change in Complex Organizations.* New York: Random House.

Health Care Advisory Board. 1992. *TQM: The Second Generation.* New York: The Advisory Board Company.

Hefferlin, J. B. 1969. *Dynamics of Academic Reform.* San Francisco: Jossey-Bass.

Keller, G. 1983. *Academic Strategy.* Baltimore: Johns Hopkins University Press.

Levine, A. 1980. *Why Innovation Fails.* Albany: State University Press.

Lewis, R. G. and D. H. Smith. 1994. *Total Quality in Higher Education.* Delray Beach, FL: St. Lucie Press.

Massy, W. F., A. K. Wilger, and C. Colbeck. 1994. Overcoming "Hollowed" Collegiality. *Change* (July/August): 11-20.

Mintzberg, H. 1983. *Structure in Fives: Designing Effective Organizations.* Englewood Cliffs, NJ: Prentice Hall.

Nordvall, R. C. 1982. *The Process of Change in Higher Education Institutions.* ASHE-ERIC Higher Education Research Report No. 7. Washington, D.C.: American Association for Higher Education.

Reger, R., L. T. Gustafson, S. M. Demarie, and J. V. Mullane. 1994. Reframing the Organization: Why Implementing Total Quality Is Easier Said Than Done. *The Academy of Management Review* 19 (3): 565-84.

Seymour, D. T. 1996. Piloting the Baldrige: Observations and Impressions from Nine Institutions. In *High Performing Colleges: Volume II—Case and Practice*, edited by D. Seymour, 282-320. Maryville, MO: Prescott Publishing.

———. 1995. *Once Upon a Campus: Lessons for Improving Quality and Productivity in Higher Education.* Phoenix: American Council of Education and Oryx Press.

———. 1993. *Total Quality Management in Higher Education: Clearing the Hurdles.* Methuen, MA: GOAL/QPC.

———. 1992. *On Q: Causing Quality in Higher Education.* Phoenix: American Council on Education and Oryx Press.

———. 1988. *Developing Academic Programs: The Climate for Innovation.* ASHE-ERIC Higher Education Report No. 3. Washington, D.C.: Association for the Study of Higher Education.

———. 1987. Out on a Limb: Why Administrators Must Take Risks. *Educational Record* 68 (spring): 36-40.

Seymour, D. T. and Collett, C. 1991. *Total Quality Management in Higher Education: A Critical Assessment.* Methuen, MA: GOAL/QPC.

Sikes, W. W., L. E. Schlesinger, and C. N. Seashore. 1974. *Renewing Higher Education from Within.* San Francisco: Jossey-Bass.

Tierney, W. G. 1988. Organizational Culture in Higher Education. *Journal of Higher Education* 68 (January/February): 2-20.

Toombs, W. and W. Tierney. 1991. *Meeting the Mandate: Renewing the College and Departmental Curriculum.* ASHE-ERIC Higher Education Report No. 6. Washington, D.C.: George Washington University School of Education and Human Development.

Tuchman, B. W. 1980. The Decline of Quality. *New York Times Magazine,* 2 November, 38-41.

U. S. Department of Commerce, National Institutite of Standards and Technology. 1995. *Malcolm Baldrige National Quality Award: Education Pilot Criteria.* Washington, DC: GPO.

Wadsworth, D. 1995. The New Public Landscape: Where Higher Education Stands. *AAHE Bulletin* 59 *(*June): 14-17.

Watson, G. 1972. Meeting Resistance. In *Creating Social Change,* edited by G. Zaltman, P. Kotler, and I. Kaufman. New York: Holt, Rinehart & Winston.

Weick, K. E. 1976. Educational Organizations as Loosely Coupled Systems. *Administrative Science Quarterl*y 47(10): 1-19.

Winstead, P. C. 1982. Planned Change in Institutions of Higher Learning. In *Effective Planned Change Strategies,* edited by G. Melvin Hipps. New Directions for Institutional Research Series, no. 9. San Francisco: Jossey-Bass.

Winter, R. S. 1991. Overcoming Barriers to Total Quality Management in Colleges and Universities. In *Total Quality Management in Higher Education*, edited by L. A. Sherr and D. J. Teeter, 53-62. New Directions for Institutional Research, no. 71. San Francisco: Jossey-Bass.

Young, K., C. Chambers, H. Kells, and Associates. 1983. *Understanding Accreditation: Contemporary Perspectives on Issues and Practices in Evaluating Educational Quality.* San Francisco: Jossey-Bass.

Part Two: Performance Criteria

The chapters in this section relate specifically to the seven categories that form the core of the Malcolm Baldrige National Quality Award evaluation process. The authors of these chapters have played key roles in piloting self-assessment projects at their institutions. In each case, the chapter authors explore the concept of the category as it relates to the education and management literatures, then reflect on their own experiences in applying the category requirements to their institution's practices. The reader is advised to review the detailed description of each category and its accompanying Items located in the appendix of this volume—before reading the associated chapter in this section.

5
Leadership:
The Driver of the System

Linda M. Thor

> *General James Longstreet, in response to General Robert E. Lee's order to remain on Seminary Ridge as the troops moved forward—an attempt to keep from losing the South's best generals—said, "A General can't lead from the rear."*

Would it have made any difference if General Longstreet had been leading that charge? No one knows. But the sentiment regarding leadership in 1863 is especially important today, 132 years later, for leaders and organizations facing the challenges of a rapidly changing world. Leaders can't lead from the rear. Soldiers don't follow their leader's example if they always have to look backwards to see it. Neither do the faculty or staff on a college campus.

It follows, then, that leaders in colleges or universities who are seeking to use the Malcolm Baldrige National Quality Award standards as a framework for improving their ability to deliver higher education services, must not skip lightly through the Leadership Criterion of these standards. The Leadership Criterion cannot be assumed as a given, but rather must be critically reviewed as a basis for the rest of the Baldrige Criteria.

In fact, in a review of traits of corporate Baldrige Award winners, Schmidt and Finnegan (1992) make the leadership case very directly: "Management leadership and commitment are essential if an organization is to establish a solid foundation for the rest of the TQManagement strategy" (149). Although educational institutions often like to envision themselves as different from the corporate world, in many ways their foundations are the same. For example, a survey of higher education institutions by Seymour and Collett (1991) showed that of the seven Baldrige Criteria, 1.0 (Leadership) and 7.0 (Customer Service) were deemed "most important" by the respondents (17). Leadership, clear and precise leadership, is essential in any educational institution striving for quality.

In the Baldrige Criteria, both for the corporate world and the new Criteria for educational institutions, leadership is first—Items 1.0 to 1.3 (see appendix for a full description of the Leadership Category). The leadership criterion makes up a full nine percent of the total, or 90 scoring points—more than categories such as Information and Analysis, more than Strategic Planning. In fact, out of twenty-four individual Items listed under the seven Criteria, Item 1.1, Senior Executive Leadership, has a higher point value (forty-five points) than 67 percent of the other items. In other words, the framers of the Baldrige Criteria agree with General Longstreet—leadership cannot be carried out from afar.

Leadership, as defined by the Baldrige Criteria, requires "personal . . . involvement." The Baldrige Criteria also require a leadership system that promotes performance excellence and examines the "highest ranking official and those reporting directly to that official"— or senior executives. Then the Baldrige approach requires that the various Items are evaluated along one, or more, of the following dimensions:

(1) Approach—refers to how the applicant addresses the Item requirements; the method(s) used.

(2) Deployment—refers to the extent to which the applicant's approach is applied to all requirements of the Item.

(3) Results—refers to outcomes in achieving the purposes given in the Item.

The Leadership Criterion requires no results, no outcomes. Only "approach" and "deployment" are evaluated and scored. And although there may be no evaluated outcomes from such leadership, the methods used and the extent to which such leadership is pervasive throughout the system are the keys to this first section of the Baldrige Criteria.

NEW NAMES FOR NEW LEADERSHIP— CHANGING LEADERSHIP STYLES

The leadership approach rewarded in the Baldrige Criteria has been called many things by many authors. John Huey (1994) refers to it as "post-heroic leadership," and asserts that "ninety-five percent of American managers today say the right thing. Five percent actually do it" (42). Huey develops the theory that there is a significant difference between good management and good leadership. He cites Harvard Business School's John Kotter in defining management as being comprised of "activities that keep an organization running, and it tends to work well through hierarchy. Leadership involves getting things started and facilitating change" (44).

Huey states that companies can no longer be successful by just doing more of what they are already doing. As corporations flatten their structures, many tasks are pushed down to workers and lower management. The result, according to Huey, is that "Upper management—often to its surprise—suddenly faced real leadership issues" (44). He sees true leadership as being aggressive in its support of the Theory Y, or empowerment, approach. In post-heroic leadership, decentralization is a key, with decision making pushed to the lowest levels. But this type of leadership requires at least one other important trait—the art of listening. Further, when a leader listens, action must follow. In the post-heroic leadership style, the risk for a leader is that listening to employees may take the organization in a direction that was not planned or desired. Huey suggests:

In post-heroic leadership, decentralization is a key, with decision making pushed to the lowest levels.

> The time when a few rational managers could run everything with rational numbers . . . was . . . part of an era very different from the fast-paced, continually shifting present. Those who cling to the past are in danger of losing their way, while the pioneers who forge ahead are most likely to claim the future. (50)

Millard (1991) applies this view to educational institutions by emphasizing that no one educational institution can hope to change all of the problems facing education today. True leadership will begin the effort of change by overcoming the obstacles to change one at a time. In other words, leadership issues are changing, and resisting that change will only further exacerbate the tensions inherent in transforming both business and educational organizations.

Even the most resistant institutions, such as the Federal Government, see leadership as the most important factor in successful improvement efforts. In a study of the eight U.S. federal agencies that have won the Presidential Award for Quality or the Quality Improvement Prototype Award, top leaders shared a passionate commitment to their job, communicated and involved others effectively, and did not merely support the quality effort, "they owned it" (*Lessons Learned* 1994). This finding bolsters Margaret Wheatley's (1994) analysis of organizational leadership in which she states that leadership attributes—such as passionate commitment, effective communications, and personal involvement in quality efforts—are poised "to replace command-and-control leadership" (20). Chain-of-command organizational charts that control contacts within the organization are not part of the new leadership style emerging through quality efforts. Wheatley concludes that "leadership that relies on such characteristics as relationship building, trust, nurturance, intuition and letting go is the leadership of the future" (20). Indeed, if the bureaucracies of the Federal Government can accept and adjust to the change described by Wheatley, anyone can.

Lee and Zemke (1993) refer to this type of leader as "the servant leader." Taking its philosophical base from Quaker thought, the servant leader is a servant first, rather than a leader first who may be responding to "an innate drive to acquire power" (22). The servant leader articulates goals, knows how to listen, inspires trust and emphasizes personal development. Or, as Peter Drucker describes it, "management's job is to find out what it is doing that keeps people from doing a good job, and stop doing it" (Lee and Zemke, 1993, 23).

This new type of leadership is dependent upon the development of individuals who desire to be "first among teammates," instead of "the boss." Such leadership is not weak. To the contrary, its strength is based on clear visions and tough goals in partnership with employees. The result is—everyone wins. Keifer and Senge (1986) see this new partnering approach come to life in what they call a Metanoic organization, in which "the rowers must row together. Translation of the individual's commitment and resources into collective accomplishment requires alignment of individual energies. There comes a rush of power as everyone recognizes how much more they can accomplish collectively" (2).

In a more detailed explanation of Metanoic organizations, Kiefer and Senge (1982) contrast Metanoic organizational leaders with more traditional leaders. In traditional organizations, the people at the top are seen in control. In Metanoic organizations, leaders are "responsible for sustaining vision . . . and evolving policy and structure. They frequently conceive of themselves as teachers, but they do not control the system" (9-10). The new leadership styles are perceived as developing partners, not czars. These partners provide vision and leadership, but they do this in closer proximity to others in a flattened organizational hierarchy.

As leadership styles are changing, so is the need for leaders to understand the changes occurring among individuals within the organization. Cleveland and Pastrik (1995), describe new answers to old questions that leaders consistently face. While the old answer may have been strong top-down organizational control, the new answer is local control, united by purpose or vision. The old approach focused on the operating unit; the new approach focuses on the entire system. Competition is replaced by cooperation and teamwork. Avoiding change is not even contemplated anymore. Expecting change becomes the norm. Information is more open with less central control. The "old" leadership styles are replaced by organizations that require leaders who emphasize information flow, teamwork, and flexibility. Cleveland and Pastrik go on to describe new assumptions about learning and how those assumptions will revolutionize the classroom and the faculty member. For educational institutions, the new leadership style and the new learning paradigm mandate that organizational concerns be addressed in an holistic manner—approaching the problem from a broader perspective, addressing its impact on numerous parts and sections of the institution simultaneously.

WHAT THE BALDRIGE CRITERIA MAY MEAN FOR ORGANIZATIONAL LEADERSHIP

Dawson (1992) reports that a study by the *Harvard Business Review* estimates that sixty to seventy percent of the climate in the workplace is credited to the managers. Further, the role of leadership in a quality organization is to complement management, not replace it (Kotter 1990). Good management is essential to the success of any large organization. According to Kotter, management organizes the chaos created in every large organization and "brings a degree of order and consistency" to the organizational efforts (104). Good leadership, in turn, is essential to the future of the organization in weaving its way through the complexities and vagaries of change which constantly affect the organization. It is the purpose of leadership to motivate and inspire, while management plans and organizes.

But the role of leadership is just not to maneuver through change, rather it is to create change and set the direction in which the organization moves. By controlling change rather than allowing the organization to be controlled by it, leadership is instrumental in shaping the future. This type of leadership requires a significant shift in thinking for both leaders and managers—new paradigms regarding change.

By controlling change rather than allowing the organization to be controlled by it, leadership is instrumental in shaping the future.

Hanson (1994) quotes Loren Ankarlo, a Colorado management consultant, who says, "In the year 2000, it's estimated that ninety percent of all American companies will structure their work forces into teams. Every member of those teams will have to know when to lead and when to follow" (2). This is what the Baldrige Leadership criterion seems to expect for the future. The aim of team leadership is foreseen by the emphasis on *personal* involvement of the senior officials "in setting directions and developing and maintaining a leadership system and an environment fostering performance excellence" (Baldrige Education Criteria, Item 1.1). The criterion requires a hands-on attitude and close, personal interaction between senior officials and employees from almost all parts of the educational institution.

Item 1.1a goes much further than just the administrative side of an educational institution and requires that senior officials be actively involved and provide direct leadership in areas such as teaching and learning and even in student-related performance and trends. Item 1.1b requires that senior officials be actively involved in the school's leadership development system and be knowledgeable about the use of continuous improvement cycles within the leadership system. Overall, Item 1.1 is much broader than just the system itself and requires that senior officials be actively involved with all communities of interest in the outcomes of the educational system, including students, parents, faculty, staff, employers, the community, and other partners.

In other words, the Baldrige Leadership criterion (1.0) is attempting to evaluate whether a leader is truly empowered or not. Is the leader able to define the institution's mission and align employees with that mission? Is the leader able to develop and maintain trust throughout the multiple layers of the institution? Is the leader able to facilitate coordination and communication at all levels in support of the mission? Does the leader ensure learning opportunities and support creativity to develop new practices, processes, and services? While numerous barriers to the creation of successful answers to each of these questions exist, the Baldrige Criteria point out the areas which must be reviewed to maintain a truly quality institution.

The Baldrige Criteria, however, should not be viewed as a set of "How To" manuals. According to Garvin (1991), "The categories are in no sense a 'to do' list, and it is simply incorrect to suggest that the Criteria specify particular programs or techniques. There is no Baldrige system to be bought off the shelf" (82). Garvin goes on to examine the Baldrige Criteria as a "roadmap" that organizations can use to determine how to reach a particular point. Many different roads can be used to reach that point, and both direct and indirect routes may be made available, with various intersections or stops along the way. The styles and theories of leadership that can work, and can meet the evaluation Criteria of the Baldrige Award, are multiple and varied. This is important to educators because as Bensimon, Neumann, and Birnbaum (1989) point out, "Each [administrator] has a picture of what ideal leaders should be like, what they should accomplish, or how they should carry out the role of leadership. Therefore, conceptions of the effectiveness of leadership depend on the theory being used" (70).

The Baldrige Criteria should not be viewed as a set of "How To" manuals.

EXAMINATION CATEGORY 1.0 LEADERSHIP —WHAT TO DO? WHAT TO BE?

It all sounds so easy. "Simply put, Total Quality Leadership is an approach to management which focuses on giving top value to customers by building excellence into every aspect of the organization," say Joiner and Scholtes (1985). This is done by creating an environment which allows and encourages everyone to contribute to the organization and by developing the skills which enable them to scientifically study and constantly improve every process by which work is accomplished" (4). That's not hard. Just a few sentences of explanation, just a few words of encouragement, just "keep your eye on the ball" and "your nose to the grindstone" and make sure "the customer is always right," and, very soon, the bank will give you a loan and the entire town will be saved—just like Jimmy Stewart in the movie *It's A Wonderful Life.*

All a leader needs to do is maintain an "obsession with quality," improve suppliers, concentrate on internal and external customers, concentrate on processes rather than individuals, create an open and extensive communications system, and create a vision which brings about constancy of purpose in every member of the educational community. A leader needs to read books and articles by Deming, Juran, Ishiwaka, Tribus, and Seymour. Just listen to your customers, rely on reliable data, break down barriers, and drive out fear. Then one will be comfortable in meeting the examination requirements of the Baldrige Leadership criterion.

But it is *not* simple. The Baldrige Leadership criterion cannot be met by hiring a consultant and holding a few meetings with top management. If there is one simple process required to implement quality leadership in an organization and, thereby, to begin the process of meeting the standards of the Baldrige Criteria, it is, simply put, TIME. It will not—it cannot—happen quickly, and the Baldrige Leadership criterion is designed to measure the "staying power" of quality leadership based on the past, present, and continued involvement of senior management in all aspects of the educational institution. As Thomson and Roberts (1992) say in a recent article on leading total quality, "Everything I read tells me that total quality has to be clearly embraced, driven, and led by the CEO and the top team. I've been trying to make ours a total quality organization for over three years. And yet, although we have a number of initiatives under way, little has changed" (46). They go on to add, "When I ask why total quality hasn't taken hold here, the people who will be candid with me say the top team and I are to blame—that we're not leading the effort like we should be. If you could just tell me what I need to do, I will do it. But on my own, I'm not sure I can figure out what else is required" (46).

As described in numerous ways by various authors, knowing the skills, using the proper terminology, holding appropriate training seminars, hiring a recognized consultant, and telling the organization that quality management is now the norm, is *not* enough.

Personal Commitment

Leadership must be personally and professionally committed to quality to make it work. It's that basic. There is no trick. There are no gimmicks. There is no one meeting that will be the turning point. There is no consultant or staff that can replace the leader's personal involvement. There is no substitute available for true leadership in implementing a quality workplace, and there is no hiding lack of true leadership from a Baldrige evaluation. As Garvin (1991) concludes, "The twin pillars of this category are symbolism and active involvement" (88).

Leadership must be personally and professionally committed to quality to make it work. It's that basic.

The Baldrige evaluation Item 1.1a requires senior administrators to be involved in creating and reinforcing values and expectations throughout the institution, using highly-visible actions to reinforce the institution's commitment to quality and to energize the employees in visualizing the institution's vision or goals. Senior administrators should set directions, goals, and measurements, maintain an environment conducive to teaching and learning, and review student and college performance and improvement trends. Is the leader in a quality educational institution aware of how the security guards deal with potential students who have to arrive on campus not knowing where to park? What does the school do to assist a student whose purse and credit cards are stolen *before* she registers for her first classes? Can distance learning classes be substituted for on-campus classes at mid-semester after a student breaks his leg skiing and cannot leave his home? There are literally thousands of questions and instances such as these that quality leadership will be aware of and, while not handling them personally, will be confident of the procedures used to resolve these issues at every level of the organization—from dean, to faculty, to receptionist, to groundskeeper.

Leaders, in the Baldrige system, are designers, teachers, and stewards. Such a perspective fits well with the type of leader that higher education so desperately needs. Indeed, Wilcox and Ebbs (1992) say in a recent ASHE-ERIC Report on leadership, "Effective leadership . . . is distinguished by vision that creates focus, by the ability to grasp the 'big picture' and communicate meaning to develop commitment, by engendering trust, and by fostering the process of renewing values, goals, energy, and human possibilities" (28).

Systems—More Than Just Leadership

The point, according to Thomson and Roberts (1992), is "that you, the leader, the beacon for the rest of your organization, must be clear about what you want and about what you, personally, are committed to make happen. Only then can you ask others to stand up and be counted, to make this choice for themselves" (52). But, in the Baldrige Criteria, a good leader, totally committed to quality leadership, will also establish a personal and broad relationship with employees throughout the educational institution, vertically and horizontally.

How much time do senior administrators spend with staff, faculty or students during the day? How accessible are they? Do they read their mail? Can employees make comments without fear of retaliation? What type and how many quality activities is senior management involved with each day? Has the President experienced the registration line this year? Does the Dean of Student Affairs understand the problems the Financial Aid Office is having with the new federal forms?

Baldrige Item 1.2 requires systematic integration of the leadership values throughout the organization so that a system exists which, when choosing and rewarding leaders, depends on performance objectives related to student development and achievement—a system that reinforces institutional values, expectations, and directions through effective and regular communications in all directions, both within the educational institution and without. This system is leader driven and is dependent on "leadership . . . living up to [the] quality mission of the organization" (Chaffee and Sherr 1992, 78).

This leadership system must be a key element of direction setting for the college. It must be based on continuous review at all levels and must be integrated to allow for all reviews to play a part in assessing strengths and weaknesses of institutional programs, with an emphasis on educational programs.

An Organizational Citizen

Even with an appropriate leadership system in place, none of the activities of the educational institution can make sense unless the institution is very clear as to who its customers are. While the identification of those customers is addressed in another section of the

Baldrige Criteria (7.0), evaluation Item 1.3 stresses the importance of a clear, institution-wide understanding of the institution's customers. This item focuses on Public Responsibility and Citizenship. Just belonging to the Rotary Club and Kiwanis is not enough. Understanding the customer, and hence being able to identify the communities which are key to the future of the college, is the foundation upon which this Criterion is built.

How does the President and senior management interact with the communities key to the institution's future? This is aimed at the evaluation of how the entire organizational unit—the college—acts as an example and as a beacon for the various communities which it serves and of which it is a part. The educational institution should serve as a role model. What leadership is evident in public interest issues? How does the college recognize, or even reward, its employees for their involvement with the community? Does the college serve as an ethical model for other institutions? How are such ethics enforced internally and how is the ethical concern for external issues projected?

This Item (1.3) is designed to evaluate the "public citizen" part of the administrative team. Do senior administrators play a role in making the community a better place to live, or are they content to be recognized at luncheons and attend social events as a spectator or passive participant? Clearly, one of the customers of any educational institution will include the community at large, made up of citizens and taxpayers and employers who may never attend a college course, take a GED program, or use an educational facility. Many major corporations understand that the definition of a customer does not stop with those who directly buy their products. As Zangwill (1993) points out, "Motorola, for example . . . requires its executives to visit its customers' firms. The executives are required to speak not just to the firms' executives, but also to the workers who actually use the Motorola product. Experience has shown that almost everyone has distorted ideas about what customers truly think, and a systematic approach is needed to overcome this" (44).

Item 1.3 requires more than just having the institution's president considered to be a "really good guy" or a "really dynamic woman" by other chief executives. Membership in organizations outside the college is not sufficient; community leadership is required. The Item examines more than just the legal requirements of the educational institution. While enforcement of non-discrimination policies and adherence to laws such as the Americans with Disabilities Act is certainly important, a quality institution cannot stop there and expect to be judged well in Item 1.3–Public Responsibility and Citizenship.

AT RIO SALADO, TQM MEANS LEADERSHIP

At Rio Salado Community College, we began to redefine leadership almost immediately upon my arrival as the new college President in Fall, 1990, and the subsequent adoption of total quality management six months later. We quickly discovered the real power of cross-functional, vertically-integrated approaches beginning with the Leadership Council, a dynamic group of administrators, faculty, and support staff members who direct the college's strategic and tactical planning and oversee the quality effort. We selected small problems to tackle first so that we could all smell the heady aroma of success together very quickly.

We selected small problems to tackle first so that we could all smell the heady aroma of success together very quickly.

After just two years of working to implement TQM philosophy, tools, and techniques in our college, Rio Salado faced an unprecedented—and frightening—opportunity. The State of Arizona created the Governor's Pioneer Award for Quality using the Baldrige corporate Criteria and opened the competition to all organizations, public and private, including educational institutions. The focus of the Pioneer Award was on sound implementation of quality principles, not necessarily sustained results over time. Should we apply? Were we ready to open our doors to external evaluation? Did we stand a chance? Was it wise to apply when we were still in a rather steep learning curve?

All of these questions plagued us. We worried and wondered. We hadn't used the Baldrige Criteria as our framework for implementing quality management. It certainly would have been easier fitting what we had been doing for two years into the Baldrige Criteria. But we had revised our mission, written and rewritten our vision, developed cross-functional, vertically-integrated teams, and had nearly every administrator personally involved in one way or another. So we took the plunge—and the bungee cord held.

Once we began examining the Criteria in detail and organizing our actions in the categories of the Baldrige Criteria, we began to appreciate how concise and appropriate the Baldrige Criteria are as a audit tool. Not only did we discover the parts of our organization that we had inadvertently neglected in our TQM leap forward, we began to understand that we had done many things correctly and, when combined with other institutional efforts, our quality activities began to take the shape of an holistic movement.

As a medium-sized institution, according to the Baldrige Criteria, with 371 Full-Time Equivalent employees, we recognized that we would be competing with private sector firms that could devote significant resources to this competition. We added no staff, hired no consultant or writer, and relied on the judgment and abilities of our staff to put the application together. And then, we got excited.

We recognized that the Baldrige Criteria allowed us to bring previously disjointed or unconnected efforts together, to make sense from disparate occurrences in different parts of our institution. Using the Baldrige Criteria as a computer uses files, we began storing information in various files and subfiles with the proper headings drawn from the Criteria themselves. Once all the material was gathered, the writing became a process of answering questions posed within each Criterion and each Item. We then faced another major concern. The Baldrige Award limits applicants to a certain number of pages, and writing specifically to the Criteria made us condense and summarize our information. Deciding what not to write was almost as hard as deciding what to write. The following is a summary of our responses to Criterion 1.0 Leadership.

Once all the material was gathered, the writing became a process of answering questions posed within each Criterion and each Item.

1.1 Senior Leadership

In the Rio Salado Baldrige application, this section begins, "There is no passive leadership at Rio Salado." We then went on to delineate the actions of the college president and senior management over the past two years. What did they do? How did they do it? Why did they do it? Specific actions of the president were included, such as, "In addition to her activity as a team member, the college president provides weekly information to every Rio Salado employee through her President's Bulletin, asks for and receives comment on various items, including the wording and development of the vision and mission statements, and holds monthly President's Breakfasts with vertically-integrated staff attendance."

1.2 Management for Quality

Rio Salado had departments and divisions still developing their mission or vision statements as we attempted to meet the Baldrige Criteria. But this section fell into place when we were able to develop an accurate flow chart that showed how the concepts and tools of TQM are used throughout the college in planning, problem-solving and decision-making (figure 1). Pareto charts showing the use of various TQM tools by operational units and by continuous improvement teams helped to make the case for college management based on TQM principles. The application also contained specific examples of how decisions were based on collected data, how team solutions were used, and how certain services or processes were streamlined or improved. Day-to-day examples of leadership exhibited by the college president were used to highlight her personal involvement in the various management systems of the college.

1.3 Public Responsibility

This section detailed the "outside" activities of the college president and other institutional leaders, both locally and nationally, and explained how the college assesses its impact on the community through focus groups, student feedback and institutional research. Information examining the college leadership's commitment to the changing community was also presented.

The Morning After—Understanding the Reviews

The Feedback Report, prepared by the external examiners, was almost as long as the college's application. The college "Scoring Summary" was brief:

> Rio Salado Community College scored in the second quartile on the written application. Under the leadership of its president, the college has taken steps to implement quality processes throughout the organization. Efforts are devoted to TQM training, development of mission/vision statements, implementation of long-term strategies, and involvement of employees in teams to assess and improve critical processes in all areas.

> While gaps still remain, there is a beginning of an overall systematic approach to quality. Deployment to the full-time staff is evident, and results show improvements in many areas.

Full-time employees are involved in improvement teams and benefits are seen. A rewards and recognition program has been initiated, based on employee input.

Student evaluations of instructors and satisfaction with the services appear positive overall. Products and services are being developed to further meet the needs of the students, businesses and the public.

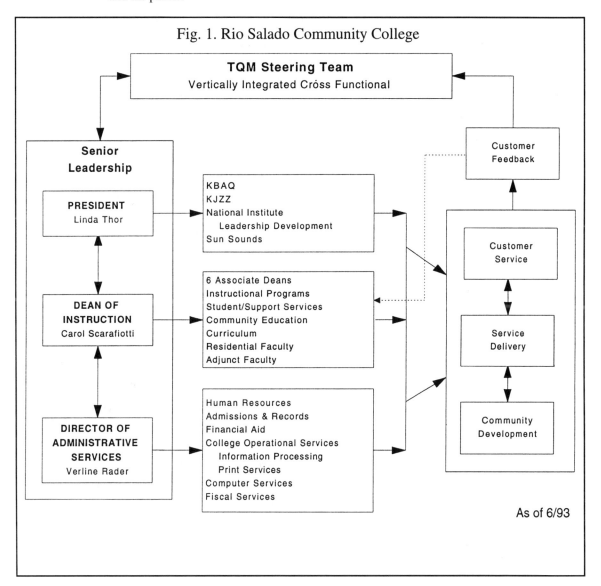

Fig. 1. Rio Salado Community College

TQM Steering Team
Vertically Integrated Cross Functional

Senior Leadership

PRESIDENT
Linda Thor

DEAN OF INSTRUCTION
Carol Scarafiotti

DIRECTOR OF ADMINISTRATIVE SERVICES
Verline Rader

KBAQ
KJZZ
National Institute
    Leadership Development
Sun Sounds

6 Associate Deans
Instructional Programs
Student/Support Services
Community Education
Curriculum
Residential Faculty
Adjunct Faculty

Human Resources
Admissions & Records
Financial Aid
College Operational Services
    Information Processing
    Print Services
Computer Services
Fiscal Services

Customer Feedback

Customer Service

Service Delivery

Community Development

As of 6/93

Critical Reviews—A Learning Tool

Within the entire application, only one item was noted as having no Areas of Improvement—Item 1.1 Senior Executive Leadership. The president's involvement was noted to be "personal" and "active." Leadership processes were described as "cross-functional" and "vertically-integrated," with membership involved in the critical decision-making processes. But review Items 1.2, Management for Quality, and 1.3, Public Responsibility and Corporate Citizenship, both contained two suggested "Areas for Improvement." Critical assessments were made regarding the inadequate use of feedback information and the lack of evidence of quality values being used in day-to-day management or supervision. A lack of a systematic approach to follow-up on needs assessments was identified and, while individual leadership efforts in the community were noted, the college was negatively reviewed because of limited evidence that the organization as a whole was providing leadership commensurate with its role as a major citizen.

Even if we had not won a Pioneer Award for Quality, we would have been pleased that we applied. We learned many valuable lessons from the application process and the feedback report gave us the opportunity to improve our processes and service delivery without having to hire outside consultants. Our own efforts at meeting the Baldrige Criteria provided us with the information we needed to

Using the Baldrige Criteria and the feedback report, Rio Salado has begun to evolve to a higher level of performance.

meet the suggested "Areas for Improvement" and make our college a better institution. Using the Baldrige Criteria and the feedback report, Rio Salado has begun to evolve to a higher level of performance.

CONCLUSION

Rio Salado Community College *did* win the 1993 Governor's Award for Quality—the only public institution to do so. The seventy-four "Areas for Improvement" that were noted in the feedback report became the basis for further improvement at Rio Salado. Our experience is consistent with findings from a study of the CEOs of the FORTUNE 100 companies in which 95 percent agreed that using the Baldrige Criteria as an internal assessment tool, even without applying for a Baldrige award, resulted in the improvement of a company's competitive position and was a positive force in increasing quantifiable success factors within the company (Knotts, Parish, and Evans 1993, 51). Using such assessment tools to improve service delivery and product reliability, whether in a corporation or in an educational institution, is absolutely necessary to the future survival of an organization.

Rio Salado Community College has been lucky. Our experience with the Baldrige Award has been, on the whole, very positive. It provided us with the basis for evolving into a true learning organization. We began with a steering team which led us through the incremental changes first associated with a quality initiative and then developed more systemic thinking which led to institutional restructuring. And now our quality efforts have become the driver to shift our institutional paradigm, to look more externally, to examine the impact of major changes in society, the economy, and the community. The original impetus, the driver of these changes, was our commitment to quality leadership as defined and examined in the Baldrige Criteria.

REFERENCES

Bensimon, E. M., A. Neumann, and R. Birnbaum. 1989. *Making Sense of Administrative Leadership: The "L" Word in Higher Education.* ASHE-ERIC Higher Education Report No. 1. Washington, D.C.: George Washington University School of Education and Human Development.

Chaffee, E. E., and L. A. Sherr. 1992. *Quality: Transforming Postsecondary Education.* ASHE-ERIC Higher Education Report No. 3. Washington, D.C.: George Washington University School of Education and Human Development.

Cleveland, J., and P. Pastrik. 1995. Learning, Learning Organizations, and TQM. In *Total Quality Management: Implications for Higher Education,* edited by A. M. Hoffman and D. J. Julius. Maryville, MO: Prescott Publishing.

Dawson, G. 1992. The Critical Elements Missing from Most Total Quality Management Training. *Performance & Instruction* (October): 15-21.

Garvin, D. A. 1991. How the Baldrige Really Works. *Harvard Business Review* (November/December): 80-93.

Hanson, C. 1994. As Companies Shrink, New Breed of Leaders Is Growing. *Chicago Tribune*, 10 April, 2.

Huey, J. 1994. The New Post-Heroic Leadership. *Fortune*, 21 February, 42-50.

Joiner, B., and P. Scholtes. 1985. *Total Quality Leadership vs. Management by Results*. Madison, WI: Joiner Associates, Inc.

Kiefer, C. F., and P. M. Senge. 1982. Metanoic Organizations in the Transition to a Sustainable Society. *Technological Forecasting and Social Change* 22.2: 18-34.

———. 1986. *Metanoic Organizations: Experiments in Organizational Innovation*. Framingham, MA: Innovation Associates, Inc.

Knotts, U. S., L. G. Parrish, and C. R. Evans. 1993. What Does the U.S. Business Community Really Think about the Baldrige Award? *Quality Progress* 26 (May): 49-53.

Kotter, J. 1990. What Leaders Really Do. *Harvard Business Review* (May/June): 103-111.

Lee, C., and R. Zemke. 1993. The Search for Spirit in the Workplace. *Training* (June): 21-28.

Lessons Learned from High-Performing Organizations in the Federal Government. 1994. Washington, D.C.: Federal Quarterly Institute.

Millard, R. 1991. *Today's Myths and Tomorrow's Realities*. San Francisco: Jossey-Bass Publishers.

Schmidt, W. H., and J. P. Finnegan. 1992. *The Race Without A Finish Line*. San Francisco: Jossey-Bass Publishers.

Seymour, D., and C. Collett. 1991. *Total Quality Management in Higher Education: A Critical Assessment.* Methuen, MA: GOAL/QPC.

Thomson, S., and C. Roberts. 1992. Leading Total Quality. *Journal for Quality and Participation* (July/August): 46-52.

Wheatley, M. 1994. Quantum Management. *Working Woman* (October): 16-17.

Wilcox, J. R., and S. L. Ebbs. 1992. *The Leadership Compass: Values and Ethics in Higher Education*. ASHE-ERIC Higher Education Report No. 1. Washington, D.C.: George Washington University School of Education and Human Development.

Zangwill, W. I. 1993. Ten Mistakes CEOs Make About Quality. *Quality Progress* (June): 43-48.

6
Information and Analysis: Managing by Fact

Valerie Broughton
and Linda Deneen

The second criterion of the 1995 Education Pilot Criteria of the Malcolm Baldrige National Quality Award, "Information and Analysis," serves as the focus of this chapter. This criterion provides a mechanism for institutions to evaluate whether they effectively produce and use information in fulfillment of their missions.

Significant documentation exists of efforts to improve higher education through systematic data collection and analysis. Several decades ago colleges and universities began adopting industrial management methods, trying to adapt them for successful use in the academy. Decision support tools were developed rapidly as computers and management software systems became available and affordable. Researchers investigated factors which could predict the ultimate usefulness of decision-support information. More recently, continuous quality improvement (CQI)—which emphasizes statistical methods—was introduced into the higher education community.

In this chapter, we document the evolution of information in support of decision making in colleges and universities, and identify problems associated with those efforts. We also discuss the contribution CQI can make towards minimizing or eliminating those problems. And finally, we describe the experience of our institution—the University of Minnesota–Duluth—in using the Baldrige Criteria to measure its progress in the area of "Information and Analysis."

THE NEED TO IMPROVE DECISION MAKING

Higher education literature reveals that for at least the last twenty-five years there have been a variety of problems plaguing our colleges and universities: budget cutbacks, accountability concerns, and public dissatisfaction. One cause cited for these problems has been the lack of rational, data-based decision making. In the 1970s university administrators were forced to consider new planning models. The models they used to help campuses accommodate the steady increase in enrollment during the 1950s and 1960s proved inadequate; enrollment and resource growth of the previous two decades slowed or halted in the 1970s and 1980s.

Two other institutional issues that required attention were the clarification of campus functions, or missions, and the lack of management concepts and instruments on most campuses. One study documenting the need for improved management practices is the National Institute of Education Study Group report, *Involvement in Learning* (1984). The study group identifies three prerequisites for excellence in colleges and universities: student involvement, high expectations, and assessment and feedback. The recommendation for assessment and feedback specifically highlights academic administrators as learners who should make a conscientious effort to collect and use better information about programmatic impacts on student learning.

A focus on the structure of data collection and dissemination, rather than on the process of decision making, guided early efforts to build a rational base for institutional data management. Sound information management systems require not only high quality data and a variety of analysis techniques, but also need an organizational structure prepared to benefit from information (Cheit 1977). A similar point has been made by McLaughlin and McLaughlin (1989), who identify five sequential steps to improving management use of information. They recommend that data selection, capture, manipulation, and delivery are only part of a solid management information process; in addition, the analyst needs to know how to enhance the value of the information. Once academic administrators accept that management techniques might improve decision making in higher education, information analysts begin building structures to provide data to academic decision makers. By necessity, the analysts in the McLaughlin and McLaughlin study focused on data collection, storage, documentation, and reporting activities. Issues of data retrieval and quality consumed most of the management information ventures. Thus, for a time, the information management systems movement in higher education was frustrated by ignoring the organizational changes necessary to benefit fully from information. Decision makers found information technology only moderately successful (Adams 1977).

Decision support tools available through mainframe systems, and eventually from more localized computer systems, fueled the information machine on many campuses. Of course, during the early 1970s and into the 1980s, mainframe computers were the most powerful tool available to information analysts. Furniture-sized machines, complicated computer language codes, and the cost of the early electronic computing equipment absorbed information users when the academy began to pursue systematic data-based decision making (McLaughlin, McLaughlin and Howard 1987). Numbers listed on computer printouts seemed to have the mystical feature of automatically providing decisive information (McCorkle 1977). Acknowledging this misperception, and advising a corrective action, Milter (1986) suggests that higher education needs "decision aids that can capitalize on the ability of computers to process information with great efficiency and consistency so as to enhance, rather than limit, the creativity, judgement, and political wisdom of administrators" (76).

Numbers listed on computer printouts seemed to have the mystical feature of automatically providing decisive information.

Studies of information utilization find that some efforts at providing data to decision makers are counter-productive. Analysts are sometimes viewed with suspicion by traditional decision makers in the academy (McCorkle 1977). Similarly, Dressel (1971) suggests that administrators who prefer to operate intuitively, and committee members with perhaps discipline- or emotion-based preferences, are not receptive to studies that might guide their deliberations.

Improving the use of information in decision making processes depends on two factors. First, the information provided must be seen as relevant to the question. Second, there must be regular dialogue and shared trust between those who gather and analyze the data and those who ultimately use it (Ewell 1989a). To maximize the likelihood that information will be useful to decision makers, information practitioners should know who is asking for the information and for what purpose, what is the most beneficial reporting mechanism, and how the information informs discussions leading to a decision (Ewell 1989a).

CQI's Impact on Decision Making

This section highlights factors that have been missing in past efforts to improve the decisions of academic administrators and discusses the degree to which CQI principles can alleviate those concerns.

Determining Data Requirements

For decades, information analysts have been trying to determine just what data and information campus decision makers need. Collecting data without carefully considering potential uses can be wasteful (Schmidtlein 1977). Data reporting systems are best developed when institutional goals are clearly identified (Keller 1983). To establish a cost-effective information system an organization must decide on its scope and complexity. In order to decide on the scope and complexity, an organization must consider who will use the data and for what purposes (Sandin 1977). Unfortunately, too often systems have been developed without even the briefest analysis of their likely use. Even if systems designers query decision makers about potential uses, unsophisticated or unpracticed academic administrators may not respond practically. If campus goals and priorities are not clear, the most sincere, rational administrator is without the means to direct system designers. McCorkle (1977) concludes: "Part of the problem with getting useful information is that we have not made the necessary top management decisions to govern the type of information to be assembled and how it should be used" (7).

Vague administrative direction results in data controlling the policy questions, rather than the policy questions dictating the data to be collected and analyzed.

Vague administrative direction results in data controlling the policy questions, rather than the policy questions dictating the data to be collected and analyzed. This "lack-of-definition" problem is minimized in a CQI organization where institutional goals are clearly specified to employees across campus and critical measures for evaluating the organization's processes have been established.

Organizational Levels

Decision support information needs vary by the levels within an institution. Historically, such complexity created dilemmas and choices for analysts. One structure of organization management activity identifies three levels: strategic, managerial, and operational.

These activities occur at all levels of a university. It is important that decision making activity and the information system function at the same level (McLaughlin and McLaughlin 1989). For example, a strategic decision made by a campus-level decision maker requires data aggregated at a much higher level than an operational decision made by a program director. Results are most positive when decisions occur at appropriate administrative levels. Schmidtlein (1977) explains:

> When upper-echelon officials do make detailed decisions on complex lower level issues, such decisions are apt to be simplistic and erroneous, leading to poor results and obstructive and evasive behavior at lower echelons. (32)

The plan-do-check-act cycle familiar to CQI institutions supports the practice of staff members gathering the data needed to make the decisions for which they are responsible, thereby minimizing the chances for decisions at improper levels.

Institutional Cultures

Colleges and universities often share common problems, but local environmental factors influence the manner in which policy questions are posed and studied. Thus, institutional cultures require analyses specific to particular campuses. The CQI process implementation requires a clarification of institutional values. Explicitly-stated values and objectives increase the likelihood that decision support information will be useful. Systematic management tools are most useful when information professionals and decision makers understand circumstances specific to their campus. Continuous improvement provides tools for identifying these important, possibly unique features.

Operating Versus Decision-Support Systems

Some early information-support endeavors in higher education made the mistake of confusing data required for successfully maintaining operating systems and data required for supporting decision making. The delineation of processes in CQI distinguishes between the two.

Management information practitioners found numerous limitations to trying to use systems developed to support daily operations for decision-support purposes. Programming against operating systems to produce information helpful to decision makers was costly and time consuming. Often a deadline was passed before the data became available. Also, most data found in operating system files are artificially segmented and difficult to link. For example, student credit hours and degrees could be in different files with different structures; one may be categorized by department and the other by degree program. Decision support systems include links to translate departments to degree programs. Operating systems by necessity are complex and comprehensive and include data at a level of detail rarely required for strategic decisions. Predetermined reports from operating systems are overly complex, and rewriting code to produce new reports may take several weeks (Sandin 1977). Operating systems must be detailed, comprehensive, and capable of handling multiple, routine tasks. Decision support systems must be flexible and easy to use.

Effective decision-support systems begin with clearly defined and well-understood processes.

CQI considerations have had an impact on the operating/decision support dilemma. Effective decision-support systems begin with clearly defined and well-understood processes. By specifying functional processes and measures to monitor and evaluate those processes, orderly development of decision support systems can be accomplished.

Benchmarking

Valid, reliable indices and trend information prepared in response to policy questions assists decision makers. Experienced administrators quickly ask for the next level of data—comparative information. The continuous improvement focus on benchmarking and studying best practices institutionalizes the need for comparative data. Historical discussion of the advantages and disadvantages of trend analysis and benchmark data provides a foundation for understanding the CQI concept of best practices.

Keller (1983) differentiates between two levels of descriptive data: those used to inform or illustrate the facts at a particular point in time, and those that use trend data to describe campus changes over time. Schmidtlein (1977), in contrast, specifies three methods of comparison and warns against the potential hazards of measuring across time or across campuses. Campus-specific data can be compared to established and accepted standards, to similar data from other institutions or programs, and to historical data from the same institution. Comparison with a standard presupposes that the ideal is a valid point of reference. For example, the current benchmarking project of the National Association of College and University Business Officers (NACUBO) includes hundreds of measures. Some measures may be valid indicators of best practices while others are more problematic. For example, cost-per-credit-hour is a commonly used indicator. A low ratio is sometimes interpreted as efficient use of departmental resources, while a high ratio is sometimes interpreted as good academic quality.

Decision-Making Style

In addition to knowledge of data structures and analytical tools, the most successful information analysts are familiar with the process or style used by the administrators for whom they prepare information. This familiarity includes a clear understanding of the goals of the institution as well. In organizations where continuous improvement is prominent, not only does the information analyst know the priorities of the campus, all campus employees do.

There are arguments both for and against tailoring decision information to specific decision makers. Hackman, for example, (1989) admonishes institutional researchers to "know your decision makers." Ewell (1989b) summarizes evaluation utilization literature and advises that information practitioners know the end users style, level of sophistication, and place in the institution. Changes in administrative styles lead to changes in organizational roles and cultures, which affect information needs. Institutional researchers need to be responsive. In practice, decision makers usually consult with others about important strategic or operational decisions. Customizing information for one person may hinder broad understanding among a group of academic administrators or decision makers. Finally, if system development is based on the preferences of one administrator, the system may need to be completely replaced when a new administrator is hired. Generally, information systems in CQI organizations are built around critical processes and measures rather than individual wishes.

Customizing information for one person may hinder broad understanding among a group of academic administrators or decision makers.

Unanticipated Information Needs

Emergencies occur in any organization. All information needs cannot be anticipated. There are predictable cycles throughout an academic year which require decision support information. Activities such as student registration, financial aid decisions, bulletin production, and faculty hiring occur regularly. However, other decisions requiring information support seem to occur without warning. For example, budget recisions, resignations of key staff, or unanticipated requests from governing bodies, require immediate action for which a decision-support system may or may not exist. While CQI principles and practices enable individuals to anticipate routine decisions, they cannot eliminate all unanticipated requests for information. On the other hand, CQI principles and practices should reduce the number of such requests through better planning.

THE UMD STORY

The University of Minnesota–Duluth (UMD) used a Baldrige analysis to support its campus quality effort in three consecutive years: 1992, 1993, and 1994. In all three years, the Minnesota Council for Quality reviewed the analysis, although UMD did not formally apply for the Minnesota Quality Award in any of these years. In all three years we used the Baldrige Criteria designed for business and industry because the Criteria for education had not yet been developed.

The 1992 Baldrige Assessment for UMD

During the winter quarter of 1992, Merlin J. Ricklefs came to UMD as the McKnight Visiting Professor in Industrial Engineering. Mr. Ricklefs was on leave from his position at IBM Rochester, where he spearheaded the effort that resulted in IBM Rochester winning the 1990 Malcolm Baldrige National Quality Award. While at UMD, Mr. Ricklefs taught a graduate course in Management Studies entitled "Total Quality Management." He assigned the job of completing the first Baldrige assessment for UMD—based on the 1991 Criteria—as a term project. (The 1991 Baldrige Award Criteria for Category 2 are shown in figure 1.)

Fig. 1. 1991 Baldrige Award Criteria for
Information and Analysis

2.0 Information and Analysis (70 points)

The Information and Analysis category examines the scope, validity, use and management of data and information that underlie the company's overall quality management system. Also examined is the adequacy of the data, information and analysis to support a responsive, prevention-based approach to quality and customer satisfaction built upon "management by fact."

2.1 Scope and Management of Quality Data and Information (20 points)

Describe the company's base of data and information used for planning, day-to-day management, and evaluation of quality, and how data and information reliability, timeliness, and success are assured.

2.2 Competitive Comparisons and Benchmarks (30 points)

Describe the company's approach to selecting quality-related competitive comparisons and world-class benchmarks to support quality planning, evaluation, and improvement.

2.3 Analysis of Quality Data and Information (20 points)

Describe how data and information are analyzed and used to support the company's overall quality objectives.

The students evaluated UMD in each category, organizing their analysis by listing strengths, areas for improvement, and recommendations for each of the subcategories. There were few strengths to note during the first year. In subcategory 2.1, they identified the Campus Data Book and the Office of Institutional Research as strengths, and they gave a score of 4 out of 20. In subcategory 2.2 they identified UMD's peer-institution data, ACT data, federal information sources, and departmental accreditation data as strengths, and they gave a score of 4 out of 30. In subcategory 2.3, they identified departments' use of survey data and analysis for quality issues as strengths, but they gave a score of 0 out of 20.

There were few strengths to note during the first year.

The students' total score for category 2 was 8 out of 70, and their overall score for the entire analysis was 149 out of 1000. The students submitted their report to the Minnesota Council for Quality for review. The Minnesota Council for Quality examiners agreed with the students' assessment and scoring of UMD's quality system.

The students also made a set of recommendations to the UMD chancellor. The chancellor shared these recommendations with the UMD senior administration. The overall recommendations are itemized in figure 2, and their specific recommendations for "Information and Analysis" are shown in figure 3.

Fig. 2. 1992 Student Recommendations for Quality Improvement

Final Overall Recommendations

1. The top administrators must demonstrate their 100% commitment to the quality program at UMD.

2. Chancellor must communicate to all UMD employees the status and direction of quality planning.

Fig. 3. 1992 Student Recommendations for Improving Information and Analysis

Recommendations for Category 2.0 on Information and Analysis

2.1a (Top Priority) Implement a continuous process to determine and review data used to analyze the quality within UMD.

2.2d (Second Priority) Develop a process to select competitive benchmarking examples that relate to UMD.

2.3b (Second Priority) Develop cross-functional groups at all levels of the organization to review and analyze quality data. Leader in the organization needs to show support for this type of activity by communicating down the organization that quality is a key concern that needs to be supported by accurate and relevant data analysis.

The students' report generated a great deal of interest among members of the UMD administration. Administrators reviewed the report and discussed it at length. We then formed a team of UMD administrators to do an assessment of UMD based on the 1992 Baldrige Criteria. We were particularly interested in determining whether an administrative team might have a better working knowledge of UMD improvement efforts and be able to describe our efforts more effectively in a Baldrige assessment. We were also interested in learning more about what we should be doing to improve quality at UMD, and we hoped that completing a Baldrige assessment would make us more aware of what we needed to do.

Fig. 4. 1992 Baldrige Award Criteria for Information and Analysis

2.0 Information and Analysis (80 points)

The Information and Analysis Category examines the scope, validity, analysis, and use of data and information to drive quality excellence and improve competitive performance. Also examined is the adequacy of the company's data, information, and analysis system to support improvement of the company's customer focus, products, services, and internal operations.

2.1 Scope and Management of Quality and Performance Data and Information (15 points)

Describe the company's base of data and information used for planning, day-to-day management, and evaluation of quality. Describe also how data and information reliability, timeliness, and access are assured.

2.2 Competitive Comparisons and Benchmarks (25 points)

Describe the company's approach to selecting data and information for competitive comparisons and world-class benchmarks to support quality and performance planning, evaluation, and improvement.

2.3 Analysis and Uses of Company-Level Data (40 points)

Describe how quality- and performance-related data and information are analyzed and used to support the company's overall operational and planning objectives.

The 1993 Baldrige Assessment at UMD

The Baldrige Award Criteria for Category 2, shown in figure 4, were slightly different from those of 1991.

The administrative team for the 1993 Baldrige self-assessment assembled early in the fall of 1992. We organized ourselves so that each team member was responsible for one section, and the team leader was responsible for combining the sections into a final report. We made a time line with a set of goals designed to get us to the final report. We agreed to submit our report to the Minnesota Quality Council for informal review, but we decided not to score it ourselves.

For Category 2 we spun off another small team, which put together a survey to send to various campus administrators and staff members most likely to use information. Some people were simply sent the survey, while others were interviewed by members of the team. (See figure 5 for a list of the survey questions.) We developed these questions by using the detailed information provided in the 1992 Baldrige Award Criteria. Our hardest job was rewriting some of the language in the Criteria so that it would be more understandable to those in an academic institution.

Our hardest job was rewriting some of the language in the Criteria so that it would be more understandable to those in an academic institution.

In section 2.2 we described data produced by other institutions and organizations that we use as benchmarks. Section 2.3 was by far the weakest of the sections; we were unable to describe any systematic way in which data and information were used in the quality improvement process.

The Minnesota Council for Quality examiners reviewed the UMD Baldrige assessment, although they did not give a formal score and UMD did not formally apply for the Minnesota Quality Award. They placed our score in the 126 to 250 range, which is described as "Early stages in the implementation of approaches. Important gaps exist in most categories." The examiners suggested two key areas in which improvement was needed:

> Two key opportunities for improvement stand out. There is no clear, consistent definition of UMD's customer, and the improvement efforts currently in place do not link together to form a cohesive system for managing product and service quality.

Fig. 5. Survey Questions for 1992 UMD Analysis

1. What major types of data do you routinely collect, assemble, or analyze?

2. How often are these data collected?

3. What major types of data do you routinely use in making decisions? Describe how each type of data is used. Where does the data come from?

4. Can your data sources be categorized in the following areas? If so, how?
> (a) Customer-related (students, parents, employers, society
> (b) Internal operations
> (c) University performance
> (d) Cost and financial
> (e) Supplier performance

5. What can you say about the quality of data that you collect or use? Are you aware of any available comparisons between your data and the data of other units or institutions? How are sources evaluated and improved?

6. How effectively does the institution use data and information to improve quality or enhance decision-making? How about your unit? How are processes to collect information improved?

7. Do you think the data you collect reflects your quality?

8. What data would you like to have available that isn't available?

9. What data are you asked to collect that you think has no value?

10. How are data analyzed? How are analysis methods improved?

Criticisms of section 2 were consistent with the Council's more general feedback:

> It is not clear how information provides the link between customer (Items 7.1 and 7.6) and internal process improvements (Items 5.1 and 5.2). There is little evidence to show that the data being kept are the critical data—either from the customer's point of view or for process improvement.

In retrospect, it seems clear that the primary problem with our evaluation was that we used a bottom-up approach to document our data and information usage. While this approach was perhaps most representative of the way in which the institution used data at that time, it was far removed from the philosophy of quality as reflected in the Baldrige Criteria. The Criteria ask us to take the top-down view—to choose measures thoughtfully at the highest levels of the institution's organization that can be used to drive the quality effort. This we had not done.

The UMD chancellor and the senior administration reviewed and discussed the UMD analysis and the report from the Minnesota Quality Council during the summer of 1993. The administration had previously developed a set of nine critical processes for the campus. In July of 1993 they added a tenth—Information Management.

As a part of the development of the critical processes, the administration also developed outcome measures for each process. Although these measures were never refined to everyone's satisfaction, they began to give us the understanding of the value of a set of high-level measures related to our quality effort. We began to believe that well-defined measures could show us the health of processes and pinpoint the need for improvement.

We began to believe that well-defined measures could show us the health of processes and pinpoint the need for improvement.

There was also a negative side to the development of measures. Many people believed that measurement would be used to allocate resources. This was a time of budget cuts at UMD, as it was at many institutions of higher education. Allocating resources based on metrics was new and unpredictable. Many feared their units would lose funding if measures were used. This led to some resistance to the development of measures at all, with many arguments given that our operations were too complex to measure or that measures told us only about quantitative, not qualitative, aspects of our performance. When we forged ahead despite these concerns, people fought hard to include the measures that did the best job of describing the strengths of their units, leading us to a large set of fairly-detailed metrics. It was extremely difficult to come up with a comprehensive set of high-level measures that accurately reflected all views of the university.

Fig. 6. 1994 Minnesota Quality Award Application Guidelines for Information and Analysis

2.0 Information and Analysis (75 Points)

This Category examines the scope, validity, analysis, management and use of data and information to drive quality excellence and to improve operational and competitive performance. Also examined is the adequacy of the company's data, information, and analysis system to support improvement of the organization's customer focus, products, services, and internal operations.

2.1 Scope and Management of Quality and Performance Data and Information (15 points)

Describe the organization's data and information system including criteria for selection, types, and purposes used for planning, day-to-day management, and evaluation of quality and operational performance. Describe also how data and information are managed to ensure appropriateness, reliability, timeliness, and rapid access, and how the scope and management of data and information are evaluated and improved.

2.2 Competitive Comparisons and Benchmarking (20 points)

Describe the organization's processes and current sources, scope, and uses of competitive comparisons and benchmarking information and data. Describe how this information and data are used to support improvement of quality and overall organization operation performance. Also, describe how the organization evaluates and improves its overall processes for selecting and using comparison and benchmarking information and data.

2.3 Analysis and Uses of Organization-Level Data (40 points)

Describe how data related to quality, customers, and operational performance, together with relevant financial data, are analyzed to support organization-level review, action, and planning. Also, describe how the organization evaluates and improves the process(es) of data analysis.

The 1994 Baldrige Assessment for UMD

In the fall of 1993 we decided to undergo another Baldrige self-assessment. We formed a much smaller team of only two people, and we agreed that we would not make major changes in the content of the previous year's report. Instead, we would address the criticisms of the 1993 analysis by improving the definition of the customer and showing how the various parts of the analysis linked together.

For this analysis, we chose to use the Criteria set down in the Minnesota Quality Award Application Guidelines instead of the Malcolm Baldrige National Quality Award Criteria. Because of the timing, we used the 1994 Criteria, although we began the process in the fall of 1993. The Criteria and points awarded were slightly different again. The word "company" was replaced with "organization" throughout, presumably to reflect the increasing interest of educational institutions and other organizations in quality improvement. There was greater emphasis placed on how data were selected and how they were used to support continuous improvement. The 1994 assessment criteria for category 2 are shown in figure 6.

To show how UMD's data and information linked to processes, we first categorized the list of data from the 1993 report according to the UMD critical processes. Then we constructed a matrix that matched each data element with the four categories in the 1994 Criteria: customer related, product/service quality, internal operations and processes, and supplier related.

The results of the analysis by the examiners for the Minnesota Quality Award were disappointing. UMD again scored in the range of 126 to 250, showing no improvement from the previous year, although actual points were not awarded. A key paragraph of the report of the Minnesota Quality Council shows how critical information and analysis are to a Baldrige assessment:

> While Vision 2000 [UMD Planning Document] contains goal statements and identifies ten core processes, the measures and quality indicators of these goals and processes do not drive a measurement system so that results can be clearly presented. For example, the database for the planning and management of quality, while clearly identified and categorized, may not be sufficient for providing system and process results given the absence of results in operational performance and customer satis-

faction categories. Since there are no measures and indicators of the goals, it is unlikely that the data that are gathered can be turned into information that is usable for improvement activities.

Despite all of our hard work and good intentions, the fundamental flaw remained. We had not developed a set of critical measures for the institution, nor had we set performance goals based on those measures.

The 1995 Education Pilot Criteria

The 1995 Education Pilot Criteria for the Malcolm Baldrige National Quality Award have now been issued. These Criteria are closely linked to the 1995 Baldrige Award Criteria, but they have been adapted for education. (See appendix for Education Pilot Criteria, 2.0 Information and Analysis.) Given our own struggle to make the language translations from the business-oriented Criteria to something that made sense for our university, we are pleased to see these pilot Criteria.

It is interesting to study a few of the changes in wording. In section 2.0, "competitive performance" is replaced with "mission-related performance." Educational institutions are comfortable with following their mission, but they are much less comfortable with the notion that they must compete in the marketplace, although of course they do. In sections 2.1 and 2.2, the emphasis falls on "selection" first of all, while "managing" and "using" information follows. This change would have helped us at UMD a great deal. As academics, we were so busy collecting and categorizing data that we lost sight of the need to select it for well-defined purposes. In section 2.3, "educational progress and business operational performance" replaces "quality, customers, and operational performance." Although some educators have grown more comfortable with the emphasis on customers, there remains a strongly-felt belief that students are not the equivalent of customers of a business. The relationship between a student and a teacher has many complexities that the term "customer" cannot capture.

As academics, we were so busy collecting and categorizing data that we lost sight of the need to select it for well-defined purposes.

The detailed instructions in the Education Pilot Criteria have been similarly revised, using language that appeals to educators. We were, at first, surprised that such translation was necessary, since the Criteria were explained using standard English. However, we have come to realize that, over time, words can become encoded with meanings that are group-specific, and that in order for communication to take place, the sender of a message must be aware of the receiver's encoded meanings. The Education Pilot Criteria should prove a great help to educators who are interested in doing a Baldrige analysis for their institutions.

Recent Activities at UMD

There will be no Baldrige self-assessment at UMD for 1995. The UMD administration decided in the fall of 1994 to let the critical processes and measures rest for awhile. At the time, UMD was beginning a search for a new chancellor, and many administrators wanted to see what direction the new chancellor would set for quality improvement. Those units most actively involved in quality-improvement efforts decided to concentrate on work in their own units rather than on any university-wide efforts.

During the 1994-95 academic year, the central administration of the University of Minnesota System embarked on the development of a set of critical measures for the system. This effort has proceeded well, led by the Office of the Senior Vice President for Academic Affairs. The system administration has produced a list of eighteen proposed institutional critical measures. Phase one of this effort resulted in five of the measures being developed and approved by the Board of Regents. During phase two, the system administration is working to develop eight additional measures. Phase three will consist of the final five measures. UMD has contributed strongly to this development process, informed by our work on our own critical processes and measures and the experience we have gained in working with the Baldrige Criteria.

SUMMARY

We have seen how the education literature reveals the need to improve decision making through the use of information and analysis. We have discussed how the principles and practices of CQI impact decision making by determining data requirements, organizational levels, institutional cultures, operating versus decision support systems, benchmarking needs, decision-making styles, and unanticipated information needs. We have described the University of Minnesota–Duluth's experience in using the Baldrige Criteria as an audit tool to support its quality improvement efforts.

We have learned that measures to drive quality must be developed with a global institutional view, that the development of measures is a difficult process that raises many fears, and that cultural change within an institution is demanding. Finally, our experience indicates that the Baldrige Criteria are valid measures of the extent to which institutions have internalized CQI practices and principles.

REFERENCES

Adams, C. R. 1977. Information Technology: Performance and Promise. In *Appraising Information Needs of Decision Makers*, edited by C. R. Adams. New Directions for Institutional Research, no. 15. San Francisco: Jossey-Bass.

Cheit, C. 1977. Challenges Inherent in the Systematic Approach. In *Appraising Information Needs of Decision Makers*, edited by C. R. Adams. New Directions for Institutional Research, no. 15. San Francisco: Jossey-Bass.

Dressel, P. L. and Associates. 1971. *Institutional Research in the University: A Handbook*. San Francisco: Jossey-Bass.

Ewell, P. 1989a. Information for Decision: What's the Use? In *Enhancing Information Use in Decision Making*, edited by P. T. Ewell. New Directions for Institutional Research, no. 64. San Francisco: Jossey-Bass.

———. 1989b. Putting It All Together: Four Questions For Practitioners. In *Enhancing Information Use in Decision Making*, edited by P. T. Ewell. New Directions for Institutional Research, no. 64. San Francisco: Jossey-Bass.

Hackman, J. D. 1989. The Psychological Context: 7 Maxims for Institutional Researchers. In *Enhancing Information Use in Decision Making*, edited by P. T. Ewell. New Directions for Institutional Research, no. 64. San Francisco: Jossey-Bass.

Keller, G. 1983. *Academic Strategy*. Baltimore: Johns Hopkins University Press.

McCorkle, C. O., Jr. 1977. Information for Institutional Decision Making. In *Appraising Information Needs of Decision Makers*, edited by C. R. Adams. New Directions for Institutional Research, no. 15. San Francisco: Jossey-Bass.

McLaughlin, G. W. and J. S. McLaughlin. 1989. Barriers to Information Use: The Organizational Context. In *Enhancing Information Use in Decision Making*, edited by P. T. Ewell. New Directions for Institutional Research, no. 64. San Francisco: Jossey-Bass.

McLaughlin, G. W., J. S. McLaughlin, and R. Howard. 1987. Decision Support in the Information Age. In *Managing Information in Higher Education*, edited by E. M. Staman. New Directions for Institutional Research, no. 55. San Francisco: Jossey-Bass.

Milter, R. G. 1986. Resource Allocation Models and the Budgeting Process. In *Applying Decision Support Systems In Higher Education*, edited by J. Rohrbaugh and A. T. McCartt. New Directions for Institutional Research, no. 49. San Francisco: Jossey-Bass.

Sandin, R. 1977. Information Systems and Educational Judgment. In *Appraising Information Needs of Decision Makers*, edited by C. R. Adams. New Directions for Institutional Research, no. 15. San Francisco: Jossey-Bass.

Schmidtlein, F. 1977. Information Systems and Concepts of Higher Education Governance. In *Appraising Information Needs of Decision Makers*, edited by C. R. Adams. New Directions for Institutional Research, no. 15. San Francisco: Jossey-Bass.

Study Group on the Conditions of Excellence in American Higher Education. 1984. *Involvement in Learning: Realizing the Potential of American Higher Education*. Washington, DC: National Institute of Education.

7

Strategic and Operational Planning: The Glue of the System

Gloriana St. Clair
and Ronald F. Dow

This chapter brings together several seemingly disparate areas—the definition and practice of strategic planning in educational institutions, the MBNQA's Education Pilot Criteria description of Strategic and Operational Planning (Category 3.0), comments from business management practitioners of total quality, and a SWOT (strengths, weaknesses, opportunities, and threats) analysis of The Pennsylvania State University's experiences with strategic planning—to provide guidance for strategic planning in a total quality educational environment. We believe, based on the evidence, that strategic planning is an essential part of high-performing organizations. We also believe that education planning practices and those required for total quality (as manifested in the MBNQA Criteria) are complementary.

Teeter and Lozier (1995), for example, emphasize the convergence of total quality management and strategic planning. In particular, they note the mission-driven nature of both processes, the importance of process orientation, the existence of information as a driver in each case, and the involvement of a broad spectrum of individuals for each process. In "The Baldrige Cometh," Seymour (1994) describes strategic quality planning as the "glue" holding the quality effort together; it must be focused, concrete, aggressive, and integrated in order to be effective. In a quality environment, such hazy language as "quality" and "excellent" must be replaced with concrete goals such as percentage improvements. Seymour particularly stresses the importance of integration—bringing employees, customers, and suppliers into the planning process. He concludes that "planning should not be dictated by leaders; it should be inspired by followers" (19).

The integration within the organization, its suppliers, and its customers must reflect prevailing conditions outside the organization. Society, and state legislatures in particular, increasingly expect educational institutions to demonstrate their effectiveness. The Baldrige process focuses on satisfactory results. In the MBNQA *Education Pilot Criteria* (US Dept of Commerce 1995), these results include delivery of ever-improving educational value to students—who are in turn developed—and the improvement of educational institutions' effectiveness and capability. Strategic and operational planning is, indeed, the glue that secures the measures needed to demonstrate improvement in key areas.

STRATEGIC PLANNING: DEFINITION AND DISCUSSION

Strategic planning is a systematic and iterative process carried out by many successful public and for-profit entities. It is designed to link management and employee actions to an assessment of operating environments by engaging senior management in broad policy, direction setting, and goal related activities. It is predicated on an extensive assessment of those environments and the stakeholders or customers. Moreover, strategic planning is designed to create a framework for organizational decision-making, and it charges operating departments with developing actions plans to meet management defined goals based upon the assessment.

Strategic planning, as practiced in educational institutions, has these characteristics:

- It represents a systematic process, based upon customer assessment, for identifying core organizational values.
- It demonstrates management's commitment to quality, as quality is identified as a core organizational value.
- It creates a framework for future decision-making that integrates management's concern for quality into departmental planning.

- It directs the creation of operational action plans focused on achieving strategic, customer-oriented goals.

- It is continuous and ongoing, dependent upon monitoring of enunciated performance standards and customer actions.

The process of strategic planning begins as senior management undertakes to define a vision for the institution. The vision statement clarifies the purpose or mission of the organization and delineates the unique fashion in which the organization responds to its stakeholders—groups or individuals who are either affected by or can affect the organization. Stakeholders include customers, employees, government agencies and legislative bodies, and in the case of colleges and universities, may also include present and future students, alumni, faculty, friends, trustees, and parents. Once a clear vision for the organization is developed, senior management formulates choices to align vision with mission.

Once a clear vision for the organization is developed, senior management formulates choices to align vision with mission.

In effect, this phase that formalizes a strategic vision for the organization involves a situational assessment of the operating environment. Most of the prescriptive literature on strategic planning, when describing this phase of assessment, cites the Harvard policy model for inspiration and proceeds to develop a plan of assessment based upon Harvard's SWOT structure (Christensen et al. 1983; Nutt and Backoff 1992; Bryson 1988). In brief, the SWOT construct seeks to build on strengths and overcome weaknesses, while exploiting opportunities, and blunting threats [SWOT].

As an initial step in the SWOT analysis, management undertakes a comprehensive assessment of the organization's external environment, seeking to identify both opportunities for growth and threats that might undermine management actions or even the life of the entity. Stakeholders are key to this assessment. Educational entities must be responsive not only to students and other perceived customers, but also to external political authorities. For public entities the external assessment must shift from a simple marketplace dependence, as in the corporate sector, to a more complex set of legal, economic, and political considerations (Nutt and Backoff 1992). Federal and state funding strategies, the scope of student aid programs, affirmative action guidelines, language requirements for instructors, legislature-set salaries for faculty, licensing requirements for the professions, even the cyclical nature of government-funded research and development all affect the vitality of educational programs and the manner in which a college or university attracts and instructs students.

As Richard M. Cyert (1988), past president of Carnegie Mellon University, has observed, "Strategic planning is necessary in order to identify the areas in which the university should be doing research and offering educational curricula, to specify the goals of the institution, and to determine the kind of university that is desired by the community" (91). The external assessment, in effect, aids in the identification of stakeholder aspirations for the organization.

Complementary to the external assessment is an internal environmental assessment. Ultimately the vision that frames the strategic questions for management must derive not only from customer needs but also from a thorough understanding of the existing organizational strengths and weaknesses (Dean and Bowen 1994). To assess internal strengths and weaknesses, the organization might describe programs, review product service mix and life cycles, or review support processes. The most significant aspect of the internal assessment, however, should be the development and review of performance measures (Bryson 1988). Without performance measures that demonstrate organizational effectiveness in terms of stakeholder criteria, stakeholder support may be withdrawn. The absence of performance information presents problems both for management and for stakeholders, and needs to be addressed in the internal assessment.

As the internal and external assessment take form, a number of fundamental policy questions will arise concerning the internal fit of the organization with its external environment. Strategic planning focuses on the achievement of the best fit between an organization and its environment (Bryson 1988). The total quality perspective on strategic decision-making consists of management deciding what strategies must be undertaken to best align the organization to meet customer expectations. Traditional planning literature focuses not only on what customers want, but also on what the organization is best prepared to deliver based upon its internal strengths and weaknesses

(Dean and Bowen 1994). With the internal and external assessment in support of their strategic decisions, senior management is ready to frame a mission statement for the organization. With a mission statement, support by the assessment documentation, and the resolution of strategic issue formulation, operating units are asked to formulate actions plans which relate the vision of senior management to day-to-day operations (Shirley 1988).

John Bryson (1988), author of *Strategic Planning for Public and Nonprofit Organizations: A Guide to Strengthening and Sustaining Organizational Achievement*, summarizes the strategic planning process in the following fashion: "[It is a] process [that] encompasses broad policy and direction setting, internal and external assessment, attention to key stakeholders, identification of key issues, development of strategies to deal with each issue, decision-making, action, and continuous monitoring of results" (30). The process is one that has been instrumental in shaping many educational institutions.

THE EDUCATION PILOT CRITERIA: CATEGORY 3.0

Strategic and Operational Planning, Category 3.0, examines how an educational institution establishes strategic directions and translates those into operations. Although this section, along with Information and Analysis, carries fewer points (75) than other sections, its importance should not be discounted. The Education Pilot Criteria Framework Dynamic Relationships diagram classifies leadership as the driver, and strategic and operational planning as a part of the system (see appendix for diagram). Inasmuch as strategic and operational planning has traditionally been a favored tool of effective leaders in moving an organization forward in a coordinated manner, it is also a driver for the institution. Yet in the most effective organizations, both leadership and strategic planning are shared far beyond the "senior administrators" defined in Category 1.0–Leadership.

Strategic and Operational Planning strongly reflects the core values and concepts of the Criteria. (See the appendix for a full description of these eleven core values and concepts.) "Learning-Centered Education" must be a prominent feature of a successful strategic planning operation. For example, "management by fact," another core value, must focus on measures of student learning, including input data, environmental data, and performance data. These data must produce trends and projections that are characteristic of learning-centered education. "Results orientation," another key for strategic planning, establishes the learning assessments that will be measured in subsequent sections of the Criteria.

Two other core values have implications for strategic and operational planning—"long-range view of the future" and "fast response." On the one hand, the planning effort itself must be a sustained one: two- to five-year projections are expected in the second section. The educational enterprise is a long-term investment with incremental payoffs; planning efforts in general require a longer view of the future than those of some other types of organizations. On the other hand, because "fast response" is also a core value, and a necessity for achieving acceptable results, the educational institution must position itself to be more agile than it has in the past.

Further, "faculty and staff participation and development," another core value, has particular implications for planning in educational institutions. Baldrige winners often point to broad participation among all employees of the organization as both an important result and as a method for achieving other results. Yet, educational institutions have typically used a more participatory management approach than many businesses due to the composition of their workforce, academic culture, and the overall nature of their enterprise. For a strategic planning operation, that already-established history of broad academic participation is an advantage; however, changing direction with a large leadership group requires a lengthy period of discussion, and thus it is also a disadvantage.

The Category contains two parts: 3.1–Strategy Development (forty-five points) and 3.2–Strategy Deployment (thirty points). For this category, educational institutions need to establish strategic directions, generate a set of annual strategic plans or their equivalent, and make sure that both broad-based participation in the creation of the strategic plan occurs and that the units affected by the plan understand its relationship to their day-to-day activities.

Strategy Development

The purpose of the first Item, Strategy Development, is to examine how an educational institution sets strategic directions and how it determines key plan requirements. Three areas are emphasized:

- How the school develops strategies and plans, including strategic approaches to students' needs and expectations; key external factors, requirements, and opportunities; key internal factors, including assessment systems; and improvement of student and overall school performance.

- How strategies are translated into critical success factors and deployed in the organization.

- How the school evaluates and improves its strategic planning process.

As discussed earlier in the chapter, each of these areas is consistent with the larger purposes and core values of strategic planning. For example, a high performing educational organization determines its students' needs and expectations (the first Area to Address) through a variety of approaches, including regular surveying or interviewing. In Category 7.0 "Student Focus and Student and Stakeholder Satisfaction," the issues of student needs and expectations are again addressed, and the results are evaluated and scored. Only planning for student and stakeholder satisfactions needs to be described in the Strategy Development section.

The more successful planning processes effectively move from consideration of a range of alternative goals and strategies to the few that become the primary focus. Educational institutions are influenced by key external factors, another Area to Address, in a plethora of different venues, such as population demographics, local political climate, technological innovations, religious activity, state and national political trends, and pedagogical advances.

The key internal factors, the next Area to Address, are also complex. Societal demands reflected in key external factors may require a rethinking of mission. Measuring that mission may require the establishment of an integrated assessment system focused on student performance for long term strategic success. To be credible, the assessment effort must be developed through and supported by appropriate benchmark data. Technological innovation, an external factor, may also require facility and equipment upgrades as well as new learning opportunities for faculty members and staff.

How strategies and plans are translated into critical success factors are measured in Categories 6.0–School Performance Results and

Societal demands reflected in key external factors may require a rethinking of mission.

7.0—Student Focus and Student and Stakeholder Satisfaction. The entire planning effort may be beautifully crafted and prepared, but unless student and school performance—as measured by facts—improves, the planning and the effect of quality on the organization fails. Benchmarking (mentioned in the notes to 3.1 and in 3.2's Areas to Address) is a tool that can be used to develop an effective system of comparing appropriate organizational results from one organization to another. While comparative analysis (comparison of results) would seem to meet the demands of the criteria, process benchmarking (a comparison of processes used to achieve results) is required to make the greatest improvements.

The final Area to Address in Section 3.1 is how the institution evaluates and improves its strategic planning process. The organization needs to be asking itself continually what it could have done better to create a more accurate and predictive plan, to make the faculty, staff, and students aware of the plan and its relevance to them, and to translate generalities into critical success factors. The methodology may be as simple as a discussion of strengths and weaknesses of the annual planning cycle. Scoring for Approach/Deployment categories allows no score over 60 percent for a planning process that does not demonstrate evidence of improvement cycles and analysis.

Strategy Deployment

The second Item (3.2) of the Strategic and Operational Planning Category—Strategy Deployment—summarizes how the institution's success factors are deployed throughout the organization and how those factors move performance ahead in the future. This section evaluates not how measures are designed but how they are spread through the educational institution.

A critical feature here is that the indicators selected should truly measure the strategic thrust.

The Strategy Deployment section has two Areas to Address; the first describes how the strategic plan has been translated into action. Key objectives and requirements are described along with associated measures and indicators. A critical feature here is that the indicators selected should truly measure the strategic thrust. For example, improving student scholastic performance might be a strategic thrust for a secondary school with scores on scholastic aptitude tests as an associated measure.

Another key objective is to achieve an organization-wide understanding of the relationships between the measures and the strategic thrust. The success of empowerment, investing employees with decision-making powers for their own processes, often hinges on a broad-based organizational understanding of the relationship between the work of individuals and the strategic direction of the organization. In a debate over the effectiveness of the Baldrige, Phil Pifer (1992), principal of McKinsey & Company, notes insufficient linkages with strategic priorities and employee confusion over how strategic priorities dovetail with unit plans as frequent flaws in unsuccessful quality programs. Further, in "How the Baldrige Really Works," Garvin (1991) contends that better plans have alignment and integration. Their important qualities include:

- Benchmarking findings
- Customer data to drive goals
- Close alignment with the resource planning process
- An umbrella for a variety of quality approaches

Anecdotes from successful Baldrige winners in non-educational categories often revolve around interviewing staff employees, such as janitors on night shifts. If these employees can articulate the strategic direction of the organization, its outlook on customers, and make such distinctions as internal and external customers, then the organization has achieved its goal. While Hillenmeyer (1994) recently estimated that only twenty-five percent of employees need to be involved for a quality-oriented culture to be in place, higher levels of deployment are necessary for success in award competition.

Student performance and faculty/staff productivity—other key objectives in the first Area to Address—should be addressed with plans and targets in this category aligned with the directions expressed in Strategy Development. Results in subsequent categories include data on student performance, school education climate improvement, research/scholarship and service, and school business performance. Many of these areas, such as climate, will cut across various administrative units of the educational institution and will require a high degree of coordination among various organizational units.

Resource plans, a final key objective, are a regular part of traditional higher education strategic planning. Resource plans allow units to see how the thrust of the plan will manifest itself in their own area. Together with the selection of key measures and indicators, resource plans allow strategic direction to be translated into concrete actions. Resource plans allow employees to see how their own operations will progress during the period covered by the plan and how their achievement of results impacts organizational success. Garvin (1991) rates close alignment with a resource planning process as a characteristic of better plans.

The Strategy Deployment section's second Area to Address requires two- to five-year projections of key indicators of student performance and business operational performance. Assessment literature findings, such as Terenzini and Pascarella's (1991) *How College Affects Students: Findings and Insights from Twenty Years of Research*, may be used as a guide to appropriate indicators of higher education's impact on students. Even though such scholars conclude that assessing the value of education is problematic, their research may provide a framework for the selection of measures suitable to a proposed strategic plan.

The second Area to Address also requires establishing a baseline for comparison from the school's past performance. Most educational institutions will have several of these standard test measurements readily available from past years. These same data may continue to be applicable as long as the character of the student body remains essentially unchanged.

Data from like educational institutions, called comparators, have long been a part of a sophisticated system of results analysis for strategic planning purposes. Most educational institutions have engaged in an attempt to develop a reliable and credible comparator list. Many belong to associations that provide extensive, carefully-controlled data about such peer institutions. These data are collected according to rigidly-prescribed definitions, are published regularly, and are good sources for basic comparative work. When such data are used, their relevance to the strategic direction should be made clear.

Key benchmarks are a final area in Strategy Deployment. Benchmarking, the search for best practices, allows the organization to know how its results compare with results in comparable organi-

HIGH PERFORMING COLLEGES

zations. As such, benchmarking may test the success of Strategy Deployment. In addition, process benchmarking provides the organization with methods for improving practices. Zangwill (1994) says that "benchmarking is a powerful concept," but believes there is fear of the benchmarking process as being threatening because it is difficult for leaders in any organization to admit that their practices are not the best.

CAUTIONS FROM THE MANAGEMENT LITERATURE

While some quality practitioners have been skeptical about the applicability of management literature to educational institutions, the management literature does offer some guidance to strategic planners in higher education. Ingeborg A. Marquardt (1992), a member of the board of examiners for the MBNQA and quality improvement process director at Siemens Gammasonics, Inc., offers a list of pitfalls for quality planners to avoid as they use the Baldrige award process to improve performance in business. These pitfalls have applicability to educational institutions as well:

1. "TQM process implementation is only a goal." For educational institutions, the focus must be on educational results—improved learning environments, better research and scholarship results (where applicable), and more effective use of resources to reach those ends. Customer satisfaction means better learning outcomes, more satisfied participants in the learning process, and a better response from successor educational institutions and from employers.

2. "The quality strategy is not tied to the business strategy." The business in an educational institution is the business of educating students. All the critical success factors must revolve around this core. An educational institution that has many quality improvement teams, is improving many processes— such as registration—and has a high level of participation in quality programs still may not be improving the core of more and better learning.

The business in an educational institution is the business of educating students.

3. "Goals, priorities, and targets are unclear." In an educational institution's strategic planning environment, this pitfall could be deadly. Stakeholders, employees, and students must all be aware of direction and priorities. In order to have a high-performing organization, all must be able to understand, articulate, and apply strategic

directions to daily tasks. In *The Fifth Discipline*, Peter Senge (1990) discusses aligning personal vision with organizational vision.

4. "Goal setting is unaggressive." This pitfall will be particularly serious as schools enter the Baldrige environment because few examples will exist of what goals might be considered regular goals and what would be required to establish a stretch goal. Seymour (1994) notes that the award criteria require that organizations establish some stretch goals, often expressed in terms of a fifty percent improvement in six months, in contrast with the more typical ten to fifteen percent goals. Baldrige winners in other competitions have set aggressive improvement goals.

5. "Goals are not quantified or substantiated." Goals must be validated through the benchmarking process. The idea of being a world-class university is a commonly articulated one, but it is not a quantifiable goal because a phrase such as "world-class" must be supported by a set of specific measures. Planners need not only ask the question "What do we want to achieve?" but also to be able to answer the question "How do we know if we are successful?" The latter question requires two sets of metrics that measure critical success factors.

6. "The process lacks customer focus." Later in this chapter, the authors define educational environment stakeholders as including present and future students, alumni, faculty, friends, trustees, parents, vendors, employees, government agencies, and legislative bodies. These are the constituents who must be consulted in establishing customer focus—a particularly thorny issue in educational institutions because few educators view their present students as customers.

7. "Customers are viewed generically." As the discussion about customer stakeholders in the next section concludes, colleges and universities have a number of target segments at their base. The needs of these different types of customers and stakeholders will drive quality efforts in different ways. Each educational institution must decide when and how to view the student as stakeholder, as customer, as partner and/or resource, and each must determine how to balance competing interests. Alumni may have a set of needs which differ from those of students' parents, which differ from those of companies that hire graduates. At various points of societal change, boards of trustees and legislators have had views diametrically opposed to

those of the current student body. Planning must reflect the results of many key decisions about who the customer is and the relative importance of competing customer needs.

8. "Company lacks perspective on competitors." Many educational institutions traditionally have not seen themselves as existing in a competitive environment. Some private colleges have been in severe competition for decades. As the college-aged population ceased to grow in the eighties, many other colleges and universities began to acknowledge the effects of competition. While the sophistication about competition is growing, educational institutions still know less about their competitors than most businesses do. In traditional strategic planning language, this situation provides an opportunity for those who have analyzed such issues as competition and a threat to those who have not.

9. "Employees are left out of the planning process." The involvement of faculty and staff in the planning process varies among educational institutions. Larger universities with a bigger cadre of professional administrators may be the least likely to include a broad-base of teachers and support staff. Smaller institutions may involve a more diverse group of employees. A great deal of energy must be spent on linking the authors of the plan with the front line personnel who will deliver it.

10. "Suppliers are left out of the planning process." The primary supplier for an educational institution is another educational institution; K-12 schools supply to colleges and two year institutions, and they, in turn, supply to graduate and professional schools. Increasingly—both on the local level and nationally—colleges are carrying on a dialogue with their K-12 suppliers about what the requirements for success are.

11. "Data insufficiently support the planning process." Educational institutions would seem to have an abundance of data about inputs and outputs in terms of standard test scores. Fewer data are available about what happens during the educational process. All of the input and output data are discussed fully in the assessment literature. The real challenge to the strategic planner is to make sense of it all, to isolate the changes that occur, and to track them back to variations in the process.

Marquardt (1992) concludes that "strategic planning is about change." She notes that no organization produces a plan saying that it intends to continue as it is. Therefore, she sees strategic planning and total quality as two change agents that work well together. Administrators in education are well aware of the existence of varied learning styles and problem-solving approaches. Some individuals see the likeness in their surroundings while others focus on the differences. Those whose mental discipline is to tie together will benefit from a brief perusal of the management literature around the strategic planning category of the Baldrige award. Others may wish to work only through the application of theory.

THE BALDRIGE AND STRATEGIC PLANNING AT PENN STATE: A SWOT ANALYSIS

The authors now provide a SWOT analysis of the strategic planning efforts at Penn State in the context of a growing commitment to continuous quality improvement and of the Baldrige criteria for the Strategic and Operational Planning Category. Like other major public research universities, Penn State faces a complex future with many applicable strengths, weaknesses, opportunities, and threats. However, for the purpose of this discussion, only one example in each SWOT area has been selected: the strength discussed is a long history of strategic planning, the weakness is the academic culture prevalent in educational institutions, the threat is the concept of customer, and the opportunity is changing the culture.

Strength: The Planning Process

The Pennsylvania State University has long had a serious commitment to an active strategic planning program with each major unit on campus producing a plan. The plans are reviewed by a strategic planning committee that often offers constructive comments to improve the plans and the planning cycle itself. This practice is consistent with quality principles as measured by MBNQA Criteria in Category 3.1. The current scenario requires a five-year strategic plan featuring a complete SWOT analysis with annual updates and reports in years two, three, four, and five to show progress and problems.

The budget shortfalls epidemic for education in the 1990s caused the university to establish a committee to examine the future of all programs and to recommend specific budget reductions. Planning units were asked to design a ten percent cut over three years and to suggest a reinvestment strategy for two and a half percent. As the University concurrently began to focus on the principles of continuous quality improvement, the Provost and members of the strategic planning committee observed that the plans contained many statements based on anecdotal evidence, and perhaps even wishful thinking. Planning units were inclined to rank themselves as "best" or "excellent" without providing data to substantiate those claims. The committee wished for better data to support the planning effort.

Planning units were inclined to rank themselves as "best" or "excellent" without providing data to substantiate those claims.

In the 1994 planning cycle, this desire for data generated a requirement that the planning units do benchmarking as a part of their planning updates. Each unit's strategic plan was to consist of a strategic update, a benchmarking plan, a resource allocation plan, and a diversity plan. The idea of comparative analysis was familiar to strategic planners at Penn State, but the concept of process benchmarking was new to most.

In the summer, the University enjoyed a corporate gift from the DuPont Corporation. One hundred and twenty Penn State faculty and administrators were invited to attend a three-day conference entitled "Continuous Quality Improvement." One of the most heavily attended sessions was on benchmarking. Penn State's Quality Council (the university-wide advisory group on quality) and the campus Quality Coordinator (the staff member who assists units with quality programs and provides overall training for the University), provided further educational opportunities on benchmarking: a panel discussion on campus, a Human Resources Department benchmarking class, and opportunities for individual consultation.

Nevertheless, the results, as judged by the benchmarking plans submitted, were uneven. Many units substituted comparative analysis for process benchmarking. These units continued to focus on inputs as represented in numbers compared across an established list of institutions. While this use of comparative analysis addressed the need for data, it did not serve as a guide to improving results.

The 1995 strategic plan guidelines called for a benchmarking plan again. The message to planning units from the Provost and the planning group focused on the value of process benchmarking. The Quality Coordinator planned a three-part series of brown bag discussions about benchmarking in the strategic planning environment, comparative analysis versus process benchmarking, and a focus on collecting and analyzing data. The results are improving, but the need to continue to teach planners how to use process benchmarking effectively remains and is being addressed by a continuous quality improvement team.

In terms of scoring an application to fulfill the MBNQA Education Pilot Criteria 3.0, this effort may be judged to provide a sound and systematic approach. Increasingly, individual units provide data, and as benchmarking becomes more effective, a greater number of unit plans should become fact-based. The strategic planning has no major gaps in deployment, but some units may be judged to be in early stages of understanding.

Weakness: The Academic Culture

Strategy Deployment, Item 3.2 of the MBNQA Criteria, focuses upon organization-wide aspects of strategic planning and looks for managed integration of quality throughout the organization in a fashion directed by the strategic focus of the planning process. However, the fabric of faculty culture that permeates educational institutions, including Penn State, compounds the difficulty of integrating a plan or even a quality focus into day-to-day operations.

Central to higher education is what Clark (1984) has referred to as the "master matrix of the higher education system." Within this matrix, faculty are grounded in discipline-based communities of interest (e.g., history, physics, chemistry) with an "assignment" to an enterprise, the enterprise being the college or university department. It has been observed that faculty frequently express far stronger allegiance to their discipline than to the organization that pays their salary (Becher 1989). Clark observes that this discipline-enterprise matrix underlies much of the organizational uniqueness of higher education, a form not found elsewhere in anything like the same scope or intensity. Similarly, Seymour (1994) notes that the structure of colleges and universities is such that "Each discipline veils itself in a lexicon that works to ensure exclusivity. Collaboration across the boundaries is discouraged" (24). While colleges and universities have long worked with a dynamic tension between loyalty to the discipline and loyalty to the institution, working through these divisions provides yet another challenge to the environment that produces a high-performing organization.

The discipline-based community evaluates faculty reputation based upon the criteria of scholarship and research as determined by each unique discipline. The college or university rewards the faculty—through academic appointment, promotion within ranks, the awarding of tenure, and financial rewards—according to the reputation that they earn within their discipline. The reputational, discipline-based system links with the college or university through the department head. It is, therefore, not uncommon for faculty, the primary interactor with the customer—to use Baldrige terminology—to view institution-based planning efforts with some disdain. They neither participate in the processes nor feel that their actions should be directed by strategic decisions. They feel this way because they view their discipline to be their organizational home. This perspective is not unique to the professoriate. Most professions function largely as relatively homogeneous communities whose members share identity, values, definitions or roles, and interests that are at times at odds with their employers (Bucher and Strauss 1960).

In education, the failure to achieve a common institutional perspective is particularly true as it relates to the curriculum. The curriculum, course content, and methods of teaching are all part of the gatekeeping function of the academic disciplines and are often considered the sole province of the faculty. The curriculum is one of the mechanics of cohesiveness through which the social structure of the disciplines is preserved (Dean and Bowen 1994). Faculty, with great stridency, object to institution-based formalized assessment of course offerings, course content, or even individual teaching ability. This perspective is consistent with the discipline-based perspective that academics bring to their employment. Reputation is based upon research and publication as recognized by the discipline and secondarily rewarded by the employing institution. Preservation of the strength of the discipline's knowledge base from intrusion by other disciplines is central to the survival of the reputation system. A field of study is frequently considered a discipline only after a curriculum has been established at a college or university by vote of the faculty. None of these has anything directly to do with customers or course

The curriculum is one of the mechanics of cohesiveness through which the social structure of the disciplines is preserved.

offerings, institutional initiatives to serve student needs, or planning initiated by an academic administrator. However, the faculty culture in higher education can be viewed as an internal threat to the survival of higher education as professional values conflict with organizational aims.

In terms of Strategic and Operational Planning 3.0, this weakness may manifest itself in several ways. For instance, in Strategy Development, agreeing on an integrated assessment system and overall measures for student and school performance may be hampered by the divided loyalties of faculty. Also in Strategy Deployment, cooperation among units contributing to the same plan elements may be difficult to achieve and issues of faculty productivity may present further challenges. For possible scoring in Approach/Deployment, the fragmentation of the academic enterprise makes an effective and consistent deployment, and thus a higher score, extremely difficult to achieve.

Opportunity: Changing the Culture

The opportunity that Penn State and other educational institutions seek through their involvement with total quality and eventually with the MBNQA is to change the culture. Educational institutions that actively scan their environments are extremely concerned about their prospects for survival. Public institutions, in particular, see themselves competing with other societal needs. In the past, educational institutions had a mystique derived from their long history as holders of valuable and secret learning, not easily understandable to the layperson. Scandals about expenditures of research and other funds, a new wave of consumerism, and such pressing demands as the need for more prisons have made legislators wary of acceding to education's increasing demands for funding. Legislators, and the public in general, want accountability. The MBNQA is designed to provide accountability for the key enterprise—Learning-Centered Education. This core value, along with Management by Fact, Results Orientation, and Fast Response, can make the dialogue between educational institutions and their legislators and other stakeholders much more productive.

Many question whether the culture of such a large, complex, and tradition-bound organization can be changed, but others believe that

---

HIGH PERFORMING COLLEGES

it must be changed and have begun to make incremental but continuous improvements. At Penn State, the focus on benchmarking as part of strategic planning is a step towards changing the culture. Planning units are encouraged to identify key processes that need improvement, to admit that the established way of doing business may not be optimal, and to learn from best practitioners. As described above, the request for benchmarking arose from a lack of data reported in existing strategic plans. Increasingly on campus, meetings of senior university administrators do focus on data, and systems to collect and interpret data are being improved to make them more useful.

Some faculty have accepted the concept of the student as a customer in the higher education enterprise. More attention is being paid to making sure that students are able to get the courses they need when they enroll. Some courses have been recognized as suppliers to other courses, and syllabi and teaching methods have been improved to meet the needs of the student "customer." Advising has been studied and is being improved. Student opinion is often sought, and the needs of students in all areas of the university are more often examined and responded to.

Strategy Deployment cannot occur in a closed organization. Penn State has gradually become more open in its approaches to key issues. For instance, heads of planning units are required to engage in broad participation in the creation of each unit plan. In addition, teamwork and cooperation are replacing competition as operational values. Continuous quality teams, benchmarking teams, self-directed work teams, and other instances of cooperation are increasing.

Organizations that compete successfully for quality awards are organizations that have succeeded in changing their culture. If the external threats to educational institutions continue at the level they have been in the 90s or increase, and if the leadership at Penn State remains strongly committed to the need for change, then in a slow and deliberate way, the culture can and will change. The reward for that would be more than a quality award in the education category; the reward would be thriving in a radically different future.

Threat: Language and Concept of Customer and Stakeholder

A dean at a major midwestern university once remarked that even naming a quality effort for an academic institution is a major challenge because the faculty don't like the words "total" or "quality" or "management." Another word that faculty don't like is "customer," especially if that might be defined to include students. If quality is defined as meeting or exceeding customer expectations, then this assumes that the customer, not the producer, defines quality, and clearly the Baldrige Criteria recognize the student as a primary customer. In the introductory section entitled "Customers," the *Education Pilot Criteria* discusses this definitional conundrum:

> The approach selected for the Pilot Program seeks to distinguish between students and stakeholders for purposes of clarity and emphasis. Stakeholders include parents, employers, other schools, communities, etc. To further clarify the requirements related to students, the requirements for **current** students are separated from those of **future** students. Requirements for current students are more concrete, specific, and immediate; determining requirements for future students is part of the school's planning, and needs to take into account changing student populations and changing requirements future students must be able to meet. A major challenge schools face is "bridging" between current student needs and the needs of future students. This requires an effective learning/change strategy.

Clearly, the award intends that both current and future students will be considered as customers. For the purposes of Strategic and Operational Planning, the needs of future students are of greater moment, and the planning effort must pay special attention to changing needs and requirements of students.

The weakness for Penn State and any other educational institution is that, for the most part, faculty do not want to see themselves as being accountable to their students. Faculty believe that they know how students need to be socialized to meet the demands of the discipline. Faculty, not students, know what knowledge is new, important, and deserving of inclusion in the course syllabus because, in many cases, those same faculty are creating the knowledge base of the discipline through their research. The whole issue of bland, brief, end-of-the semester student evaluation of teaching efficacy has been the subject of such endless debate in educational institutions that its value is often marginal. The idea that a professor might give over some time weekly or even daily to a discussion of teaching effectiveness is unthinkable to many faculty, and a significant weakness in meeting the criteria of the MBNQA.

Understanding how stakeholders might define "customer" perhaps sheds some further light on the idea of customer as a weakness in educational institutions. Students and their parents are clearly important stakeholders in higher education, but more and more these stakeholders view higher education as a training ground for professional careers. For this category of stakeholder the most important customer of higher education is the future employer. The course of instruction and classroom assessment might best be designed to accommodate the needs of employers, to assure good job offers and high starting salaries for the students upon graduation, or to gain entry to professional programs in graduate schools, where an M.B.A., M.D., or J.D. degree might guarantee even greater career rewards. For the legislator, the customer might well be the taxpayer whose dollars contribute to the ongoing operations. These customers want to know that their money is being well spent to produce better citizens, winning sports teams, an improved standard of living for their children, and so forth. Legislative actions that seek to address teacher quality or faculty workload address the concept of taxpayer as customer. On campus the customer is frequently identified as next year's student. Faculty in large research universities want to attract the best graduate students to their programs. These students enhance the reputation of their departments and upon graduation lend to the mentoring faculty's overall reputation within the discipline.

Other stakeholders exist and could be considered, but throughout academia, today's student is seldom seen as a customer. Although some effort on every campus is directed at retaining students, only at the community college, trade school, or preparatory school level is curricula tailored to attract students. Those in education argue that teaching is designed to impart new knowledge and explore new ideas; higher learning is tailored to socialize students to the methods of the disciplines; and the social good of higher education is the creation of an educated human being. It is not about customers' self-defining outcomes.

Other stakeholders exist and could be considered, but throughout academia, today's student is seldom seen as a customer.

This threat is a significant one for meeting the requirements of Strategic and Operational Planning. At a large institution with a cadre of planning professionals, a strategic plan using language not accepted by faculty might be written, but it could not be successfully deployed into a community accustomed to open discussion. Neither could the many planning units of a large university be expected to write about concepts they questioned, written in language that they considered inappropriate. The support side of many universities does accept both the concept and the language of the student as customer. Much progress can be made in improving those areas, but even discussing, much less changing, the key teaching/learning enterprise, the faculty-dominated classroom, presents an ongoing challenge to planning for quality.

CONCLUSION

One cynical view of both the Strategic and Operational Planning Category and any educational institution's strategic planning effort is that they are not very important. The number of points assigned to the category is small, and educational planning often results in a document that is placed on the shelf and ignored. However, any organization that has engaged in productive strategic planning will attest to its value, especially if that organization has successfully deployed the plan to employees, customers, and stakeholders and has coordinated operational plans in a fact-based environment. A well-conceived plan can do much to hold an organization together, to make leadership effective, and to achieve the results necessary for high performance.

Strategic planning is a systematic and iterative process that requires management and employee to link their decision-making and actions to a strategic assessment of operating environments to achieve a competitive edge. The total quality approach holds that the competitive edge can only be maintained as organizations strive to meet or exceed customer expectations. Strategic planning is significant to the Baldrige Award because it provides a framework that forces leadership to define the core attributes of an organization and links those attributes to action; it supports the Baldrige focus on customer by addressing the needs of stakeholders and defining strategies in terms of stakeholder concerns. Strategic planning also supports the Baldrige's focus on process because it engages the total organization in action.

REFERENCES

Becher, T. 1989. *Academic Tribes and Territories*. Bristol, PA: Society for Research into Higher Education and Open University Press.

Bryson, J. 1988. *Strategic Planning for Public and Nonprofit Organizations: A Guide to Strengthening and Sustaining Organizational Achievement*. San Francisco: Jossey-Bass.

Bucher, R. and A. Strauss. 1960. Professions in Process. *American Journal of Sociology* 66(2): 325-34.

Christensen, R., K. Andrews, J. Bower, R. Hammermesh, and M. Porter. 1983. *Business Policy: Text and Cases*. Homewood, IL: Irwin.

Clark, B. 1984. The Organizational Conception. In *Perspectives on Higher Education*, edited by B. Clark, 106-31. Berkeley: University of California Press.

Cyert, R. 1988. Carnegie Mellon University. In *Successful Strategic Planning: Case Studies*, edited by D. Steeples, 91. New Directions for Higher Education, no. 64. San Francisco: Jossey-Bass.

Dean, J. and D. Bowen. 1994. Management Theory and Total Quality: Improving Research and Practice Through Theory Development. *Academy of Management Review* 19(3): 392-418.

Garvin, D. 1991. How the Baldrige Award Really Works. *Harvard Business Review* (November/December): 80-92.

Hillenmeyer, S. 1994. Baldrige Assessment for Education. Presentation at Penn State University, 15 December.

Marquardt, I. 1992. Inside the Baldrige Award Guidelines Category 3: Strategic Quality Planning. *Quality Progress* (August): 93-96.

Nutt, P. and R. Backoff. 1992. *Strategic Management of Public and Third Sector Organizations: A Handbook for Leaders*. San Francisco: Jossey-Bass.

Pifer, P. 1992. Does the Baldrige Award Really Work? *Harvard Business Review* (January/February): 137-38.

Senge, P. 1990. *The Fifth Discipline: The Art and Practice of the Learning Organization.* New York: Doubleday.

Seymour, D. 1994. The Baldrige Cometh. *Change* (January/February): 19.

Shirley, R. 1988. Strategic Planning: An Overview. In *Successful Strategic Planning: Case Studies,* edited by D. Steeples. New Directions for Higher Education, no. 64. San Francisco: Jossey-Bass.

Teeter, D. and G. Lozier. 1995. Total Quality Management Principles and Strategic Planning. In *Strategic Planning: A Human Resources Tool*, edited by K. Alvino. Washington, D.C.: College and Universities Personnel Association.

Terenzini, P. and E. Pascarella. 1991. *How College Affects Students: Findings and Insights from Twenty Years of Research.* San Francisco: Jossey-Bass.

U. S. Department of Commerce, National Institute of Standards and Technology. 1995. *Malcolm Baldrige National Quality Award: Education Pilot Criteria.* Washington, DC: GPO.

Zangwill, W. 1994. Ten Mistakes CEOs Make About Quality. *Quality Progress* (June): 43-48.

8
Human Resource Development and Management: Helping People Grow

Kathleen A. O'Brien, William McEachern, and Elizabeth A. Luther

Recently the American Association of Higher Education sponsored its third annual conference (1995) on faculty roles and rewards with the theme "From 'My Work' to 'Our Work': Realigning Faculty Work with College and University Purposes." This theme captures much that is problematic about the function of human resource development and management in higher education, especially when focused on the faculty. The culture of higher education has long nurtured and rewarded the work of individual faculty, particularly in creating new knowledge—the "scholarship of discovery" to use Boyer's (1990) categories. In many institutions, faculty are encouraged to function as independent entrepreneurs, focusing their efforts on their own scholarly work. Yet all across the country there has been a realization by faculty themselves, as well as by many outside academia, that this model of faculty work has decreased collective responsibility for contributing to the institution's mission and purposes. No where is this more evident than with the mission of teaching and learning (Boyer 1990; Riordan 1993). Since faculty goals and institutional missions are frequently not aligned, a coherent human resource or faculty development agenda is difficult to achieve.

But this isn't the only dilemma associated with human resource development and management in higher education. On the staff side of the equation, another kind of discontinuity occurs. In "The Age of Paradox," a provocative and reflective essay on modern society and its organizations, Charles Handy (1994) writes: "There must be more to life than being a cog in someone else's great machine, hurtling

God knows where" (xx)—a lament that many employees of colleges and universities may recognize as their own. Many staff not directly involved in teaching or research experience their work—no matter how significant to the mission and purposes of the institution—as unconnected, unrecognized, and unrewarded. Not having a clear sense of their relationship to the mission and purposes of the institution, or to each other, college operations such as accounting, plants and grounds, and food service may become narrowly fixed on immediate goals and oblivious to the impact of their efforts on the quality of teaching and learning and other important institutional goals.

This chapter is focused on ways the Baldrige criterion—Human Resource Development and Management (4.0)—may help analyze and even serve as a means to transform these discontinuities into productive forces that lead to the accomplishment of mission and purposes. First, we will briefly review the management literature on human resource development and management (HR) to examine its compatibility with quality improvement principles and practice. We will also take a look at the experience of Baldrige Award winners and applicants from business and industry, examining their human resource practices for lessons learned. We'll then turn our attention to how the Baldrige human resource criterion for education might serve as a framework for analyzing and improving the HR function in higher education, describing, too, the problematic elements in applying the Baldrige. Finally, we will set forth our own experience in applying the Baldrige criterion to the HR function at Alverno College, noting what we've found to be helpful and what has assisted us to analyze and plan for necessary improvements at the College.

HUMAN RESOURCE THEORY AND PRACTICE IN RELATION TO CONTINUOUS QUALITY IMPROVEMENT

As conceptualized in the management literature (Heneman and Schwab, 1982; Schuler, Beutall, and Youngblood, 1989) the HR function in organizations seeks to accomplish two major objectives: (1) obtaining and retaining a workforce and (2) ensuring the effectiveness of that workforce. Although interrelated, the first objective is associated most directly with activities such as planning, forecasting, recruitment, selection, and staffing, while the second is associated with training and development, performance appraisal systems, compensation and reward structures, safety and health procedures, and labor management relations.

Recent analyses of the research, theory, and practice of human resource management compared to the developing theory and practice of continuous quality improvement (CQI) approaches, reveal a significant overlap between the two (Dean and Bowen 1994). Both the HR literature and the writings of proponents of CQI focus on human resource planning, employee involvement, education and training, performance and recognition, and employee well-being and satisfaction. Both highlight the significance of the systems approach to evaluating the HR function in organizations and the role of human resources in providing a competitive advantage for the firm (Lado and Wilson 1994).

Despite these commonalities, there are several significance differences between the theory and practice of HR described in the management literature and the principles and practices of continuous improvement. Each places different weight on the importance of the individual employee as a determinant of organizational quality. W. Edwards Deming, the founding father of statistical quality control methods and quality improvement efforts adopted in Japan (and later in the U.S.), believed that much of employee performance is determined by system factors beyond the individual's control (Walton 1986). Deming estimated that only ten to twenty-five percent of performance problems are due to employees and the rest are due to management and the way work is organized.

Consequently, CQI approaches place less emphasis on individual motivation, individual performance appraisal systems, or pay for performance and other individually focused compensation arrangements, emphasizing instead teamwork and recognition rewards. From this perspective, quality outcomes are derived from collective efforts and cross-functional work, so CQI efforts stress team or group-based rewards and cooperation as opposed to competition (Blackburn and Rosen 1993).

The HR management literature, on the other hand, focuses on the individual as the primary determinant of performance. It stresses the interaction of person and situation and focuses attention on solving performance problems by analyzing individual employee ability, motivation, and role clarity. For instance, there is voluminous research literature on performance appraisal (see Landy and Farr 1983; Bernardin and Beatty 1984; Berk 1986; Latham and Wexley 1994), but much of it is focused on developing reliable and valid performance appraisal instruments for individual employees. Similarly, there has been significantly more focus on the individual performer in relation to topics such as motivation, selection and reward systems than in CQI (Blackburn and Rosen 1993).

One of the reasons for the differences is that continuous improvement stresses the significance of systems and organizational structure as determinants of performance whereas conventional approaches focus on the individual. Another major reason is the changing nature of work in organizations. Most U.S. corporations today face much stronger global competition and more complex technological changes than ever before, and these require a more flexible, knowledgeable, and team-based workforce. Companies have also responded with flatter, less hierarchical organizational structures, emphasizing the quality of product or service as a means to remain competitive. It is not surprising, then, for human resource management and development approaches to be characterized by the differences noted above in quality driven companies.

THE BALDRIGE AND HUMAN RESOURCES IN BUSINESS AND INDUSTRY

Given the general description of human resource approaches in CQI organizations, the Baldrige Award can provide a vehicle for highlighting best HR practices in participating companies. In a study of the practices of eight Baldrige Award winners, Blackburn and Rosen (1993) found that the HR policies in these companies formed a constellation of supportive and interdependent processes. Based on interviews with award winners, the researchers reported fourteen ideal HR strategies that are important contributors to CQI. Those that are most salient to human resource managers in higher education are set forth in figure 1.

All the award winners in this study stressed the importance of: changing the culture of the organization to support quality efforts, replacing environments of distrust with ones of openness and trust, moving from rewarding individuals working alone to those working in teams, helping departments move from separate isolated units to seeing their connections with other units, moving from autocratic management styles to styles based on coaching and facilitation. Each also underscored the importance of the award *process* rather than the award *itself* as being instrumental in improving the quality of products and services.

Of particular interest to colleges and universities is the emphasis on training and the de-emphasis on promotions as symbols of corporate achievements. All of the companies invested significant amounts of time and money on training all employees and managers, to support quality measurement, problem solving, and teamwork. Such training is costly; however, in one of the few studies on the impact of training (Blackburn and Rosen 1993), Motorola estimated that thirty dollars were earned for each dollar spent on quality training.

Blackburn and Rosen also found that TQM-driven companies are structurally flatter, and less hierarchical and bureaucratic. Consequently, career development strategies de-emphasized promotions as signs of success and achievement and instead emphasized horizontal moves to challenging cross functional problem-solving positions.

The Baldrige self-evaluation process, of course, does not ensure quality practices. Even those that have applied for Baldrige recognition have shown tendencies to avoid or minimize several important quality practices. For instance, one experienced Baldrige examiner (Easton 1993) noted that many companies that have applied for the Baldrige Award have teams that do not effectively use team processes such as problem solving methods, do not provide the most basic quality training, do not measure the impact of training on employee work, and do not align the company performance evaluation system with the quality system. However, the most important lesson for higher education is that the Baldrige process revealed these inconsistencies, providing a framework and criteria that point out the structures and policies that do, as well as do not, support quality practices.

The Baldrige self-evaluation process, of course, does not ensure quality practices.

Fig. 1. Selected HR Policies that Support TQM
Lessons from Baldrige Winners

• Systems that allow upward and lateral communications are developed, implemented and reinforced.

• TQM training is provided to all employees and top management shows active support for such training.

• Employee involvement or participation programs are in place.

• Autonomous work groups are not required, but processes that bring multiple perspectives to bear on quality issues are imperative.

• Employees are empowered to make quality-based decisions at their discretion. Job design should make this apparent.

• Performance reviews are refocused from an evaluation of past performance only, to an emphasis on what management can do to assist employees in their future job-related quality efforts.

• Compensation systems reflect team related quality contributions, including mastery of additional skills.

• Non-financial recognition systems at both the individual and work group levels reinforce both small win and big victories in the quest for total quality

• Employee recruitment, selection, promotion, and career development programs reflect the new realities managing and working in a TQM environment.

Blackburn, R. and B. Rosen. 1993. Total Quality and Human Resources Management: Lessons Learned from Baldrige Award-winning Companies. *Academy of Management Executive* (Aug): 49-66.

CAN HR IN HIGHER EDUCATION BENEFIT FROM BALDRIGE SELF EVALUATION?

Some who question the value of higher education's conventional evaluation practices believe that the Baldrige Award process could become a tool to assist colleges and universities to improve, focusing attention on those systems that cause, reinforce, or diminish the quality of institutional commitments (Seymour 1994). Lessons learned from businesses who have used the Baldrige provide some support for this perspective.

However, although there are similarities, there are significant differences between the business world and the academy—differences in underlying values, organizational structures, and whom each serves. Who is the customer in a college or university? Should we think of our students primarily as consumers? Is using the language of business and commercial exchange appropriate, or does such use undermine the very heart of the human interchange we call teaching and learning? Might we use the concepts and principles without using the language?

All these questions confronted the staff of Alverno College as we took up the quality debate. We explored what we could learn from various quality initiatives in business, finding that many of the underlying values of CQI are similar to those we hold, particularly those values that encourage collective responsibility for college goals, fact-based problem solving, and continuous improvement (McEachern and O'Brien 1993). Believing that actively exploring new ways to improve the quality of our mission and purposes is worth the effort, we convened a quality council to begin the process. What follows is a description of our efforts to apply the Baldrige Criteria—especially the human resource function—to activities at the college.

APPLYING THE BALDRIGE TO HR PRACTICE AT ALVERNO COLLEGE

Although Alverno College has been dedicated to continuously creating and maintaining a quality educational program—particularly in regard to teaching, learning, and assessment—the more formal discussion of specific CQI concepts, their application to education, and their congruence with College assessment principles began approximately four years ago. In fact, the discussion grew out of several College initiatives in the human resources area. In the early '90s several milestone events occurred within a relatively short period of time:

- Impressed with the achievements of a major Wisconsin corporation's TQM effort in the area of employee policies, a College representative met with company representatives to learn more about their TQM effort.
- A steering committee was formed to systematically and institutionally promote and implement the principles behind Deming's philosophy and 14 points. The steering committee in collaboration with department heads and department employees developed a continuous improvement statement and 12 supporting points that together became known as "Implementing the Mission."
- Human resource policies and practices, as well as some benefits, were revised in light of the philosophy underlying "Implementing the Mission."
- "Implementing the Mission" points were presented to all non-faculty employees, followed by workshops on team building, mutual respect, and achieving goals for all administrative department heads.
- The Quality Council was formed.

From 1991 to 1994 the Quality Council was involved in the planning and coordination of a variety of campus quality initiatives. For some time the Council had been seeking a meaningful framework for quality activities, a stimulus that would focus related efforts on the academic and administrative sides of the institution, and a means of integrating and communicating the congruence of quality principles and Alverno's assessment-as-learning principles. The Baldrige Award Criteria appeared to fill these needs as well as provide the opportunity to more systematically identify the extent to which quality principles were being applied and deployed across the College.

Alverno had, in the early '70s, implemented a matrix form of organization on the academic side of the College—a structure whereby faculty held joint appointments in their discipline departments and ability departments. This matrix structure was introduced when the College initiated its ability-based educational program, a program that requires all students to demonstrate eight abilities (communication, analysis, problem solving, valuing in a decision making context, social interaction, global perspective taking, effective citizenship, and aesthetic response) as part of their graduation requirements. Since these abilities are integrated into disciplinary courses throughout the curriculum, it became necessary for faculty to work in interdisciplinary teams to develop new ways to teach and assess the abilities. For instance, a biology department faculty member may also be a member of the Effective Citizenship Ability Department. Or a faculty member in the nursing department may also be a member of the Social Interaction Department.

This matrix structure provided an opportunity for faculty to work collaboratively on teaching, learning, and assessment issues in interdisciplinary workgroups. It also supported the deployment of assessment-as-learning principles college-wide. The challenge remained to replicate this structure on the administrative side of the College as a means of deploying quality principles across the College. The Baldrige assessment process, with its potential for identifying a large number of improvement projects, provided an opportunity to identify strategies to achieve this goal.

The Baldrige assessment process, with its potential for identifying a large number of improvement projects, provided an opportunity to identify strategies to achieve this goal.

Given limited College resources for a pilot project, the Quality Council decided to focus on one of the Baldrige categories. It chose the Human Resource Development and Management Category (4.0) because it concentrates on two critical elements: the examination and documentation of how an organization's work force is developed to enable them to pursue the organization's quality and performance objectives, and the examination and documentation of how an organization creates and maintains an environment conducive to the full participation in their own and the organization's growth and development. These processes are explored by focusing on human resource planning and management, employee involvement, employee education and training, employee performance and recognition, and employee well-being and satisfaction.

These areas of focus were of particular interest to the Quality Council since they would enable evaluation of previous college-wide efforts in creating an environment of mutual trust and changes in human resource policies and practices. Also, Alverno had a new director of human resources who brought with her some quality and Baldrige experience, which we hoped to capitalize on as we moved through the self-evaluation process.

self-eval proc

The Council also selected the human resource category because of the College's practice of faculty development that emphasizes a collaborative approach to teaching and assessment, believing that this approach would be congruent with the underlying emphasis of the Baldrige. We recognized, too, that because of the needs of our students and our ability-based curriculum, we had, in effect, changed the nature of faculty work; as a consequence, we needed a continuously improving faculty development program.

Specific goals of this program include assisting faculty:

- in acquiring and maintaining strong skills in teaching and assessing student learning.
- in continuously re-conceptualizing and refining their understanding of the core curricular abilities and how to effectively teach for them across the curriculum.
- to continuously further their understanding of the needs of a changing diverse student population and to develop a wide range of effective strategies for developing student learning.
- in exploring the changing nature of their disciplines in relation to their ever growing understanding of teaching, learning, and assessment.

For all these reasons, we decided to use the Human Resource Category (4.0) in our testing of the Baldrige framework. We formulated a question we hoped the Baldrige process would answer: Do we have the structures in place college-wide, particularly in the human resource area, that support our on-going efforts to create and maintain quality in our educational program?

The Quality Council, with its cross-College representation, assumed major responsibility for data gathering, analysis, and drafting the Baldrige self-assessment. Academic and administrative sub-committees were formed to gather initial data regarding the College's approach to Human Resource Management and Development. The Council as a whole reviewed the preliminary data to identify errors or omissions regarding deployment of our approaches across the institution. A primary writer drafted the self-assessment and presented it to the entire Council for review and comment.

Through this experience we developed insight in three areas that had significant impact on our on-going quality efforts:

A primary writer drafted the self-assessment and presented it to the entire Council for review and comment.

Observations Regarding the Baldrige Itself

We returned to the consideration of the core values and concepts, and raised the question of whether they should be reshaped for education—and if so, how? Alternative models exist (for example, see the 1993 Report of the Wingspread Group on Higher Education, *An American Imperative: Higher Expectations for Higher Education,* for values/core concepts such as taking values seriously, putting student learning first, creating a nation of learners). We continue to engage in a conversation regarding the appropriate values and concepts in relationship to our own principles of assessment-as-learning.

Observations Regarding Our Process

We experienced a general dissatisfaction with the process we went through in completing the self-assessment. It is easier to respond to the "Areas to Address" than capture the uniqueness of an organization and its processes. While we addressed the areas relevant to each item within the category as we worked through our self-assessment, the end product did not capture the Alverno culture, environment, or processes in their richness and complexity.

We recognized the need to continue to experiment with alternative ways of communicating our processes to ensure we captured their richness and complexity. One such alternative is the faculty development map we developed to explain this process. Another is the diagram illustrated in figure 2. It begins with the College mission and purposes, then moves to the transformation of objectives into human resource development and management outcomes for indi-

---

HIGH PERFORMING COLLEGES

179

CONCORDIA COLLEGE LIBRARY
BRONXVILLE, N.Y. 10708

viduals, departments, and the entire College (for example, one such outcome might be effectively using problem solving and interaction methods and application of work standards to the achievement of job, department, and college goals). It then depicts the opportunity to articulate the principles and assumptions out of which we operate, and diagrams and describes the causal (albeit somewhat chaotic) process by which the outcome is achieved. In effect, this model does not start from the Baldrige category, but from our own themes, values, and organizing principles.

Observations Regarding Alverno College

We learned that the movement from college mission to human resource development and management outcomes in a small but complex educational institution was not a linear process, but rather a somewhat chaotic one. Figure 2 attempts to capture this complexity, and hints at an additional observation made elsewhere regarding the need for alternative models to articulate and communicate this complexity.

We became ever more aware of the need to integrate the academic and administrative activities of the College—to, in effect, make the institution whole. The answer to this problem found its first expression in a chapter written for *Continuous Quality Improvement: Making the Transition to Education* (Hubbard 1993) in which the authors attempted to articulate, for the College and others, the congruence between the quality principles we were attempting to implement and the assessment-as-learning principles we had so long embraced. The most recent expression of the congruence solution to this integration problem is found in the definition of Alverno Quality, "Toward A Definition of Quality at Alverno College":

> Quality occurs at Alverno College when all of our resources and processes are appropriately directed toward learning how to improve and improving in ways that result in benefits to our students, our faculty and staff, our colleagues in higher education, and all the other stakeholders in our educational mission. This is an ongoing quest that involves the application and integration of quality principles, the principles of ability-based education, and the principles of assessment-as-learning.

Fig. 2. Themes, Values, and Organizing Principles

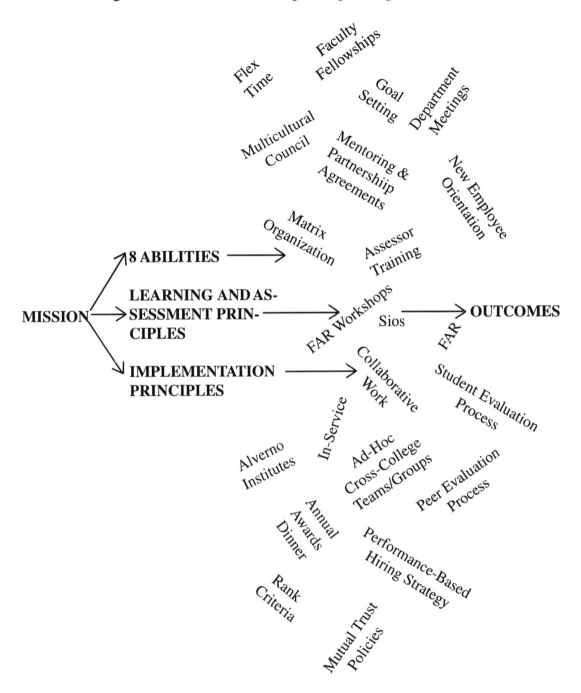

Alverno's quality efforts are customer-driven by directly focusing these resources and processes on the needs of the student-as-learner, the needs of students for timely and reliable services, the needs of the community and society within which we operate, and the needs of all the internal support services that contribute to the achievement of our educational mission. We meet these diverse needs through inquiry, dialogue, conversation and assessment.

Through the integration of quality principles that are applied primarily to administrative processes and the ability-based education and assessment-as-learning principles that are applied primarily to teaching and learning processes, Alverno has created a college-wide approach to the achievement of Alverno Quality.

At the end of this pilot project we recognized two potentially serious shortcomings in our self-assessment. The first relates to the role examples serve in the write-up. Do they come across as anecdotal evidence or as a genuine reflection of how Alverno College does things? This point relates to a second and more serious concern—the absence of readily available data as a basis for measuring our results. These observations led the Quality Council to establish a 1994–95 goal related to improving measurement College-wide.

CONCLUSIONS

These observations led the Quality Council to establish a 1994–95 goal related to improving measurement College-wide.

Colleges and universities haven't escaped the pressures facing many businesses today and need to find new ways of approaching complex problems that range from improving student learning to reducing overall costs. Unlike many businesses, however, much of the cost of higher education involves faculty and staff compensation. Like their for-profit colleagues, colleges and universities realize that these same human resources are also the primary drivers of improvements and solutions. Higher education, then, needs to focus its effort on ways to improve its own human resources—thinking through the nature of faculty and staff work, how this work supports the institutional mission, and how HR strategies and structures support and enhance the alignment of work and mission.

Continuous quality improvement practices in business—particularly those in the HR area—may prove to be helpful in higher education, too, but only if they are adapted to the values and culture that underlie the educational enterprise. On the other hand, this translation is likely to be ineffective if college and university faculty do not rethink the nature of their work in relation to the major problems facing higher education. How can we improve teaching and learning unless we work together? How will we contain the costs of education unless we rethink the nature of faculty roles and rewards? How do we ensure that technology is used to enhance the quality of education, not merely to reduce costs or numbers of faculty?

The faculty and staff at Alverno who have studied and experimented with CQI practices and the Baldrige Criteria concur with the conclusions of a recent review of books on this subject by De Villo Sloan (1994):

> If the various scholars from gender studies, leadership studies, and other disciplines were to look beyond the "management fad" they envision when they hear the language of TQM, they would find a holistic philosophy that supports and enhances their ideas. . . . Those very faculty members who express reservations about TQM because it represents yet another instance of corporate infiltration into campus life might be genuinely amazed at the iconoclastic and egalitarian implication of its practice. Even though it is a product of the politically conservative business world, the widespread implementation of TQM in higher education would have the impact of an egalitarian revolution. (462)

We have found that the Baldrige is a helpful process, pointing up the discontinuities as well as the coherence in our College-wide systems that are charged with supporting and enhancing our educational program. We have also found that the Baldrige needs thoughtful translation into the culture of the College. Whether revolutionary or not, the Baldrige holds promise for improving the important work we do in educating our own students and developing the other significant goals of higher education.

REFERENCES

Bernardin, H. J., and R. W. Beatty. 1984. *Performance Appraisal: Assessing Human Behavior at Work.* Boston: Kent Publishing.

Berk, R. A., ed. 1986. *Performance Assessment Methods and Applications.* Baltimore: Johns Hopkins University Press.

Blackburn, R., and B. Rosen. 1993. Total Quality and Human Resources Management: Lessons Learned from Baldrige Award-Winning Companies. *Academy of Management Executive* 7(3): 49-66.

Boyer, E. L. 1990. *Scholarship Reconsidered: Priorities of the Professoriate.* Lawrenceville, NJ: Princeton University Press.

Dean, J. W., Jr., and D. E. Bowen. 1994. Management Theory and Total Quality: Improving Research and Practice through Theory Development. *Academy of Managment Review* 19 (3): 392-418.

Easton, G. S. 1993. The 1993 State of U.S. TQM: A Baldrige Examiner's Perspective. *California Management Review* (spring): 32-54.

Handy, C. 1994. *The Age of Paradox.* Boston: Harvard Business School Press.

Heneman, H., and D. Schwab, eds. *Perspectives on Personnel/ Human Resource Management.* Revised edition. Homewood, IL: Richard D. Irwin.

Lado, A. A., and M. C. Wilson. 1994. Human Resource Systems and Sustained Competitive Advantage: A Competency Based Perspective. *Academy of Management Review* 19 (4): 699-727.

Landy, F. J., and J. L. Farr. 1983. *The Measurement of Work Performance: Methods, Theory and Applications.* New York: Academic Press.

Latham, G. P., and K. N. Wexley. 1994. *Increasing Productivity through Performance Appraisal.* 2nd edition. Reading, MA: Addison-Wesley.

McEachern, W., and K. O'Brien. 1993. Constancy of Purpose: Ability-Based Education and Assessment-as-Learning. In *Continuous Quality Improvement: Making the Transition to Education,* edited by D. L. Hubbard. Maryville, MO: Prescott Publishing.

"My Work" to "Our Work": Realigning Faculty Work with College and University Purposes. 1995. Third AAHE Conference on Faculty Roles and Rewards, 19-22 January, Phoenix, Arizona.

Riordan, T. 1993. *Beyond the Debate: The Nature of Teaching.* Milwaukee: Alverno College Institute.

Schuler, R., R. Beutall, and F. Youngblood. 1989. *Personnel and Human Resource Management.* 3rd edition. St. Paul, MN: West Publishing.

Seymour, D. 1994. The Baldrige Cometh. *Change* (January/February): 16-27.

Sloan, De Villo. 1994. Total Quality Mangement in the Culture of Higher Education. *Review of Higher Education* (summer): 447-64.

Walton, M. 1986. *The Deming Management Method.* New York: Pedigree Books.

9

Educational and Business Process Management: The Work of Work Flows

Susanna B. Staas and Mary Ann Heverly

Category five in the Education Criteria of the Malcolm Baldrige National Quality Award, "Educational and Business Process Management," is fundamental to the core value of continuous improvement and organizational learning, which says in part: "Achieving ever-higher levels of school performance requires a well-executed approach to continuous improvement. A well-executed continuous improvement process . . . focuses primarily on **key processes** as the route to better results." (See appendix for a full description of this core value). The reasoning, which extends from a manufacturing paradigm, is that if the process for manufacturing a product—or producing a service—can be made to meet or exceed a standard, then consistent quality can be assured. (The thrust of the Baldrige and of continuous quality improvement is that the standard must meet the customers' needs. Those needs continuously change, of course, which lead the producer to continuously improve.)

This chapter begins with a series of definitions surrounding process management and details a brief history of the process management concept. The discussion then explores higher education questions—*Does process management apply to higher education? How does process management fit the higher education community's heritage of individual effort and scholarship?* Throughout this discussion we weave the issue of Baldrige's role—specifically, Category Five, "Educational and Business Process Management"—in bringing a systematic approach to the management of processes and continuous quality improvement. Finally, we reflect on our experience in attempting to bring a process management perspective to Delaware County Community College.

DEFINING MANAGEMENT PROCESS

According to Mehan (1993), a process can be defined as a "bounded group of interrelated work activities providing output of greater value than the inputs by means of one or more transformations" (15). A process orientation is essentially an invention of the industrial revolution. As industry developed, division of labor and skill specialization followed. Adam Smith in *Wealth of Nations* espoused dividing a single productive task into a series of discrete tasks requiring specialized skills as a basis for increasing productivity and efficiency. By 1800, the Soho Engineering Foundry was applying the concept of sequential steps to manufacturing, and in 1832, Charles Babbage added to these concepts by pointing out the value of analyzing work processes to establish product costs (Mehan 1993). In the U.S., the transition to the factory system after the Civil War saw the development of manufacturing processes—a repetitive series of discrete tasks each adding value to an input and producing a desired output—whose management was first described by Frederick Taylor in *Principles of Scientific Management.*

The concept of a manufacturing process, as epitomized by the (automotive) assembly line, persists to this day and has served as a foundation for total quality control and for process management (Feigenbaum 1961). Indeed, work processes are perceived as the foundation of an enterprise; for example, according to Rummler and Brache (1991) in *Improving Performance: How to Manage the White Space on the Organization Chart,* "an organization is only as effective as its processes" (45). In *Process Management,* Harrington (1991) concurs with this assessment when he calls the manufacturing and business processes, not the people, the key to error-free performance. And finally, there is the often-quoted conclusion reached by Deming (1986): "I should estimate that in my experience most troubles and most possibilities for improvement add up to proportions something like this: 94% belong to the system (process) and 6% are special" (315).

How does process management translate from the assembly line to today's service and knowledge-based enterprises? The two books already cited—*Improving Performance: How to Manage the White Space on the Organization Chart* and *Process Management*—provide cogent descriptions of business and service processes and how to manage them. The easiest method for experiencing the concept that all work involves processes is to list the steps involved in accomplishing the output of the work. Those steps, each of which should add value to the output that is developing, form the backbone of the process. Once the process steps are listed, the process can be depicted in a simple diagram or flowchart. When a process is flowcharted, the nature of "work as process" becomes visually clear; it also becomes clear that the hand-offs—from one step of a process to the next—offer many opportunities for errors.

The assumption underlying process management is that an enterprise is essentially a web of processes whose purpose is to produce products or services that meet customers' needs. The assumption underlying process management is that an enterprise is essentially a web of processes whose purpose is to produce products or services that meet customers' needs. Rummler and Brache (1991) suggest that the best way to truly understand how customer-satisfying work gets done is to view an organization horizontally (as a system), rather than vertically (as a hierarchy of functions). In an effective web of business processes, the output-to-be moves smoothly through the web, gathering value as it goes, until it is completed. Instead of pushing or pulling the output through the web by any means available, process owners (management) and process operators concentrate on keeping the web intact, with no tears or snarls, so that the output-to-be can move through easily. To keep the process web intact, the people operating the processes need a structure and individual skills that will allow them to connect the steps of a process smoothly, that will enable them to move outputs smoothly between processes, and that will allow them to improve process steps and interfaces as the opportunity arises.

Mehan (1993) states that "fundamentally, all processes operate within the framework of a sociotechnical system" (230). This is a critically important statement because it affirms that the seamlessness of the process web depends upon both the structure of the process, the technological assists that may be available, and the interpersonal skill and good will of the owners and operators of each process.

More specifically, the structure and skills have the following characteristics:

- Built-in feedback mechanisms that allow process owners and operators to monitor customers' needs and the ability of the process to deliver products or services that meet those needs.
- Measurement points in the process that allow operators to monitor the consistency of the process.
- Structure that lowers barriers between functional departments enabling the process operators to implement smooth hand-offs between steps in the process.
- Training that develops process operators' skills in collecting and measuring customer feedback.
- Structure and training that encourage all employees to focus on designing and improving the system (process) for producing good output, rather than on heroic efforts to produce good output despite the process.

Does process management apply to higher education? Is the education of individuals a process? How does process management—a concept that is founded on the assumption that 90 percent or more of error lies within the system, not with individual error—fit the higher education community's heritage of individual effort and scholarship? Although the literature is sparse, the evidence is beginning to accumulate that process management not only can be applied to higher education, but that its application has the potential of assisting our enterprise to become more responsive to our students and to the communities we serve.

PROCESS MANAGEMENT AND HIGHER EDUCATION

Five years ago there were few publications describing process management and its application to college and university settings. The literature has grown since then, and today a variety of books and articles provide schematic diagrams of process management, along with illustrations of how such diagrams can describe the work conducted in these settings. For example, Chaffee and Sherr's (1992) monograph, *Quality: Transforming Postsecondary Education*, depicts the core elements of a process and shows how such a schema can be used to understand the process of conducting an algebra class. Other examples are included in Hubbard (1993), Lewis and Smith (1994), Seymour (1992), and Teeter and Lozier (1993). This developing literature emphasizes the importance of focusing on process management and describes how to depict a process, gather data on it, analyze the data, and improve or standardize the process. More importantly, the literature contains a rich variety of examples showing how process management can be applied in colleges and universities: in individual jobs, in work units, across departments and divisions, in college-wide process study teams, and in strategic planning.

At first glance it might appear that we have begun to delineate how colleges and universities can practice the "process management" described in the Baldrige guidelines. Various authors (Lewis and Smith 1994; Seymour 1993; Teeter and Lozier 1993) have shown how the model fits and have offered diverse illustrations of how it could be (or has been) applied. However, the Baldrige does not ask for a laundry list showing the application of process management at various places throughout the organization. Rather, it asks about the infrastructure that supports the use of process management throughout an organization. It also asks about the plan and method for deploying process management throughout the organization. It seeks validation that process management is an integral part of organizational functioning, not something that occurs in organizational pockets where it is supported or tolerated. The existence of such an infrastructure could make process management become part of what we do, rather than a special activity to which one can point. In a sense, we succeed with process management when it begins to disappear from view as a special activity worthy of notice and becomes part of the fabric of daily work life.

The literature has little to offer on developing an infrastructure, especially if examples specific to education are sought. In part, the lack of progress on this front simply reflects that continuous quality improvement (CQI) efforts are in an early developmental stage. Higher education is just beginning to learn how to adapt CQI so that the pieces fit its organizations. Weaving an infrastructure that synthesizes these pieces into an organic whole will be one of the next frontiers.

HIGH PERFORMING COLLEGES

Aside from the short history of CQI in higher education, colleges and universities face other barriers to creating an infrastructure for process management, including cultural and linguistic barriers. According to Lewis and Smith (1994), structural barriers include the division of higher education into parallel sides—the academic and the administrative—that often operate with little sense of shared purpose. This fragmentation extends to the divisional or departmental level, where faculty tend to identify with a particular discipline or specialty, rather than with the entire enterprise. Fragmentation also occurs at the leadership level, where events in the external environment can easily monopolize attention.

The cultural barriers identified by Lewis and Smith include the idea that education is so different from other sectors that CQI's process approach cannot be adapted, the tendency to value and to reward individualistic effort, and the notion that quality has already been attained and that participatory governance already exists. Chaffee and Sherr (1992) cite as a barrier higher education's "culture of authority through expertise" (90). CQI requires all participants, including faculty, to be willing to give up some authority and power.

CQI requires all participants, including faculty, to be willing to give up some authority and power.

Lewis and Smith cite several linguistic barriers. Higher education's difficulty with the terms "customer" and "control" have been discussed widely in the literature (Chaffee and Sherr 1992; Seymour 1992). Lewis and Smith also point out that the drive to "minimize variation, encourage standardization" (15) can be misconstrued as an attempt to stifle the creative process and force everyone to teach in regimented ways and to produce cookie-cutter outputs. However, the drive to reduce variation and standardize processes should properly focus on unwanted, negative variation in processes (such as rework, steps that add no value, and other sources of "noisy" variation that distract from the process goals). Minimizing these sources of variation frees time and effort that can more profitably be spent on the real work of processes.

The list of barriers to CQI—and hence, process management—can appear daunting. However, it is possible to view the structure and culture of higher education through a rosier lens. Carothers' (1992) examination of higher education reveals some features that could facilitate the use of CQI. The fact that higher education does not have the hierarchical structures found in business and that it is decentralized, for example, can be seen as a positive factor. Faculty value quality, they value lifelong and continuous learning, and they are accustomed to self-directed work that provides a large degree of autonomy.

Whether we view the glass as half full or half empty, the lack of models for developing the process management infrastructure remains. Rummler and Brache's (1991) model is one that might be adapted to higher education. While other sources provide road maps for implementing CQI, Rummler and Brache offer a road map for managing and improving processes throughout an organization—from the macro level of the strategic goals to the micro level of the individual worker. Their model suggests specific areas to address and questions to ask at each of three levels within the organization: the total organization level, the process level, and the job or performer level. They view these levels as analogous to the anatomy of an organism, with the organizational level representing the skeletal system, the process level representing the muscular system, and the job/performer level representing the individual cells. At each of the three levels, three factors are responsible for how well the system functions; each level must have goals, an efficient design, and management of the system. This 3 x 3 matrix provides the framework for asking questions that assess how well the system is functioning. Rummler and Brache outline criteria designed to insure that a measurement system ties together the systems represented in the 3 x 3 matrix.

A primary goal of the infrastructure described by Rummler and Brache is to enable the organization to be adaptable to changing situations and needs inside and outside the organization, much as an organism adapts to the dynamics of its internal functioning and its external environment. Although their model would require adaptation to fit education, it contains sufficient detail to provide a model that would address the Baldrige criterion on process management.

Does higher education need to develop an infrastructure to support process management? In some ways it can be suggested that process management is already being addressed within the assessment movement in higher education. Ewell (1991) has delineated several parallels between the assessment movement's "best practices" and CQI. For example, the assessment movement has evolved from a primary focus on outcomes to the realization that studying processes is equally important. Assessment approaches such as those employed in the Harvard Assessment Seminars (Light 1990) and in classroom assessment as described by Angelo and Cross (1993) focus on the process of student learning, using data on the process and how it operates, in order to improve the process.

Although the philosophy and methods of assessment and CQI have many features in common, Ewell (1993) also sees key differences. One is that "the *reach* of (CQI) is from the outset more comprehensive" (50). According to Ewell (1993), assessment results at many institutions have not been used to benefit the institution and its students, in part because "a structure of utilization was assumed, not created" (50). He sees a similar situation with classroom assessment, which looks very much like CQI at the micro level. At the macro level, however, classroom assessment lacks an "infrastructure to support wider institutional improvement" (47).

In the Baldrige Criteria, process management is comprehensive, systematic, planned, documented, and supported by an infrastructure designed to move an organization toward its strategic goals. This feature, which runs through all of the Baldrige Criteria, offers to bridge the structural gap Ewell discerns in assessment as practiced in many institutions. However, Ewell also warns that it is easy to avoid these key elements and to adopt individual pieces of CQI that neatly fit into its institution or that can be adapted narrowly without disturbing the existing fabric. This pitfall, or piecemeal implementation, is the easy route to take. The power of the Baldrige is that it reveals the inadequacy of this piecemeal approach. Before embarking on CQI, institutions could profit from consulting the Baldrige Criteria, to gain an understanding of the depth and breadth of commitment required by the "total" approach that Ewell suggests.

Process management also fits well with the "value-added" model of assessment and accountability.

Process management also fits well with the "value-added" model of assessment and accountability. Astin (1991) advocates the value-added model as an alternative to evaluating institutions of higher education based on criteria describing their inputs, resources, and outputs—criteria traditionally used by evaluators and accrediting bodies. The value-added model examines *process*, or "what happens to students during their stay at a college or university." It focuses on student change between entry and exit, particularly on change that can be tied to the experience of attending that college or university. The value-added model is supported by an extensive review of the literature on how college affects students. Terenzini and Pascarella (1994) find little evidence linking the traditional indicators of "quality" with student growth and change. Included among these traditional indicators are such measures as educational expenditures per student, student/faculty ratios, faculty salaries, percentage of faculty holding the highest degree in their field, faculty research productivity, size of the library, admissions selectivity, or prestige rankings (Terenzini and Pascarella 1994, 29).

Demands for accountability in higher education typically emphasize traditional indicators—outcome measures and input/output ratios designed to assess efficiency and return on investment. Process measures, which attempt to quantify value that has been added, are rarely requested by state or federal governing bodies interested in assessing higher education. Accountability standards proposed by external stakeholders (federal and state governmental entities) take a "one size fits all" approach to evaluating quality. (see Hittman, "The View From the Top: Accountability and Improvement" in the Quality Assurance section) The standards describe a single set of indicators that attempt to assess quality across institutions with diverse missions. Sometimes, specific numeric standards are set as requirements for continued funding.

The flaw in this approach is described by Tribus and Tsuda's (1985) critique of management by objectives: "Setting such targets removes from the manager the responsibility to improve the system" (35). Tribus and Tsuda posit the perversity principle as a basic tenet of quality management: "If you try to improve the performance of a system . . . by setting numerical goals and targets for their performance, the system will defeat you and you will pay a price where you did not expect it" (35). The Baldrige Criteria, on the other hand, are not prescriptive and do not presume to force a standard set of indicators or outcomes across diverse organizations. Instead, the Criteria focus first on "Approach" and "Deployment"—how the organization systematically proceeds to carry out its mission, using its own defining structure, functions, and resources. Outcomes or results are not ignored—they are a key part of Criteria 6 and 7—however, they

HIGH PERFORMING COLLEGES

are not the starting point for assessing an organization. Instead, they flow from the approaches and deployment of the first five Criteria.

LESSONS LEARNED BY USING BALDRIGE CRITERIA 5.0

At Delaware County Community College (DCCC), understanding work as process rather than as a collection of many discrete tasks proved to be a difficult hurdle to clear. When the college was introduced to continuous quality improvement in 1986, the concept of work as process (defined as a *series* of value-adding steps beginning with an *input* and ending in a *product*) was utterly foreign. The philosophy and values of our institution were based on a deeply-held belief in the importance of providing individual service to our students. Individual service and caring defined Delaware County Community College. Viewing our work as processes that were, by definition, repetitive, seemed to contradict our very soul!

Viewing our work as processes that were, by definition, repetitive, seemed to contradict our very soul!

Since 1986, we have learned that our work is indeed a system of processes. We have learned that by analyzing and measuring each work process against customers' expectations, we can improve the process—and by improving the process, we can improve the results. We have learned that we can develop processes that enable us to provide individualized service that is more responsive to each student's needs far more reliably and effectively than before our enlightenment.

For example, by studying the effectiveness of the teaching/learning process in their classrooms, our faculty are learning how to modify that process to address the individual learning needs of the students. Faculty use classroom assessment techniques (Angelo and Cross 1993), collaborative learning (Johnson, Johnson, and Smith 1991), and Project Learn techniques (Baugher 1992)—all of which focus on the teaching/learning process—to improve systematically their classroom processes. In 1995, faculty members are conducting studies designed to correlate use of these techniques with student retention and success. Our belief in the importance of individual caring for our students is as strong as ever. We now understand that process management in every aspect of the work we do is critical to our success in providing the individualized and responsive care we value.

The next transition we must undertake—from identifying and managing individual work processes (i.e., processes that are under the control of an individual or functional work unit) to managing the institutional system—is critical, and foretells another cultural shift. This time, the college must move away from its hierarchical, functional organization to a structure that facilitates movement of nascent products/services through the web of processes, and that enables rapid continuous improvement in response to customers' feedback.

Gradual, incremental change is a hallmark of the culture at DCCC. And true to form, we are slowly addressing the challenge of managing the College as an integrated system instead of as a collection of quasi-independent functions.

For example:

- The nursing curriculum has developed a process for curriculum design and redesign that is linked with the college's processes for collecting feedback from students, graduates, and employers on one end and with feedback from the teaching/learning process and student outcomes on the other (Boyer and Lillis 1995).
- Student registration, course scheduling, accounting and advising processes are linked.
- Academic hiring processes are linked with the evaluation process for nontenured faculty to provide feedback to improve the hiring process.
- The faculty development process supports the faculty's efforts in the classroom by providing inservice training in response to needs, and by providing a regular forum for faculty members to share their work.
- Perhaps the most exciting effort to link processes is the computer networking project that is currently underway at the college. Networked computers will be accessible to every staff member. To implement this project, many departments and levels of employees are engaged in examining how their processes will be affected by the advent of the network. When the network is in place, information flow will be expedited and responsibilities for many routine college processes (such as entering and monitoring purchase orders, registering students, etc.) will be

decentralized, leading to a realignment of departmental responsibilities.

In 1991, administrators at DCCC diagrammed the college's key processes. Many of those processes—such as teaching/learning, student certification and placement, and student intake—flow across departmental lines. The challenge that we face—and which Criterion 5.0 of the Baldrige addresses—lies in organizing the structure of the college so that the ownership of a given process is clear and so that the process linkages that are pictured in the diagram become seamless.

CONCLUSION

Given the escalating expectations of our stakeholders, and the rapidly changing needs of both our students and the employers of our graduates, it seems inevitable that higher education must adopt a philosophy and a method of operation that will enable us to be both mission-driven and responsive. It is the position of those quoted in these pages that the philosophy and methods of quality management, including the use of process management, will enable us to meet these challenges.

However, if quality management—as suggested by Rummler and Brache (1991) and represented by the Malcolm Baldrige Award—is to truly take hold in higher education, the hierarchical structure that is the foundation of our enterprise must change. Horizontal process management and hierarchical, top-down management as we know it are contradictory. We must ask ourselves, "What will be the new paradigm of management in higher education? How will the teaching/learning process be managed? How will educational administration function? How will we—as faculty members, administrators, or students—be expected to change? We believe many of the answers to these questions are found in the core values, framework, and criteria of the Malcolm Baldrige National Quality Award.

REFERENCES

Angelo, T. A. and K. P. Cross. 1993. *Classroom Assessment Techniques: A Handbook for College Teachers*. 2nd edition. San Francisco: Jossey-Bass.

Astin, A. W. 1991. *Assessment for Excellence*. New York: ACE MacMillan.

Baugher, K. 1992. *LEARN: The Student Quality Team Process for Improving Teaching and Learning*. Birmingham, AL: Samford University.

Boyer, M. J. and C. Lillis. 1995. Quality Approaches for Curriculum Redesign Using a CQI Framework. *The Chronicle of CQI* (May).

Carothers, Robert L. 1992. Translating Quality for the Academy. *AAHE Bulletin* (November).

Chaffee, E. E. and Sherr, L. A. 1992. *Quality: Transforming Postsecondary Education*. ASHE-ERIC Higher Education Report No. 3. Washington, D.C.: George Washington University School of Education and Human Development.

Deming, W. E. 1982. Out of the Crisis. Cambridge, MA: Massachusetts Institute of Technology Center for Advanced Engineering Study.

Ewell, P. T. 1991. Assessment and TQM: In Search of Convergence. In *Total Quality Management in Higher Education*, edited by L. A. Sherr and D. J. Teeter. New Directions for Institutional Research, no. 71. San Francisco: Jossey-Bass.

Ewell, P. T. 1993. Total Quality and Academic Practice: The Idea We've been Waiting For? *Change* (May/June).

Feigenbaum, A. V. 1983. *Total Quality Control*. 3rd edition. New York: McGraw-Hill.

Harrington, H. J. 1991. *Business Process Improvement*. New York: McGraw-Hill.

Hubbard, D. L. 1993. *Continuous Quality Improvement: Making the Transition to Education*. Maryville, MO: Prescott Publishing.

Johnson, D. W., R. T. Johnson, and K. A. Smith. 1991. *Cooperative Learning: Increasing College Faculty Instructional Productivity*. ASHE-ERIC Higher Education Report No. 4. Washington, D.C.: George Washington University School of Education and Human Development.

Lewis, R. G. and D. H. Smith. 1994. *Total Quality in Higher Education.* Delray Beach, FL: St. Lucie.

Light, R. J. 1990. *The Harvard Seminar on Assessment: Final Report.* Cambridge, MA: Harvard Graduate School of Education.

Mehan, E. H. 1993. *Process Management.* New York: McGraw-Hill.

Rummler, G. A. and A. P. Brache. 1991. *Improving Performance: Managing the White Spaces on the Organization Chart.* San Francisco: Jossey-Bass.

Seymour, D. 1993. Quality on Campus: Three Institutions, Three Beginnings. *Change* (May/June).

Seymour, D. 1992. *On Q: Causing Quality in Higher Education.* Phoenix, AZ: ACE Oryx Press.

Teeter, D. J., and G. G. Lozier, editors. 1993. *Pursuit of Quality in Higher Education: Case Studies in Total Quality Management.* New Directions in Institutional Research, no. 78. San Francisco: Jossey-Bass.

Terenzini, P. and E. Pascarella. 1994. Living with Myths: Undergraduate Education in America. *Change* (January/February).

Tribus, M. and Y. Tsuda. 1985. *The Quality Imperative in the New Economic Era.* Cambridge, MA: MIT Center for Advanced Engineering Studies.

10
School Performance: Making Things Happen

Susan G. Hillenmeyer

The Malcolm Baldrige National Quality Award asks companies to respond to questions about how quality has been advanced. Moreover, Category 6.0–Business Results focuses specifically on product and service quality results, operational and financial results, and supplier performance results. In *The Corporate Guide to the Malcolm Baldrige National Quality Award,* Steeples (1992) offers several explanations for how Category 6.0 is viewed:

> As might be expected, evaluators look for documentable results of a company's quality improvement. Is the company's product more reliable? Have levels of defects, scrap, and rework decreased? Are services improved? Is efficiency improved? Has the company improved the quality of its suppliers as well as its own quality?

> Evaluators also look at the appropriateness of a company's measures of quality, depending on factors such as the company's size, types of products and services, and competitive environment. Are the measures sufficient to support overall improvement and to establish clear quality levels and comparisons? (181)

Such traditional quality language and concepts are problematic if one tries to use the same questions to improve educational activities. The whole notion of education's "products," "operational results," and "suppliers" makes Category 6.0, as detailed in the business Criteria, virtually untenable for higher education. Indeed, Category 6.0 in the Education Pilot is largely centered on assessment information—of the 230 possible points for the category, 100 of them

HIGH PERFORMING COLLEGES

are designated for student performance. Primary improvement objectives and student assessment results are reported here. Climate improvement results, also included, refer to results from overall general policies and practices that contribute to progress. These might include faculty and staff satisfaction with elements of worklife. Category 6.0 also requires that schools provide results of how they contribute to the world of knowledge through research, scholarship, and service.

Finally, Category 6.0 responses summarize school business operational and financial performance. The more traditional measures of improvement in personnel, materials, energy, and capital are reported and compared with results from other organizations.

In order to understand a "Baldrige results focus," it is important to grasp the systemic nature of the Criteria. For both sets of Baldrige Criteria—that is, education and business—scoring is built around *approach, deployment,* and *results.* The premise is that if an organization has good approaches which are well-deployed, it will deliver strong results. Within both the education and business sets of Criteria, dynamic relationships exist. In them, leadership "drives" the system of process management, human resource development, planning, and information and analysis. The "products" of such a system are customer/stakeholder satisfaction and performance results. In short, the ultimate challenge in continuous quality improvement is measurably improved quality results.

The premise is that if an organization has good approaches which are well-deployed, it will deliver strong results.

Underlying Category 6.0's results focus is a deeper Baldrige value, that of managing by fact. In order for organizations to be managed by fact, the whole notion of measures, data, results, and indicators becomes consequential. From the business perspective, companies are looking to answer the question, "How do we provide superior value of offerings as viewed by customers and the marketplace, and superior company performance reflected in productivity and effectiveness indicators?" For the Education Criteria, we can ask the question as follows: "How do we provide superior education value as viewed by stakeholders and the public? How do we provide superior performance reflected in student performance, educational climate, research, scholarship, service, and efficient use of resources?"

For those who form answers to these questions, there is an underlying not-so-subtle distinction between data and results. The education Criteria state that "Data are numerical information; results are the outcomes of activities" (U.S. Dept. Commerce 1995b, 36). For example, an institution might have several years of data on percentages of students who complete courses within a certain time frame. Results come from some activity or intervention on the part of the university to change the time frame. What resulted from such an intervention? Because Category 6.0 deals with results, the responses an institution makes to items calling for results require data using measures and indicators. For example, direct measurements are available for retention and placement rates, but other types of data serve as indicators of performance. An ACT score may indicate an ability to succeed in completing coursework. For those who are used to using the terms interchangeably, such distinctions require study in order to apply the Criteria.

A REVIEW OF 6.0–RESULTS

There are five issues that influence how we should look at Category 6.0: (1) the importance of results and the controversy over whether the Baldrige is results-oriented enough, (2) benchmarking, comparisons, and goalsetting, (3) competitiveness, (4) the cost of quality, and (5) gains beyond the measurable ones. Each of these issues warrants further discussion.

Importance and Controversy

There is ongoing debate in both the business press and government studies about whether or not the Baldrige does indeed lead to improved results. The General Accounting Office completed the first study of Award effectiveness in 1991. It questioned whether quality practice, as defined in the Baldrige Criteria, fostered results such as greater customer satisfaction, improved human relations among employees, increased market share and profitability, and higher productivity. The GAO study (1992) concluded that Baldrige practices did, in fact, lead to improved performance measures.

Harvard's David Garvin (1991), a noted author on quality topics, interviewed Baldrige judges and examiners; his study affirmed that the "Baldrige Award is positioned exactly where it should be—as an agent for transforming U.S. business" (92). The American Society for Quality Control (ASQC) developed a survey to determine what the U.S. business community thinks of the Baldrige Award. The organization surveyed *Fortune* 500 industrial and service firms, and a similar survey was sent to 120 small manufacturing firms and 120 small service firms. Results of those surveys indicated that "the benefits gained from using the award Criteria for internal assessment and from participating in the award process were well worth the resources invested" (Knotts et al. 1993, 52).

In 1991, quality expert Philip Crosby and Curt Reimann, director of the Baldrige program for the National Institute of Standards and Technology, squared off about the intent of the Award. Crosby was sharply critical of it and asserted that the Criteria focused too much on quality process and not enough on results. Reimann, in a response to Crosby's comment that the Baldrige is not results oriented, said, "There is major emphasis throughout the Criteria on results—results that lead to customer satisfaction. Indeed, a central premise in the Criteria is that companies should improve quality primarily to improve customer satisfaction. In addition, they improve quality to reduce operating costs" (Crosby and Reimann 1991, 43). Further, Reimann differentiated the Baldrige Award from other Criteria and quality standards because it has a major focus on results and customer satisfaction.

Reimann's assertion seems well-supported by others. In a study of several award processes—the Deming Prize, Baldrige, and European Quality awards—the Baldrige award was found to base eighteen percent of its point value on quality and operational results (Nakhai and Neves 1994). Further, according to the 1995 Criteria, the title of Category 6.0 changed from "Quality and Operational Results" to "Business Results" to "reflect greater emphasis on business-oriented results to encourage companies to report data that demonstrates impact on customers, markets, and business financial performance" (U.S Dept. Commerce 1995a, 19). Overall, Category 6.0 has been strengthened by the reporting of human resource results and employee satisfaction, thus providing a more "holistic" focus for the entire category. As a consequence, the Category 6.0 point value now constitutes twenty-five percent of the total points available.

Benchmarking, Comparisons, and Goalsetting

It isn't enough to conclude that the Baldrige positively affects organizations' results. We must also consider whether those results are significant when compared to those of others. Benchmarking, or comparison results, is a key part of Category 6.0. Often companies think the benchmarking process is too expensive or time consuming, but results can depend on chosen strategies. According to Micklewright (1993), "In reality, small companies cannot afford not to benchmark. Because of the fewer number of employees in a small company, there are fewer employees entering the company with knowledge of the latest technology and methods" (68). He goes on to add—"Smaller companies can get left behind, operating the same way they always have and designing virtually the same products over and over" (68).

Texas Instruments, a previous Baldrige winner, echoes the value of finding comparative results:

> The Baldrige Award process introduced two radical new ideas: benchmarking and stretch goals. Benchmarking—comparing one's own processes to the best processes in the world—can deflate arrogance. Nothing is more sobering than having patted oneself on the back for making 5 % to 10 % improvements only to discover that the competitor does things twice as well." (Judkins 1994, 58)

Moreover, the Baldrige process is credited with helping Texas Instruments achieve its long term results: "Throughout Texas Instruments, it has been found that it takes about five years of dedicated pulling in the same direction to begin seeing measurable results" (Judkins 1994, 58).

Not only is benchmarking a part of the results focus of Category 6.0, goalsetting is part of the standard as well.

Not only is benchmarking a part of the results focus of Category 6.0, goalsetting is part of the standard as well. There is considerable emphasis in Category 6.0 on comparison to others. While the category does not specify goalsetting results, the benchmarking emphasis is a strategy the Baldrige Criteria uses to increase the rate of improvement. Marquardt (1992) recommends quantifying the results of aggressive goalsetting as a key way to benefit from the Baldrige process.

HIGH PERFORMING COLLEGES

Competitiveness and the Cost of Quality

The issue of quality and its costs is part of the results focus in Category 6.0. Businesses may report, for example, prevention costs including quality planning, training, and design improvement (Radhakrishnan and Srinidhi 1994). These costs are then contrasted with competitor and industry information as evidence of performance.

In a letter to *Quality Progress*, quality engineer Rao (1993) reported that Baldrige results and financial success are linked. He opposed an argument by Stratton, the editor, that a Malcolm Baldrige National Quality Award winner might likely show financial loss because the award Criteria do not take into consideration the financial performance of a company and because a company's business performance is not determined by quality control alone. He contended, "My observations indicate that a prosperous company working toward winning the Baldrige Award should also compare the marketplace position of its own products to that of its competitors' products" (6).

Organizations that win the Baldrige find that their marketing research fits into Category 6.0. By 1994, Orsini (1994) saw that the results of quality studies such as J. D. Powers' Initial Quality Survey and Cadillac's winning of the Baldrige Award involved marketing issues. In an analysis of the Criteria and the possibility of marketing expertise, he found that Category 6.0, Quality and Operational Results, had the third highest potential use of marketing expertise in the Baldrige Award. Such factors as research methods, consumer behavior, market and competitive assessments have high capacity for marketing involvement.

Certainly, the process of applying the Criteria leads to deep understanding of an organization's improvement system, but there may also be fortuitous unintended results. Joseph Juran (1991), the well-known authority in designing and implementing quality systems, authored an article for *Quality Progress* describing the results Baldrige Award winners have shown. He characterized the results as "stunning achievements" and listed the following results-related information:

- Customer service response time reduced by an order of magnitude.
- Deficit levels reduced by an order of magnitude.

- Productivity doubled.
- Costs reduced by 50%. (81)

Juran discussed the results as a by-product of making other improvements. He asked how winners could achieve such results and posited an explanation: "One obvious difference was that the companies established 'stretch goals,' such as tenfold quality improvement in four years, fourfold improvement in reliability, and twelve-month reduction in the product development cycle" (82).

Beyond Measurable Gains

For those businesses who make continuous quality improvement a "way of corporate life," there can be extensive gains beyond measurable results. In his study of Baldrige winners, Juran (1991) pointed out the by-product of making improvement habitual and measuring results—widespread success, financial profitability, and teamwork.

Small companies often reorganize after studying themselves using the Baldrige Criteria. Unintended gains sometimes result in changes in employees' perspectives. Award-winning Marlow Industries changed when the inspection process and test functions that had been conducted by a quality assurance division were given to manufacturing, where employees checked their own results. COO Chris Witzke recalled:

> Our QA department now only consists of two engineers and two hourly employees. We took all the inspection and test functions that were conducted by QA and gave them to manufacturing. Manufacturing is responsible for quality. During our site visit, an examiner asked one of the QA engineers, "What department are you in?"
>
> "QA," the engineer replied.
>
> "How many people are in the QA department?"
>
> "One hundred and sixty."
>
> The examiner, who normally tries not to smile, just broke into a grin and said, "Good answer." (Bemowski 1991, 45)

WHY MEASURE RESULTS? WHAT SHOULD WE MEASURE?

College and university administrators and faculty members have two fundamental questions when using the Malcolm Baldrige Education Criteria as an assessment framework: "Why measure results?" and—if we find satisfactory answers to that question—"What should we measure?" The "why measure?" question can be answered by echoing what Deming often asked of his students, "How do you know?" Although Deming never supported the Baldrige Award, he often quoted Lloyd S. Nelson in saying that "The most important figures are unknown and unknowable." If students are not learning what they need, how will we know? Ted Marchese asked a similar set of questions during a recent trip to my institution, Belmont University. He said: "Do your students know, and can they do, what their degrees imply? Further, how do you know?"

Historically, we have used numbers in fundamentally different ways from those the Criteria addresses. At the very worst, systems of promotion and tenure, of resource allocation and planning were based on ranking. We rank people, ideas, plans, expenditures. Tenure systems, ranks within pay grades, and hierarchies often miss the real intent of "quality numbers" as measures of progress. Price (1993) says, in a recent article, "You can't sustain continuous improvement without measuring progress. Anecdotal success stories, heroes and missionaries can generate enthusiasm and a lot of impetus for change, but . . . without meaningful measurement of progress, partners will tire of the effort" (101). The Baldrige Criteria encourages us to see numbers as indicators of the progress of an improvement system.

The Baldrige Criteria encourages us to see numbers as indicators of the progress of an improvement system.

Unfortunately, higher education has not operated this way. History, popular magazines, and our accreditation standards have encouraged "counting" as a way to measure results. We have counted books in the library and used the result as the key indicator of good collections, when, in fact, it is the content of the collection as well as the number of volumes that is important. Further, the AGB Higher Education Issues Panel (1992) reported that quality "is measured more by the kinds of students excluded and turned down than by the kinds of students included and turned out . . . not by how much value is added to students' knowledge, but by the size of the endowment, the range of scores and the number of doctorates produced" (22).

Our inability or unwillingness to measure performance in a meaningful way has created a problem. Seymour and Collett (1991) in *Total Quality Management in Higher Education: A Critical Assessment* point out that the inability of colleges and universities to measure quality has led to boards' and state legislatures' efforts to mandate quality through various accountability measures. Peter Ewell of the National Center for Higher Education Management Systems and others have worked to develop new measures to indicate a school's progress. Studying assessment trend information, Ewell (1992) concluded that unless university administrators capture and report relevant information, government agencies will step in to determine what is relevant.

It is difficult for educators to focus on measuring results. Again, Seymour and Collett (1991) conclude—"There is a general, well-established perception that much of what we do is not really measurable" (18). Truthfully, we may never know whether the graduate appreciates a Beethoven sonata nine years from now differently and better than she would have had she not completed a course in music appreciation. There is much, however, that can be measured to show improvement results. Quality requires measurement; higher education is like all other organizations in this regard. The changing times and societal scrutiny make school performance results even more important. The "results focus" in many ways keeps us from just being good storytellers, from merely describing our efforts at improvement and the activities in which our people engage. Indeed, Price (1993) asserts, "It is possible to approach the whole subject of measuring progress by means of the Baldrige process. However, that in and of itself does not solve the measurement problem. Rather, it highlights the need for effective measurement and evaluation processes for each major function involved in delivering the end service or product" (109).

The "What should we be measuring?" question is a tricky one. In Category 6.0 we are asked for the following types of results:
- Student Performance
- Educational Climate
- Research, Scholarship, and Service
- Efficient Use of Resources

At the individual level, student performance is difficult to measure. Dean Hubbard (1993), president of Northwest Missouri State University, comments that "there is the temptation to focus on what is easily measurable. In education, that often means the lower-order cognitive skills of recall and understanding, as opposed to the higher-order skills of analysis, synthesis, and evaluation. In fact, since creative thinking may not blossom until several years after the student has graduated from college, test results must always be viewed somewhat tentatively." "Furthermore," Hubbard adds, "it is difficult to establish cause-effect relationships between particular curricula or teaching strategies and higher-order cognitive skills. Nonetheless, assessment lies at the heart of CQI" (xiii).

This assessment focus is being used in the state of Minnesota, which has adopted seven indicators of quality for schools: preparation for higher learning; higher-order thinking; multicultural sensitivity; global awareness; scientific and quantitative literacy; readiness for work; and citizenship in a global society. At Bemidji State University, for example, faculty added "a sense of community" to the list. It is significant that the Bemidji students and alumni report results on how their educations prepared them to "do something" rather than on what they learned (Baer et al. 1993). If these are the types of quality indicators in schools, then corresponding measures and performance indices are needed. In Category 6.0, for example, applicants examine student performance and improvement around measures and indices. In the Minnesota model, applicants would report on student progress around those indicators in Category 6.1–Student Performance Results.

Continuous quality improvement (CQI) may offer a more fruitful way to assess educational progress. Many traditional assessment methods report performance results at the end of the educational process. This end-of-the line inspection is of little help to current students. Evans and Krueger (1993) assert that the use of quality indicators shifts the focus to process and continuously monitors progress. They argue eloquently that "what is valued is what is measured and what is measured is what is funded" (378-79). Seymour and Collett (1991) conclude there is a tendency to avoid measuring results. Experience and hunches often substitute for real data around performance. Early practitioners of quality methodology often find themselves searching for helpful benchmarks.

The assessment movement in higher education and the Alverno model of learning has a much different way to examine results. Alverno has educational values and a curriculum which emphasizes expected learning outcomes. The outcomes represent a set of statements of what students can do with what they know and are developed out of what contemporary life requires and the faculty's experience with students. According to McEachern and O'Brien (1993), they are "benchmarks that learners can use to measure their own development" (464).

At the broader institutional level, there seems to be a faulty "production model" which means administrators study results that are not as meaningful as they might be. As Baer et al. (1993) report, "Universities must leave the production model of higher education in which success is based on head counts, credit generation, grades, and degrees and move toward a learning environment which emphasizes an involvement that will empower students with a high-quality 'tool kit' to meet new challenges" (201).

Robert M. Price (1993), an ex-industry executive, challenges us to think differently about the nature of the information we collect and report in Baldrige applications. Further, he believes there are opportunities to collaborate for better measurement systems:

> Devising effective measurements may be one of the most fruitful areas for collaboration. Nor is this a one-way street. Experience shows that business struggles with this measurement problem as much as educational institutions do. Much of the data gathering and analysis for a typical Baldrige assessment is brute force and expensive. In short, metrics for and "instrumentation" of the soft processes of business and industry is, at best, poorly understood and would greatly benefit from widespread collaboration. (103)

Studying the language of Category 6.0 is helpful as applicants plan responses. For example, there is a request for "trends and current levels." As Case and Bigelow (1992) point out, "current level implies one number, a trend implies a pattern based on a minimum of three data values (preferably five or more)" (49). "Key measures and indicators" are the characteristics for which data are generated. "Comparisons are anchors; for each result, they answer the question, 'Compared to what?' " (49). A company (or school) might have only low levels and modest trends but be the best in the business. Finally, "basis for comparison" asks where and how did the company gets its data? There must be a reason the comparative school or business data was chosen. This benchmarking is a critical requirement to answer.

Ewell's work on longitudinal student data systems provides some guidance on how the results of student performance can be reported and tracked. He advocates graphical presentations of reports, likening them to control and Pareto charting in business. Such data systems provide the data needed to support continuous instructional improvement. According to Ewell (1992), "Several major multi-institutional student tracking systems, for instance, have been explicitly designed to provide comparative performance data in subsequent college-level work for students who, (1) were assessed as deficient in a particular basic skill area and who were later fully remediated as defined by the institution, (2) assessed as proficient on entry" (44). Such comparisons address the request for "benchmarking" results in Category 6.0.

Dean Hubbard, at a congressional forum on quality in education, told the assembled legislators, "Comparing one's students or programs with those from other institutions is the best antidote for the inertia that plagues most campuses." He contended that, "compared to other techniques, benchmarking is the easiest and most important tool in education, because it raises expectations and helps create broader goals and change" (Axland 1992, 67-68).

Comparing one's students or programs with those from other institutions is the best antidote for the inertia that plagues most campuses.

Finally, Case and Bigelow (1992) studied Category 6.0 and reported in *Quality Progress* on what they termed the "simplest" language in any part of the Criteria, "requests that the applicant quantitatively assess how it is doing in areas that are ultimately important to the customer and identify trends in those results" (47). For both the education and business applicant, the questions Case and Bigelow posit are helpful in checking whether a proposed measure is a good one:

- Does it relate, directly or indirectly to the ultimate goal of customer (stakeholder) satisfaction? Every measure should.

- Is the measure operationally defined? Is it understood the same way by all concerned?

- Is the measure considered important? Do all parties agree that this measure needs to be watched closely and acted on if its performance is less than desirable? Is it something that can be continuously improved? Does it affect another important measure? Does the benefit exceed the cost of taking the measurement? If the answer is "no" to any of these questions, you should reevaluate why you are measuring it. (47)

They include helpful guidelines for responding to Category 6.0 including:

- Use graphs and tables whenever possible.

- Show trends over several years.

- Illustrate competitors and benchmarks on the same graph or table.

- Show a goal and discuss your plan for reaching it.

- Use clear graphics and make sure they are understandable.

- Put multiple graphs and tables on a page.   (49-50)

LESSONS FROM BELMONT UNIVERSITY

Like most institutions of higher education, much of the information we collect at Belmont University is not useful. It will take time to develop the kind of results from approach and deployment of quality systems that will be useful in our improvement. In our third year of using the Baldrige Criteria as a framework for assessment, we have made some progress but are not nearly where we aspire to be. Our two Tennessee Quality Achievement Awards indicate progress, but the overall challenge of measurably improved quality is a daunting one.

There are major lessons which seem to emerge from three years of applying the Category 6.0. They can be summarized as follows:

1. The more you know, the more you need to know.
2. Looking in the rear-view mirror to see what worked and reporting on that is far easier (but much less rewarding) than designing an improvement system and measuring its results.
3. A good benchmark is a rare and valuable thing.

One of the fundamental changes we began to make at Belmont was in the management of processes. Instead of always focusing on the "bottom line" numbers, we looked at "in process" numbers. Those examinations led us to deeper and deeper study of results. As we studied student performance results, it became clear that the value of information collected at the department level was varied. For example, we discovered data showing increasing numbers of student internships in several of our degree programs, but we were still unsure whether all those internships were preparing students to "perform" better on the job after graduation. Before the Baldrige application we really had no idea about the overall increases in internships campus wide, whether they were a function of enrollment, or whether they were department specific. Now we know. What has happened, however, is that those data have led to further study of internship usefulness in job preparedness and the nature of the internships in predicting student performance. Indeed, the more you know, the more you need to know.

Looking in the rear-view mirror to see what worked and reporting on that is far easier than designing an improvement system and measuring its results. Three years ago, as we met in our writing teams, gathered information from across the campus, and quizzed each other on,—*Now what does this mean?*—there was a tendency to find some aggregated data somewhere, try to ascribe a process to it, and claim it as results. We did, in fact, report on our low campus crime rate as compared to Vanderbilt University just down the street (or in the rear view mirror). It was a number we could report; we had comparative information, and it looked good.

Looking in the rear-view mirror to see what worked and reporting on that is far easier (but much less rewarding) than designing an improvement system and measuring its results.

This year, there were many instances when we could point to a real process that produced improving results over time as compared to other institutions. Student loan processing time has gone from almost thirty days to fewer than twenty-four hours with the first electronic funds transfer protocol in the nation, winning the Financial Aid Office an award from Sallie Mae. Belmont Central, one-stop-shopping for almost all student administrative processes, is in full swing with cross-trained service employees whose motto is to give "unparalleled student service." (And results say they *are* giving it.) Undergraduate student research is up almost fifty percent over 1991 figures, due to an explicit process to improve undergraduate scholarship. A focus on results does pay dividends.

Finally, benchmarking and finding valuable comparisons is particularly difficult. We are not used to sharing with our competitors and tend to use only easy-to-find published information. In our first two Baldrige assessments—both self assessments and site visits—we had significant gaps in reporting comparison results. Our "areas for improvement" in the feedback reports contained multiple references to "no reported benchmark information." It wasn't that we didn't try; they just weren't out there. For example, Belmont now has several years of survey results about employee satisfaction, much of it related to our CQI effort. Four years ago, the only usable comparisons we could find were among businesses, most of them large service industries. Now, however, we've made serious pushes to find partners—those universities who, like us, want to examine results and learn best practices. We must shorten our learning cycle for improvement—not copying, but learning what is applicable for us, modifying and even improving on it.

Belmont University and University of Minnesota–Duluth have a three-year sharing history with real benchmarks. We have come to know several of their processes with almost the same depth of knowledge as we know our own. The Baldrige assessment has held up the standard, and the result of such initiatives is real learning. This kind of information is vital to knowing whether results reported in 6.0 are merely acceptable, or whether they are "world class."

Finally, this chapter is subtitled "Making Things Happen"—and certainly the concentrated effort of putting together a team that learns the Criteria, completes an internal assessment, and writes an application will indeed make things happen. There will be questions about whether the results are sound or whether they are just good stories. People will ask, "Why do we collect that information? We never use it." Engaging colleagues in the rich dialogue that surrounds the results Category 6.0 can be productive, and it can help you grapple with Deming's challenge to all of us—"How do you know?"

REFERENCES

Axland, S. 1992. Congressional Forum on Quality Education. *Quality Progress* (October): 67-68.

Baer, L., B. Knodel, J. Quistgaard, and I. Weir. 1993. Partners in Progress: An Integrative Approach to Educational Quality. In *CQI: Making the Transition to Education*, edited by D. Hubbard, 199-220. Maryville, MO: Prescott Publishing.

Bemowski, K. 1991. Baldrige Award Winners Pause to Celebrate Their Success. *Quality Progress* (December): 44-45.

Case, K. and J. Bigelow. 1992. Inside the Baldrige Award Guidelines. *Quality Progress* (November): 49-51.

Crosby, P. and C. Reimann. 1991. Criticism and Support for the Baldrige Award. *Quality Progress* (May): 41-44.

Evans, G. and D. Krueger. 1993. Quality Quest: A Community's Catalyst for Progress. In *CQI: Making the Transition to Education*, edited by D. Hubbard, 369-91. Maryville, MO: Prescott Publishing.

Ewell, P. 1992. Longitudinal Student Databases: A Critical Tool for Managing Quality in Higher Education. In *Quality Quest in the Academic Process*. Birmingham, AL: Samford University.

Garvin, D. 1991. How the Baldrige Really Works. *Harvard Business Review* (November/December): 80-93.

General Accounting Office, National Security and International Affairs Division. 1992. Management Practices: U. S. Companies Improve Performance Through Quality Efforts. Washington D.C.: GPO.

Hubbard, D. 1993. Is Quality a Manageable Commodity in Higher Education? In *CQI: Making the Transition to Education*, edited by D. Hubbard, 72-89. Maryville, MO: Prescott Publishing.

Judkins, J. 1994. Insights of a Baldrige Award Winner. *Quality Progress* (March): 57-58.

Juran, J. 1991. Strategies for World-Class Quality. *Quality Progress* (March): 81-85.

Knotts, U., L. Parrish, and C. Evans. 1993. What Does the U.S. Business Community Really Think About the Baldrige Award? *Quality Progress* (May): 49-53.

Marquardt, I. 1992. Baldrige Award Guidelines. *Quality Progress* (August): 94.

McEachern, W. and K. O'Brien. 1993. Constancy of Purpose: Ability-Based Education and Assessment-As-Learning. In *CQI: Making the Transition to Education*, edited by D. Hubbard, 454-73. Maryville, MO: Prescott Publishing.

Micklewright, M. 1993. Competitive Benchmarking: Large Gains for Small Companies. *Quality Progress* (June): 67-68.

Nakhai, B. and J. Neves. 1994. The Deming, Baldrige, and European Quality Awards. *Quality Progress* (June): 33-37.

Orsini, J. 1994. Make Marketing Part of the Quality Effort. *Quality Progress* (April): 43-45.

Price, R. 1993. Forging Effective Business-Academia Partnerships. In *CQI: Making the Transition to Education*, edited by D. Hubbard, 90-116. Maryville, MO: Prescott Publishing.

Radhakrishnan, S. and B. Srinidhi. 1994. Should Quality Be Designed In or Inspected In?: A Cost-of-Quality Framework. *Quality Management Journal* (fall): 72-85.

Rao, T. 1991. Letter to the Editor. *Quality Progress* (December): 63-66.

Seymour, D. and C. Collett. 1991. *Total Quality Management in Higher Education: A Critical Assessment.* Methuen, MA: GOAL/QPC.

Steeples, M. 1992. *Corporate Guide to the Malcolm Baldrige National Quality Award.* Milwaukee: ASQC Quality Press.

Trustees and Troubled Times in Higher Education. 1992. A report prepared for AGB Higher Education Issues Panel. Washington, D.C.: The Association of Governing Boards of Colleges and Universities.

U. S. Department of Commerce, National Institute of Standards and Technology. 1995a. *Malcolm Baldrige National Quality Award: 1995 Award Criteria.* Washington, DC: GPO.

U. S. Department of Commerce, National Institute of Standards and Technology. 1995b. *Malcolm Baldrige National Quality Award: Education Pilot Criteria.* Washington, DC: GPO.

11
Student Focus and Student and Stakeholder Satisfaction: Expectations and Requirements

Gary M. Shulman and Marian L. Houser

Quality improvement approaches embrace the view that students and other stakeholders (external and internal customers) should be actively involved in educational processes. In the *Chronicle of Higher Education*, Katherine S. Mangan (1992) states that a quality improvement effort "which stresses total staff commitment to 'customer' satisfaction, is reported at increasing numbers of colleges and universities. A survey of 22 institutions found employees felt better about their jobs, students were happier, and communication was improved" (25). For example, Belmont University reported their emphasis on continuous quality improvement in terms of the financial effect:

> We calculate in dollar amounts the value of each major customer to our institution. Participants spent time actually multiplying known figures (tuition, housing, food revenue, average alumni contributions) by the number who enter. We calculate the dollar impact of a lost student, a lost business-community customer, a lost employee. These numbers bring into focus how important the service dimension is to our financial well being. (Hubbard 1993, 524)

The trend of focusing on students and stakeholders in academe is said to be driven by university trustees who come from the corporate sector (Chait 1993). In the corporate sector the focus on customers is equivalent to the student and stakeholder orientation of academic institutions. It is noteworthy that even in corporations customers do not run the business. Similarly, academic institutions should not abdicate management responsibility but rather shape their services in response to student and stakeholder needs. The challenge is to identify such needs and create programs, services and products to meet them.

The corporate experience, however, has on many occasions been characterized by good intentions leading to hastily devised actions that lacked adequate theoretical grounding, planning or resources. In fact, nearly two-thirds of the quality improvement initiatives in organizations are dropped after less than two years (Fuchsberg 1992; Doyle 1992). The net result has been many abandoned or redesigned quality programs that led to confusion for employees and customers. The academic community, nevertheless, stands to benefit by learning from both the successful and unsuccessful corporate experiences.

By providing a conceptual framework for understanding the student and stakeholder focus criterion and describing an example of its application, this chapter will help academe to avoid the misguided and expensive corporate experiences. The Malcolm Baldrige National Quality Award was developed to recognize organizations that excel in quality management and achievement where quality is judged by customers. It is our view that in order to evaluate the quality of the service that educational organizations provide to its customers, it is necessary to first determine a conceptual basis for student and stakeholder evaluation. Equity theory provides a foundational perspective from which we can understand how students and stakeholders view their experiences with educational systems.

Therefore, the first section introduces equity theory and explains the nature of the student and stakeholder relationship to the college or university. In the second section the explicit linkage of equity theory to Baldrige Category 7.0 is drawn to demonstrate that the assessment is grounded in behavioral theory. The final section of the chapter provides excerpts of an application of Baldrige Category 7.0 by a Miami University assessment team. Equity theory provides an explanation for why student and stakeholder perspectives are featured in the Baldrige assessment. The reader can apply this knowledge immediately to a critical analysis of the case study example, and eventually to the implementation of the assessment methodology to other institutions.

EQUITY THEORY FOUNDATION

Although the Baldrige Award criteria has seven Categories, the "Student Focus and Student and Stakeholder Satisfaction" component is of critical importance by virtue of its high point value allotment. No matter how many quality improvements are made in a college, or how impressive they are, it is the students' and stakeholders' perceptions that are most important in determining what quality is.

The business environment is no longer alone in its goal to serve and satisfy the customer—that is, the user or beneficiary of a service or product. Institutions of higher education maintain this goal as well. Colleges and universities serve a broad group of people, both internally and externally. Primarily they have been envisioned as institutions dedicated to the sole purpose of providing learning to their students, but they serve many more constituencies. In fact, everyone in contact with systems of higher education is a customer or a stakeholder: state agencies, alumni, employer, community groups, faculty, staff, prospective students, and countless others.

What makes the individuals in these groups customers? And what must occur to create their support in the first place? Can institutions of higher learning assume that if they open the doors of their classrooms, there will always be students to fill them? Forgive us for borrowing a line from the film *Field of Dreams*, but can we be sure that "If we build it, they will come?" Our customers (students) and other stakeholders do have options, and like the business environment, they also realize that they can take their business elsewhere.

Can institutions of higher learning assume that if they open the doors of their classrooms, there will always be students to fill them?

This idea is closely akin to equity theory, a social comparison theory of motivation as proposed by Adams (1965) and Weick (1966). Equity theory has been applied to both interpersonal relations and business. In both fields, this theory proposes that people evaluate their jobs, situations, relationships, or experiences by comparing what they put into it (inputs) and what they get out of it (outcomes) with the experiences of others. If people perceive that they are experiencing a basic inequity (an unequal ratio of inputs to outcomes), they are motivated to alter the conditions or situation. However, since inequity is a relative phenomenon, individuals will compare their circumstances with others they perceive to be in a similar situation before they take remediating action.

Adams' (1965) initial presentation of equity theory took a business perspective and was expressed in the form of three axioms: (1) People evaluate their relationships with their organizations by comparing what they give to the organizations with what they get in return; (2) When what people give does not equal what they get, they feel distress or dissonance; and, (3) People who feel distressed because they are under-rewarded will try to restore equity. From a very practical point of view, equity theory explains why employees perform the way they do and acknowledges them as (internal) customers. This motivation theory claims that organizational members are driven by their desire to be equitably treated in their work relationships. Thus, employees/customers expect to receive benefits at a fair exchange rate for their services, and they determine their equity through a comparison to other employees/customers. As Huseman and Hatfield (1990) conclude, "Although equity theorists have identified many ways in which people may restore equity, two stand out: reducing inputs and increasing outcomes . . . the studies show that people who have tried but failed to restore equity may simply quit their jobs" (99).

The concern for a fair rate of exchange can be seen with equity theory in the interpersonal realm as well. All people are inclined to react according to their self-interests; this notion is put forth by Walster, Walster, and Berscheid (1978) who argue that individuals will try to maximize their relational outcomes. In this context, outcomes equal psychological or social rewards minus psychological or social costs associated with an interaction or relationship. Thus, people will seek to develop and maintain relationships in which the ratio of costs and rewards is equal to their partner's. If not, relational dissatisfaction is imminent. This dissatisfaction with relational rewards to costs ratio may lead to redefining or dissolving the relationship. The perception of the equity of the cost-reward ratio in a relationship may change when one of the parties engages in social comparison. If there are fewer perceived costs or greater perceived rewards associated with an alternative relationship partner, the current relationship may be redefined or dissolved.

For example, one partner may be perfectly happy performing *all* of the household cleaning chores until he or she discovers that a neighbor *shares* those burdensome responsibilities with a spouse. Clean-

HIGH PERFORMING COLLEGES

ing toilets increases the perceived costs of maintaining the current relationship, and inequity may exert pressure to redefine the relationship to include sharing chores. If the gap between rewards and costs grows too large, it can lead to divorce, or the end of the relationship.

The basic assumption in all "Social Comparison Theories" is that the focus is on the perceptions of individuals. They are concerned with evaluating and comparing their treatment with what others are receiving. It is human nature to socially compare.

Equity theory is a social comparison theory which relies on two basic assumptions of human nature. First, individuals compare their relationships and success from an economic perspective. As Homans (1961) states in his "rule of distributive justice": "A man in an exchange relation with another will expect that the rewards of each man be proportional to his costs—the greater the rewards the greater the costs—and that the net rewards, or profits, of each man be proportional to his investments—the greater the investments the greater the profits" (75). Homans uses the term investment in reference to the time and effort an individual puts into an activity or job.

The second assumption is that people do not view their personal equity in a vacuum. They are constantly comparing the inputs and outputs in their social and business environments to determine their relative balance. In a work environment there are many inputs which are commonly observed—educational background, previous experience, work hours, and effort expended are a few. Outputs are equally important in the equity theory because these are the items in the exchange that individuals expect to receive based on their inputs: pay raises, compensatory time, promotion, verbal or written praise, and employment benefits.

Ultimately, individuals compare the ratio of their inputs and outputs to the ratios of other individuals. These then become the reference points for their determination of equity.

Students and stakeholders enter into a relationship with colleges and universities. All parties in a relationship evaluate the ratio of their psychological as well as financial costs and rewards. A perceived inequity may lead to a dissolution of the relationship. For example, if a student fails to meet minimum academic standards, the college may expel the student due to a lack of sufficient outcomes or "rewards" to justify the continued "costs" (financial and psychological) associated with the teaching-learning relationship. An example from a stakeholder perspective may apply to the college-employer relationship. If an employer perceives that the cost of training new graduates exceeds the reward of what those employees contribute, the employer may try to change its relationship with the university by requesting revisions to curricula, or may sever the relationship and hire graduates from another college.

Other stakeholders of higher educational institutions may include parents of students, alumni, the local community, state legislators, and society. These are people who do not *directly* receive the service or product of colleges and universities but whom, nonetheless, indirectly benefit from those services or products and consider themselves interested constituents. For example, parents and alumni do not typically find themselves in the classroom to receive educational services yet remain interested parties in the activities and outcomes of the college or university. Parents and alumni may be directly involved (e.g., paying fees, attending sports events) with some university activities, but typically form impressions vicariously through their children or the media. Parents are likely to be satisfied stakeholders if they believe that their children have received sufficient educational benefits to justify the time and cost investment at the institution. Alumni want the reputation of the institution to be favorable so as to make their degree valuable for future employment or self-esteem purposes.

Local communities and state legislators are often concerned with the economic, political, and social dividends emanating from the public's investment in institutions of higher learning. Similarly, society benefits from a well educated work force that contributes to a higher standard of living for all of its members. Satisfying various stakeholders directly affects the financial well being of the institution.

Satisfying various stakeholders directly affects the financial well being of the institution.

THEORETICAL UNDERPINNINGS OF BALDRIGE CATEGORY 7.0

With the importance of stakeholder perceptions of equity in our educational institutions established, it is critical as well to consider a means for observing and measuring this quality. This section will introduce Baldrige Category 7.0 for educational institutions and each of the six items that comprise it. Each Item is classified as emphasizing approach, deployment, or results. "Approach" means that systems are in place to improve quality as well as student and stakeholder satisfaction. "Deployment" means that the approach is implemented throughout the college or university. "Results" are essentially data or outcomes that assess effectiveness. After describing the intent of each component of this category, we will discuss how it is linked to equity theory.

The Student Focus and Student and Stakeholder Satisfaction Category examines how the college determines student and stakeholder needs and expectations. In addition, trends over time and comparisons with other colleges are analyzed using key satisfaction measures. The general thrust of Category 7.0 is consistent with the principles of equity theory. The trend data allow the college to track its relationship with students and stakeholders over a period of time. If it is determined that there may be a perceived inequity in the relationship, the college can choose to alter the cost rewards ratio in the relationship in order to avoid its dissolution. Trend data will show whether the relationship is in equilibrium or imbalance, and whether there is movement toward strengthening or weakening the relational ties. The comparative data analysis is an acknowledgment that relational partners have alternatives and are likely to seek them out when they perceive inequity in their current relationships. Students and stakeholders may abandon their college if they perceive inequity and if another college has a more favorable perceived cost-reward ratio. Remember that costs and rewards are not limited to financial measures and include psychological and social dimensions as well.

Item 7.1, Current Student Needs and Expectations, describes how the college develops and maintains awareness of the needs and expectations of current students and seeks to create an overall climate conducive to active learning, well-being, and satisfaction for all students. The direct costs for students include tuition, other financial fees or expenses, time, effort, and energy. Indirect costs might be the lost opportunities of being somewhere else or doing something different. For example, forgone wages from working full time somewhere else might be considered an opportunity cost to a student. Thus, the total cost to the student would include those costs directly incurred while pursuing an education plus those rewards that are lost by choosing to be a student rather than an employee. To avoid inequity, colleges must determine what rewards students need or expect so that they can justify the expenditure of various costs. Retention issues are related to equity theory and this Item. Current students may terminate a relationship with a college by dropping out, flunking out, or transferring to another college when they feel the rewards received do not justify the personal costs. By knowing what current students value as rewards, the college is in a better position to manage the cost-reward ratio and avoid the hardships associated with inequity. This is an approach and deployment item.

Item 7.2, Future Student Needs and Expectations, describes how the college determines the needs and expectations of future students and maintains awareness of the key factors affecting these needs and expectations. Whereas Item 7.1 focuses on *maintaining* current relationships between the college and its students, Item 7.2 focuses on *developing* future relationships. Relationships are dynamic and must be adapted to the specific parties constituting them. As students' values change over time, the college must be prepared to provide rewards that meet those new needs and expectations. Failing to do so could result in falling enrollments when the new generation of students do not value the perceived rewards of the previous generation. For example, an outdated curriculum that does not include technology may create an inequity in the minds of prospective students who will then choose to attend another college that provides a more technologically sophisticated educational opportunity. This is an approach and deployment item.

Item 7.3, Stakeholder Relationship Management, describes how the college provides effective linkages to key stakeholders to support and enhance its mission-related services and to meet stakeholder needs and expectations. Stakeholders are those who have an interest in the success or failure of college practices or outcomes. Their interest is such that they may gain or lose something they value as a result of a change or the maintenance of the status quo. Of course, some stakeholder groups and individuals have more at stake than others in any given situation. Thus the elements in the cost-reward ratio analysis will vary from stakeholder to stakeholder and situation to situation.

To maintain relationships and avoid inequity among diverse stakeholders means that a college must learn to identify and manage the perceived costs and rewards of its various constituencies. This is an approach and deployment Item.

Item 7.4, Student and Stakeholder Satisfaction Determination, describes how the college determines student and stakeholder satisfaction, including their satisfaction relative to students and stakeholders of comparable colleges. This Item identifies the strategy for seeking the costs and rewards contributing to the perception of relationship equity. Moreover, by requiring a comparative analysis with other colleges, it embodies the equity principle of social comparison. Students and stakeholders will compare the cost-reward ratio of one college with another and search for the most favorable relationship. This Item recognizes that even if colleges do not compare themselves with others, students and stakeholders will. The key in this item is selecting the same colleges for comparison as the students and stakeholders will. This is an approach and deployment item.

This Item recognizes that even if colleges do not compare themselves with others, students and stakeholders will.

Item 7.5, Student and Stakeholder Satisfaction Results, summarizes the institution's student and stakeholder satisfaction and dissatisfaction results using key measures and/or indicators of these results. The resultant satisfiers measured in this Item are related to equity theory rewards and the resultant dissatisfiers are related to costs. By applying metrics for costs and rewards the college can determine whether the overall relationship with students and stakeholders is in equilibrium or inequity. This is a results item.

Item 7.6, Student and Stakeholder Satisfaction Comparison, compares the college's satisfaction results with those of comparable schools. Here the college—mindful of social comparison in equity theory—compares actual data measuring the cost-reward ratios with other relevant colleges. This provides a broader context for understanding how much of a gap in the cost-reward ratio may be tolerated before it leads to inequity for students and stakeholders. It is mindful of the alternatives available to students and stakeholders. This is also a results item.

MIAMI UNIVERSITY CASE STUDY

Recently, Miami University embarked on a Baldrige-guided self-assessment with the help of two expert consultants from a corporate partner. The motivation for undertaking this project was to establish a baseline of current practices and performance so as to guide and track the effectiveness of continuous improvement strategies. Since the Education Pilot Criteria did not exist at the time of the assessment a faculty team worked with the consultants to translate the business language into terms deemed more "user friendly" for academia.

The remainder of this section highlights excerpts from our Baldrige assessment followed by key learnings from our experience with Category 7.0, Student Focus and Student and Stakeholder Satisfaction. (See appendix for a full description of 7.0, its Items, and their corresponding areas to address.)

7.1 Current Student Needs and Expectations

Miami University seeks input on student expectations and requirements through a wide variety of advisory councils. First and foremost, there are a wealth of student advisory councils throughout campus which provide feedback and direction to departments, divisions, admissions, and student services.

Second, student services participates in the Cooperative Institutional Research Program (CIRP), which compares entering Miami freshmen to students across the nation. This survey assesses reasons for attending college, reasons for selecting Miami, demographics, goals, and attitudes. The regional campuses will begin an additional survey of newly enrolled students this fall to help assess expectations, customer requirements, and satisfaction.

Third, short term trends are continuously assessed within both the academic and support services divisions. For example, academic departments engage in constant fine-tuning of the curriculum (the major product offered to our students) through course evaluation, revision, and program change. Programmatic efforts such as summer orientation and freshman advising are consistently evaluated by participants and subsequently adjusted to meet student needs. The Career Planning and Placement office maintains an ongoing dialogue with employers concerning their needs and the adequacy of Miami's programs and graduates.

The registrar's office gathers information on a regular basis from advisors to help determine customer expectations and satisfaction. The College of Arts and Sciences routinely evaluates the effective-

HIGH PERFORMING COLLEGES

ness of its advising efforts. Many offices also regularly conduct on-going customer service surveys.

Complaints are handled throughout the university through both formal and informal processes (outlined in greater detail in 7.2). Such complaints are informally used by each department or office in recalibrating the system to be more responsive to customer expectations. Complaints are one piece of the assessment data utilized in the Support Services Review process.

Gain/loss data are specifically used by the Office of Admissions in assessing their efficacy in appealing to new markets. The office routinely assesses the reasons why students do not choose Miami; this information is informally utilized as feedback into the system. For example, admissions has noted that one reason students do not choose Miami is the financial aid package offered—this information is shared with the Office of Financial Aid, and with the President's Council for future action in developing new avenues of financial aid. The regional campuses have also begun an assessment of non-enrolled applicants.

Product and service performance is assessed primarily through academic program and support services reviews. Each academic department and office providing support services is evaluated every three to five years. The academic review assesses program quality, viability and centrality. The support service review assesses planning processes and continuous improvement, centrality, and effectiveness. These reviews provide key feedback on the degree to which customer expectations and requirements are being met.

7.2 Future Student Needs and Expectations

The university maintains a relatively long term horizon—approximately five years. The primary means for evaluating and improving processes for determining student expectations are program and support services reviews. These reviews are conducted every three to five years, and require the program or support office to articulate mission, goals, objectives, quality of service, quality of teaching and scholarship, and centrality to the university's functional mission. After completion of an extensive self-study, the program or office is reviewed by a team of at least three peers from within the university. The team outlines strengths, and makes concrete recommendations for improvement, which are forwarded to the appropriate vice president.

Both Admissions and the regional campuses maintain guidance counselor advisory groups which provide advice and information about student expectations, how Miami is perceived by the community, and community needs.

As a part of strategic planning, many programs and divisions in the university meet regularly with external advisory councils (some of the offices/divisions with advisory councils include Career Planning and Placement, School of Business, School of Education and Allied Professions, School of Applied Science, Hamilton campus, Middletown campus). The councils provide key information on long-term trends and student requirements.

Students of our competitors are considered in multiple ways. We analyze where the students in our pool are going to college, through a subscription to ACT's yield analysis and surveys of accepted students who do not enroll on the main and regional campuses. This lets us know how many students are going to each competitor and why students may choose another college.

We conduct follow-up contacts with employers who were unsuccessful in recruiting from Miami, and with employers who have discontinued use of our placement center.

We conduct exit interviews with students who withdraw from the university, to assess the role of competitors in drawing away our current students. We conduct follow-up contacts with employers who were unsuccessful in recruiting from Miami, and with employers who have discontinued use of our placement center.

Future trends in product/service features and in market segments are determined and projected through the use of the advisory councils (both student and external) described earlier. In addition, changing and emerging market segments are considered most broadly in the strategic planning process and in the development of the University's functional mission. Recently, this process has emphasized the importance of recruitment and retention of a more diversified population.

Key features of the programs that are offered to our primary students are determined within departments and divisions through analysis of trends in each discipline. This analysis takes place on many levels, including assessment of trends outlined in professional journals and books, discussions with colleagues at national professional conferences, discussions with employers and active professionals, and discussions with current and former students. The recent changes in the Liberal Education Program are an excellent example of how identifying students' long term needs can translate into a programmatic focus on critical thinking, understanding contexts, engaging with other learners, and active learning.

Many divisions and offices use external advisory councils (composed of alumni, employers, leaders in the profession) to provide information on stakeholder expectations as well as short and long term market trends.

7.3 Stakeholder Relationship Management

Overall, throughout the university, contacts between employees and stakeholders occur in similar ways. Our most important contacts for students (prospective, current, and recent graduates) occur at admission, registration, graduation, placement, as well as in teaching and advising interactions. Our employer and graduate school contacts occur primarily under the career planning and placement umbrella and academic divisional units, and secondarily through the alumni and development offices. The following describe the key requirements for maintaining and building stakeholder relationships:

- Accessible faculty and staff.
- Ability to provide accurate and comprehensive information.
- Provision of graduates appropriate to the needs of employers and graduate institutions in terms of academic preparation, maturity, and readiness for employment or advanced study.
- Assurance that all services are provided in a professional, competent, caring and effective manner.

Employees have a well-defined sense of purpose to be constituent driven within the framework of their departmental responsibility.

Employees have a well-defined sense of purpose to be constituent driven within the framework of their departmental responsibility. Almost all units evaluate or gather feedback from their stakeholders. The method for receiving feedback is varied and includes surveys, focus groups, exit interviews, etc. It is not clear how they respond to this information, or whether standards for improvement occur as a result. Teaching evaluations are one of the only university-wide standard methods for gathering student feedback.

The Statement of Good Teaching Practices is a written commitment for standards of good teaching. Unless defined at the unit level, there are no other service standards—among the groups interviewed for this report—set at the university-wide level.

The publications office responds to all letters to the editor of the alumni magazine. Complaint letters are handled on a case-by-case basis and are often circulated to the appropriate offices for follow-up. The president's office is part of the routing loop.

The registrar's office trains staff to handle as many complaints or problems as possible at the point of customer contact; if resolution is not achieved, the problem is only then referred up to the next level in the office hierarchy.

Formal processes—such as the grievance procedure, petitioning process, or sexual harassment claim procedure—allow for a systematic way of dealing with complaints or disagreements. These are tabulated within individual units, but do not appear to be reviewed centrally.

All the academic units of the university provide new faculty orientation. A component of these is teaching effectiveness. Some academic departments also include a peer mentoring program for new faculty. Probationary faculty are evaluated annually by the chair and dean. Information gleaned from these evaluations is used to improve both teaching and scholarship.

There are lots of sporadic means for rewarding employees for effective customer relations. Examples include effective/distinguished educator awards created by student government and by some academic divisions. The "STAR" award has been an attempt to recognize any special effort made by employees to assist students and is done through a nomination process which is later published in "The Miami Report." Further recognition is given in "The Miami Report" for publications, presentations, and any special awards for all employees. Most of these formal means of recognition are directed to the faculty.

A systematic approach to evaluation is not used throughout the university. However, there are a multitude of departmental/unit examples of evaluation of customer relationships. These range from teaching evaluations and graduate surveys at one, five, and ten-year intervals, to academic advising evaluation done by first year and College of Arts and Science advising. Certainly the Program Review Process and the Administrative Support Review process touch on this as well. The upcoming North Central Accreditation Review has also been a catalyst for cultivating programmatic data.

The question is: are these data used to improve customer relationships? The best example is the promotion and tenure process, where data regarding teaching effectiveness are used to make recommendations and final decisions. The classified staff annual evaluation is another example of feedback that is designed to improve stakeholder/staff relationships.

7.4 Student and Stakeholder Satisfaction Determination

Miami uses multiple methods for capturing information about our student and stakeholder satisfaction levels. We determine customer satisfaction through personal contacts, independent third-party studies, and our own multi-faceted on-going assessment efforts. For our key constituents, prospective students, current students, recent alumni, employers, and graduate-professional schools, these include:

Prospective students: The admissions office collects data on the percentage of Ohio high school graduates that apply to Miami, the number of applications from minority students, and the yield rate (ratio of the number of students who actually enroll over the number of applicants accepted for admission). All accepted students who do not enroll are surveyed about why they chose not to come to Miami and where they went instead. The Hamilton campus also surveys high school guidance counselors and campus visitors (prospective students and their parents).

Current students: The division of student affairs conducts evaluation and opinion surveys as part of the Student Research Program which is part of a comprehensive effort to improve the quality of programs and services offered to students. For example, many aspects of dining and residence halls are studied. The Student Research Program and various divisions have systematically studied student satisfaction with advising. Other aspects of student satisfaction are measured through end-of-term course evaluations, annual third-party CIRP surveys, annual divisional surveys, interviews or focus groups, and decentralized department-initiated assessments. Current students are also considered in Academic Program Review and Support Service Review which takes place on a three to five-year cycle. The registrar collects information on graduation rate, class retention rates, and course scheduling satisfaction rate. CPPO tracks monthly the number of students who register for its services and attend its instructional programs. It also measures monthly the number of students making counseling appointments.

Recent alumni: Satisfaction of recent graduates is measured annually through the percentage of alumni donating money to Miami, the amount donated, the percentage participating in Senior Challenge, and the amount pledged to and ultimately collected for Senior Challenge. Departments and divisions conduct their own exit interviews and three to five-year post-graduation surveys (procedures are not systematized university-wide).

Employers: CPPO collects office evaluations by visiting recruiters, conducts annual surveys of all employers who recruited on campus to ascertain how many students received offers of employment from on-campus recruitment, makes follow-up calls to employers who were unsuccessful in their recruitment efforts at Miami, conducts yearly assessment of organizations that have or have not returned to campus to recruit, and measures monthly the number of organizations scheduled for recruiting visits, the number of organizations to which referrals are made, and the number of job notices reported to CPPO.

Graduate-Professional Schools: Divisions have their own formal and informal procedures for collecting information. For example, the College of Arts and Sciences annually collects data on the number of Miami students applying and accepted for advanced study.

Comparative Data: We are investigating methods to create a database warehouse that would allow us to compare customer satisfaction with our performance versus our competitors'. Currently, we participate in surveys conducted independently by professional organizations (e.g., NACUBO and CIRP) that provide comparative information between Miami and specific other universities (Kent State, OSU, Akron, and Wright State, or an aggregate composite of comparable universities). The independent nature and large sampling of NACUBO and CIRP studies assure reliability and validity.

Information Dissemination: Evaluation data are regularly summarized, published, and disseminated in the Miami University Fact Book. Many key stakeholders automatically receive this information and others may receive it by request. "Through the Arches" is issued periodically through student affairs and contains information about the Miami student body together with results of evaluation and opinion surveys. Using a decentralized process, we use customer feedback to evaluate the data collection process and recommend improvements. Students withdrawing from the university participate in exit interviews. This allows us to determine if there are additional important issues to include in other objective measures. We regularly upgrade our questions to improve clarity, understandability, explicitness, and relevance. The data warehouse committee is, in part, studying data collection strategies (their concerns go beyond customer satisfaction). There is no university-wide process used to review the evaluation results and develop an action plan for improving our approach to measuring customer satisfaction. There is no university-wide evidence that improvements have been made in the measurement of customer dissatisfaction indicators. However, each unit in the university has been encouraged to develop and communicate a grievance procedure to their customers.

7.5 Student and Stakeholder Satisfaction Results

Miami University uses a variety of measures to gauge its effectiveness in serving its broad constituencies. The University's key constituent groups include prospective students, currently enrolled students, alumni, employers, and graduate and professional schools. Therefore, its primary performance measures focus on these key student and stakeholder groups.

Prospective students: There has been a steady increase in both the number and percentage of Ohio high school graduates who have applied for admission to Miami during the past three years (from 4.23 percent to 5.62 percent). Were the University not considered attractive, these figures would have fluctuated or declined during this three-year period.

Likewise, Miami has sought to diversify its student body by attracting greater numbers of applicants from ethnic minority groups. While there have been variations from year to year in applications from specific minority groups, the overall trend has been upward over the past three years (from 464 to 549). This application flow data from minority groups confirms that Miami is increasingly becoming attractive to prospective students from minority groups.

In addition, the yield rate, or the number of accepted students who enroll, can be considered a performance measure when reviewing trends pertaining to prospective students. Yield rates for the past three years fell from 46 percent to 42 percent.

A number of measures are used to ascertain students' satisfaction with their educational experiences at Miami.

Currently enrolled students: A number of measures are used to ascertain students' satisfaction with their educational experiences at Miami. Some of these measures are university-wide indicators, while many others are maintained exclusively by the various academic and administrative support units of the University.

A key measure of satisfaction among currently enrolled students is retention data. According to records maintained by the Office of the Registrar, four-year retention rates for classes entering Miami in 1987, 1988, and 1989 range from 81.1 percent to 82.6 percent.

A measure closely related to retention rate is graduation rate. Four-year graduation rates for classes entering Miami in 1986, 1987, and 1988 range from 74.6 percent to 75.3 percent.

Likewise, another measure of students' satisfaction with the University pertains to their ability to register successfully for courses they need. This "course scheduling satisfaction" data is highly related to shifting enrollment patterns and the ability of the University to adjust faculty staffing in response to enrollment changes. In any case, figures from the Office of the Registrar reflect course scheduling satisfaction levels measured in 1991, 1992, and 1993 range from 90.4 percent to 92.9 percent.

It should be further noted that course evaluations are widely used by virtually all of the academic departments of the University and that these data are used at both the divisional and departmental levels to assure high quality classroom learning experiences for Miami students.

Alumni: Most of the major academic divisions survey their new graduates annually to determine their placement status. Each year, the Career Planning and Placement Office (CPPO) aggregates this divisional data in order to develop a broader profile of the University's new alumni. The aggregated divisional placement data calculated by the CPPO the past three years indicates an unemployed rate (not employed or in graduate school) ranging from 3.4 percent to 4.3 percent.

According to these aggregated divisional placement reports, Miami students enjoy a high placement rate. However, since there is wide variation among the academic divisions as to the interval between graduation and the solicitation of their graduates' placement status, the CPPO conducted a survey of new graduates in the fall of 1992 and the fall of 1993. This pulse survey includes a random sample of 100 new graduates who were registered for placement services during their senior year. This survey provides a measure of standardization in placement-related data across academic divisions. Two key dimensions of customer satisfaction provided by this report include graduates' responses to the questions of whether a college degree is required for their present positions and the extent to which their positions are related to their college major(s). Results for the surveys of the Classes of 1992 and 1993 show that the range of those agreeing that a college degree was required for their job was between 57 and 68 percent. The range of responses to whether their position was related to their major was 68 to 73 percent.

Another important indicator of graduates' overall satisfaction with their Miami experience includes the extent to which they participate in the University's fund-raising efforts. Alumni giving amounts and percentages for the past three years range from $11.4 million to $9.8 million and 34 to 25 percent. Alumni giving is exceptionally strong, especially when considered in light of the 18 percent annual average for all public universities.

Employers: Articulation and cooperation with prospective employers is an ongoing, University-wide endeavor among Miami's various academic divisions and departments, and several meet regularly with advisory councils comprised of key employers and prominent alumni as a means of assuring that both their students and their curricula are responsive to employers' needs. The Career Planning and Placement Office is charged with the responsibility for serving as the principal servicing unit for businesses, government agencies, and school districts seeking Miami graduates. As such, it maintains a variety of reports that track utilization of its services by employers.

Miami has enjoyed a relatively high level of on-campus recruitment activity over the past three years, despite a sluggish economy. With a ratio of 3.72 employer interviews per graduating senior, Miami's on-campus recruiting program is approximately two-and-one-half times larger than the national average, according to a benchmarking study conducted by the National Association of College and University Business Officers (NACUBO) in 1992.

Graduate/Professional Schools: A relatively high percentage of Miami graduates seek admission to graduate or professional programs immediately after graduation. In recent years, nearly 26 percent of our graduates have gone on to advanced studies. The graduate school attendance rates of graduates from the College of Arts and Science for the past three years are particularly illustrative (ranging from 33 to 43 percent).

While the tight economy has had an impact on the number of students who have elected to go on to graduate programs, the steady increase in the number of graduates enrolling in graduate and professional schools is also an indicator of the high regard in which Miami graduates are held by these institutions.

These data are further supported by acceptance rates for Miami graduates seeking admission to medical and law schools. Acceptance rates over a three year period for first-time applicants from Miami University to medical school range from 57 to 80 percent compared to the national acceptance rate ranging from 44 to 55 percent. The acceptance rates over a three year period for Miami seniors who applied to law school and the corresponding national average acceptance rates range from 74 to 79 percent and 60 to 64 percent, respectively.

7.6 Student and Stakeholder Satisfaction Comparison

As mentioned in Items 7.2 and 7.4, while there is a great deal of emphasis at the divisional level and below with identifying and meeting student and stakeholder expectations and providing a high level of satisfaction, these efforts are decentralized in nature and the data which are gathered is rarely shared with other units. Moreover, even the data which are gathered as a result of a particular office's or division's decentralized efforts is rarely measured against a standard or target for improvement. Rather, the information is used more often as a means of triggering corrective action rather than to produce continuous quality improvement. Having said this, individual service units do use a wide variety of different measures to monitor the quality of their service to the key customer groups which have been identified previously, as seen in Item 7.5. We also compare that data against other institutions in the field of higher education, though not in a consistent manner. The following customer satisfaction comparison data are organized by key student and stakeholder groups.

Current Students: Key measures for current student satisfaction levels include retention and graduation rates, course scheduling satisfaction rates, course evaluations, full-time faculty to FTE student ratios, and information gathered from students regarding their perception of their college environment and their overall satisfaction with their college.

Using data regarding retention rates from the NACUBO/Coopers & Lybrand Benchmarking Project for FY93 indicates that 91.62 percent of Miami freshmen return for their sophomore year. Miami's figure sets the benchmark for that year for the five Ohio Universities which also provide data to the NACUBO project. On the other hand, Miami's retention figure of 65.08 percent for sophomores is the lowest of the five schools. The NACUBO project, while very promising, is a relatively new effort. Therefore, adequate trend data are not available.

NACUBO data regarding graduation rates for the same five Ohio state assisted universities shows that, once again, Miami sets the benchmark with a six-year graduation rate of 82 percent. Using data gathered by the National Collegiate Athletic Association for Division I universities in Ohio, as well as for Mid-American Conference schools outside Ohio, Miami ranks highest in its percentage of graduates for the years reported.

Recent Graduates: Key measures for the satisfaction of recent graduates with Miami University are both the percentage and number of its alumni who contribute to the University. According to the office of Planned Giving, approximately 25 percent of Miami Alumni contribute to the Annual Campaign compared to a national average of 18 percent for publicly supported universities.

Employers: The key measure used to evaluate employer satisfaction is the number of employer interviews per graduating senior.

The key measure used to evaluate employer satisfaction is the number of employer interviews per graduating senior.

According to NACUBO Benchmarking data from FY92, Miami enjoys a level of on-campus recruiting that is two and one-half times greater than the national average and two times larger than the Ohio average. More specifically, Miami provides an average of 3.72 employer interviews per graduating senior while the national mean is 1.43 and the Ohio mean is 1.89. No reliable trend data are available for this measure.

Graduate/Professional Schools: Currently, there is no readily available University-wide data which provides a measure of the satisfaction level of graduates from Miami's graduate and professional schools. Some data does appear to be available at the divisional level, but is not consistently gathered.

Key Learnings

After the Baldrige assessment was written, it was distributed to selected members of the university community and reviewed by our corporate partner consultants who were Baldrige examiners. The consultants subsequently facilitated a discussion with selected members of the university community to identify key learnings from the assessment process. The strengths and areas for improvement enumerated below were abstracted from this reflection phase.

Strengths:
- Miami has identified its market segments and has a good understanding of the qualifications of its incoming students.
- Miami has successful processes to determine near-term student and stakeholder requirements—student and external advisory councils, the Cooperative Institutional Research Program, assessments within the academic and support services division, extensive analysis of the gains and losses of students to understand why students do not choose to attend Miami, exit interviews of students who leave Miami, and follow-up interviews with employers who have discontinued the use of the placement center.
- Miami periodically reviews its processes for determining student and stakeholder requirements using peer reviews within the university.

- Almost all Miami units gather feedback from their students through surveys, focus groups, teaching evaluations, etc.
- Miami has a decentralized/informal process that results in a very personalized approach to handling complaints.
- Miami is committed to providing students with a quality, affordable education.
- Miami has achieved good results and shows improvement in some key student satisfaction areas. Miami has achieved good student retention levels, graduation rates, and course scheduling satisfaction ratings. The percentage of students obtaining a job related to their major and requiring a degree have improved. The acceptance rates for first-time applicants to the law and medical schools have improved.
- Miami has achieved superior levels of customer satisfaction in some key areas. It has earned the reputation as a public ivy, a best buy. The overall level of employee interviews and acceptance into medical and law school are high relative to national averages, as are student perceptions on four out of five areas of student development emphasis. Graduate giving to the annual campaign is higher than the national average. The graduation rate of 82 percent is the highest among the National Collegiate Athletic Association Division I and Mid-American Conference schools.

Areas for Improvement:
- It is not clear how Miami validates assessment of needs after students graduate, other than through occasional alumni surveys.
- It is unclear how Miami considers technological, competitive, environmental, economic and demographic factors in addressing the future requirements and expectations of students and stakeholders.
- Service standards, except the Statement of Good Teaching Practices, have not been reported. A formal system for aggregating complaint data for root cause analysis,

strategic planning, and systematic improvement does not appear to exist.

- No system exists for special training of employees who fill student and stakeholder contact roles. Similarly, no system exists to evaluate and measure the student and stakeholder relationship management process.
- Trends of objective student and stakeholder perception data is fairly limited. Some data relates more to internal quality results. For example, there is an absence of data of satisfaction level of grad schools with graduates, direct employer satisfaction data, etc.
- An opportunity exists for university-wide student and stakeholder satisfaction data analysis as part of the strategic decision making and planning process.

We learned from the Baldrige self-assessment process to view the university as a system of interrelated parts that exist to serve the needs of multiple constituencies or stakeholders (e.g., students, faculty, staff, employers, alumni). Going through the assessment process helped us appreciate that student and stakeholder satisfaction can be understood by studying the interaction among university operations or processes, faculty and staff performance, and student or stakeholder expectations. The challenge is to integrate these components into a coordinated system. The assessment moved us closer to such a system by encouraging cross-functional conversations among disparate parts of the university community that did not communicate on a regular basis. These conversations helped sharpen the shared vision of the university and focus it on serving students and stakeholders. Moreover, it led to the realization that no single constituency can unilaterally determine what "satisfaction" means. The assessment team learned that there were opportunities for improving key processes and data collection methods. Sometimes we could not adequately assess a process because there was insufficient information readily available. This experience fulfilled our goal for providing a baseline measurement from which to mark our progress in improving the quality of our processes.

CONCLUSION

The Baldrige National Quality Award Education Criteria provide a basic blueprint for implementing a quality process. Of all the Baldrige Criteria, none are more important than Student Focus and Student and Stakeholder Satisfaction. The assumption is that what these constituencies judge to be the meaning of quality cannot be ignored. The intended interdependencies among the seven Baldrige categories bring every aspect of the institution under scrutiny through the eyes of students and stakeholders. The relationship between educational institutions and their students and stakeholders can be described systematically using the items comprising Category 7.0. Equity theory helps us understand how students and stakeholders view their experiences with educational institutions for each of these items. Combining the knowledge of equity theory with the application of the Baldrige items in the case study will prepare readers for assessing the progress of their institution's quality journey.

The authors gratefully acknowledge the following Miami University faculty and staff who contributed to the preparation of the case study material: Linda Dixon, Rick Hearin, Sally Lloyd, Claudia Scott-Pavloff, Dick Pettitt and David Stonehill.

REFERENCES

Adams, J. S. 1965. Injustice in Social Exchange. In *Advances in Experimental Social Psychology*, edited by L. Berkowitz. Vol. 2. New York: Academic Press.

Chait, Richard. 1993. Colleges Should Not Be Blinded by Vision. *Chronicle of Higher Education*, 22 September, B1-2.

Doyle, Kevin. 1992. Who's Killing Total Quality? *Incentive* 166 (August):12-19.

Fuchsberg, Gilbert. 1992. Quality Programs Show Shoddy Results. *Wall Street Journal,* 14 April, B1.

Homans, G. C. 1961. *Social Behavior: Its Elementary Forms.* New York: Harcourt, Brace, & World.

Hubbard, D., ed. 1993. *Continuous Quality Improvement: Making the Transition to Education.* Maryville, MO: Prescott Publishing.

Huseman, R. C. and J. D. Hatfield. 1990. Equity Theory and the Managerial Matrix. *Training & Development Journal* 4: 98-102.

Mangan, K. S. 1992. TQM: Colleges Embrace the Concept of Total Quality Management. *Chronicle of Higher Education* 38: 25-26.

Mowday, R. T. 1979. Equity Theory Predictions of Behavior in Organizations. In *Motivation and Work Behavior*, edited by R. M. Steers and L. W. Porter. 2nd edition. New York: McGraw-Hill.

Walster, E. H., G. W. Walster, and E. Berscheid. 1978. *Equity: Theory and Research*. Boston: Allyn & Bacon.

Weick, K. E. 1966. The Concept of Equity in the Perception of Pay. *Administrative Science Quarterly* (September): 414-39.

Part Three: Quality Assurance

These chapters offer the reader a different view of the Malcolm Baldrige National Quality Award and its application to the higher education community. While the previous section focused on institution-based issues that were operational in nature, these chapters reflect other perspectives. State legislators, trustees, and accrediting agency officers perceive colleges and universities in broad sweeping terms. They care about developing and maintaining policies and procedures that assure their various constituencies of proper and efficient use of scare institutional resources. The authors of these chapters explore how the Baldrige Award evaluation process relates to the current array of quality assurance approaches.

12

What Accreditation and the Baldrige Can Learn from Each Other

Thomas E. Corts, John P. (Jack) Evans,
John W. Harris, and James T. Rogers

The traditional system of accreditation and the Baldrige approach to evaluation have one common, major concern: quality. While the two do not conflict or compete, they do represent different conceptualizations and different approaches. Accreditation assesses compliance with a set of standards which educators associate with good practices in education. A Baldrige evaluation diagnoses an organization against a general framework designed to increase understanding of its activities and provide guidance to improve those activities and their results (e.g., student learning and stakeholder satisfaction). These differences allow those engaged in either approach to learn from the other.

As we think about the advantages of mutual, cooperative learning between the Baldrige pilot in education and the accreditation system, our thoughts center around four questions and possible responses to those questions:

How does the Baldrige evaluation process differ from accreditation self-studies and site visits?

What can a college or university learn from a Baldrige review that it might not learn from an accreditation review? And what can an institution learn from an accreditation review that it might not learn from a Baldrige review?

What can the Baldrige Education Pilot effort and traditional accreditation practice learn from each other?

How can the Baldrige influence accreditation in the future?

HOW DO THEY DIFFER?

The original Malcolm Baldrige National Quality Award Criteria developed for business evolved from a focused and integrated conceptualization of quality. For the Baldrige approach, as applied to business, quality means value added to the customer, largely judged by the customer. The core values of the Baldrige Business Criteria obviously shape the Baldrige Education Pilot Criteria 1995. (If interested in comparing the two, one can compare the Education Pilot core values shown in the appendix with the core values of the Business Criteria.)

The Education Pilot Criteria, adapted from business to suit the field of education, comprise an integrated system with a driver, processes, and results.

Driver:
1.0 Leadership *drives* a subsystem composed of:

> **Processes:**
> **2.0** Information and Analysis
> **3.0** Strategic and Operational Planning
> **4.0** Human Resource Development and Management
> **5.0** Educational and Business Process Management

> This subsystem *yields*:
> > **Results:**
> > **6.0** School Performance Results
> > **7.0** Student Focus and Student and Stakeholder Satisfaction

A Baldrige assessment links the *approaches*, the *deployment* of the approaches, and the *results* of the approaches and their deployment. Seymour summarizes the Baldrige system as follows:

> Its core values—continuous improvement, fast response, partnership development, and so on—are the soul of the enterprise. The core values, in turn, are embedded in seven Criteria that form the vital organs. The Criteria work within a framework, a skeleton if you will, that gives the enterprise structural integrity. Lastly, the examination items provide the necessary measures and feedback, much like a nervous system, that enable the enterprise to adapt and grow. (1994, 21)

Accreditation criteria reflect views held by academics of what constitutes academic quality. They include such factors as admissions policies, advising practices, curriculum content, grading practices, faculty credentials, library holdings, quality of physical facilities, administrative efficiency, and financial stability. In other words, accreditation criteria emphasize resources, or viewed another way, inputs.

In addition to its traditional emphasis upon resources, higher education embraces the concept of assessment by outcomes. In 1986, the report "Task Force on College Quality" urged states to go beyond "resource measures" and insisted that colleges and universities develop programs that measure what students really learn (Edgerton 1990, 4). By 1990, according to data from the American Council on Education, eighty-two percent of all colleges were reporting "assessment activities underway" (Hutchings and Marchese 1990, 14). Even so, accreditation criteria rarely reflect a system linking inputs, processes, and results. In fact, most accreditors continue to require adherence to certain standards, regardless of results.

In fact, most accreditors continue to require adherence to certain standards, regardless of results.

Academics resist attempts to quantify educational results. Even W.Edwards Deming, the mathematical physicist turned statistician *extraordinaire*, who certainly believed that evaluation could be useful, ultimately doubted numbers as an exclusive means of understanding business. (Although most of Deming's views on organizational improvement were developed before the Baldrige Criteria were designed, the latter were not intended to reflect the views of any one individual.) Educators would no doubt agree with Deming (1982) as he cites Lloyd Nelson:

One cannot be successful on visible figures alone. Now, of course, visible figures are important. There is payroll to meet, vendors to pay, taxes to pay, amortization, pension funds, and contingency funds to meet. But he that would run his company on visible figures alone will in time have neither company nor figures.

Actually, the most important figures that one needs for management are unknown or unknowable . . . but successful management must nevertheless take account of them. (121)

To the extent that "visible figures" serve as useful proxies for overall educational objectives subject to continuous improvement, it makes sense to track them for accreditation and assessment. However, visible figures (meaning things that are most readily quantified or otherwise measured) rarely provide comprehensive or thorough evaluation of the performance of an organization, whether a business or an educational organization. This is particularly true if the measures are limited to end-results divorced from important process evaluations that contribute to those results.

Basically, educators believe tests of student achievement and surveys of stakeholder satisfaction, however well done, cannot capture the core intent and outcome of their efforts. They see the value of their work going beyond assessment by numbers, beyond precise measurement, to something much less tangible though of supreme importance. This is consistent with Deming's reference to visible figures. The challenge of reducing intellectual growth, which is inherently gradual and complex, to "visible figures" feeds academic skepticism of weighing educational effectiveness by numbers.

Actually, the Baldrige does not load everything on quantified results. Two-thirds of the Baldrige's 1000 points are assigned to approach and deployment. The Baldrige framework seeks a high level of integration and consistency among: (1) overall educational objectives, (2) the approaches and deployment employed to achieve those objectives, and (3) the results that are achieved from those activities—whether evaluated via quantitative measures or more subjective judgments.

An illustration might serve to clarify the distinction. One of the regional accrediting bodies requires that anyone teaching at the baccalaureate level have at least eighteen graduate hours of credits related to that field. This standard was determined by consensus, not empirical research. In contrast, the Baldrige Education Pilot Criteria on Human Resource Development and Management requests a college or university to address faculty training in performance requirements and performance assessment methods and to describe how the school evaluates the effectiveness of faculty development efforts. If results do not meet expectations, then changes are aimed at improving results. No prior standard or process is assumed to be correct; rather, processes that do not produce desired results are targeted for revision and improvement.

Baldrige assessment techniques and accreditation processes differ in the degree of integration of process and results. Accreditation, for a century and a half, focused on input—institutional resources, faculty credentials, library holdings, and so on. Yet as a culture influenced by pragmatism, we tend to hold the feet of any practice to the fire of empirical validation. Nevertheless, until we have such validation—which we often do not in education—it is wise to observe common practice. Common usage does not prove the validity of a practice; yet, one can learn by applying judgment to common practices among professionals or craftsmen. On one hand, we should be skeptical enough about the validity of any practice so that we will change if results indicate the practice does not work. On the other, observing common practices when there is no empirically validated best practice appears to be prudent. Clearly, both approaches have value. Inevitably, higher education must use both approaches in its continuing efforts toward better quality and service.

WHAT CAN THEY LEARN FROM EACH OTHER?

As noted, the Baldrige and accreditation differ significantly in their approach to evaluating performance. The institution learns from traditional accreditation about the *adequacy* of its resources, structures, and programs, in comparison to standards developed over time. From the Baldrige, it learns about the *effectiveness* of those programs and resources. Only in recent years have some accreditation agencies added new criteria on "institutional effectiveness." Attention to the integration of processes, results, and improvement efforts is still not a strong theme of accreditation.

We also need to look at the reliability of the two systems. While most accrediting associations strive for consistency in applying their criteria, we believe from our collective experience that accreditation reviews vary greatly. Two different teams visiting the same campus and reviewing the same self-study can come away with different judgments. We can best explain why accreditation reviews seem less reliable, by comparing them with the Baldrige system.

The way the Baldrige prepares its examiners to evaluate and score an organization's quality against the Baldrige Criteria contributes to its reliability. The Baldrige program intensively trains its examiners by having them apply the Criteria to realistic case studies. The training requires the examiner to evaluate a case independently against the Criteria, following a defined process for evaluation and scoring. The trainee-examiner then participates in three days of training, discussing evaluation of each item with other trainee-examiners as well as with senior examiners. To continue as a Baldrige examiner, one must re-train every year.

Accreditation site visitors do not typically receive as much training. The Southern Association of Colleges and Schools (SACS) trains chairs of accrediting teams, and a professional accrediting officer accompanies every team. While team members receive some pre-visit guidance through print and video materials, they are not trained in detailed assessment procedures. Nor are the accreditation teams required to do the extensive homework (20-30 hours) in order to contribute to the painstaking and detailed consensus judgment before any site visit occurs. Baldrige examiners do all of this.

The Baldrige scoring techniques also provide more definitive comparisons. The accreditation approach determines an institution's compliance with each of the criteria and makes recommendations when compliance is not met. A report of an accreditation team may have any number of recommendations. Some indicate minor changes that can be easily met; others relate to major flaws in the structure, resources, or processes of the institution. Comparing the number of recommendations one institution receives with those of another is essentially meaningless. Accreditation reviews produce no numbers or scores that can be used for comparative purposes.

A Baldrige review, on the other hand, provides an institution a score derived from Criteria and a scoring template constructed as an

The way the Baldrige prepares its examiners to evaluate and score an organization's quality against the Baldrige Criteria contributes to its reliability.

integrated system. Institutions can determine where they stand on a numerical scale of quality. The Baldrige yardstick is less elastic and more precise than that of accreditation. When asked about the rigor of the Baldrige, Curt Reimann, who directs the Baldrige, said, "Maybe the Nobel Prize is more rigorous, but not much else" (Keenan 1994, 70).

Accreditation serves as a gatekeeper, while the Baldrige seeks the very best for recognition and learning. Accreditation has two basic purposes: (1) to assure a reasonable floor of quality, and (2) to stimulate improvement above the floor. Consequently, its criteria and practices cannot resemble those designed to identify the very best.

A Baldrige review may prompt breakthroughs in quality improvement or cost reduction. The Baldrige encourages breakthroughs because practices must stand the test of actual results. The very structure of the Baldrige prompts an institution's leadership to think outside its boxes and to view its processes in light of their consequences.

In summary, then, what can we conclude that a college or university can learn from the Baldrige that it is unlikely to learn from the accreditation process? And what can an institution learn from the accreditation process that it is unlikely to learn from the Baldrige?

From the Baldrige:
1. Because of the common training experience of examiners, Baldrige assessments appear to be more reliable than accreditation reports. That is, two Baldrige teams would likely assess one institution similarly.

2. A Baldrige report can provide an agenda for overall, comprehensive improvement of the institution as a system.

3. Out-of-the-box thinking leading to breakthroughs is a more likely result from a Baldrige assessment.

4. A team preparing a Baldrige report is more likely to discover missing links between approach, deployment, and results than those who write or review accreditation self-studies.

5. A Baldrige evaluation provides detailed feedback to an institution's leaders on each element of their organization along with a numerical score, providing a clear baseline for comparison to future assessments.

6. Baldrige feedback reports and scoring show an institution how it can improve systematically. Accreditation's Pass-Fail approach provides little discrimination and little incentive to improve except in "failing" areas required for compliance. Baldrige feedback reports provide a comprehensive summary of strengths and areas for improvement, but they do not prescribe specific actions nor usurp institutional prerogatives.

From the Accreditation Process:
1. A college or university is more likely to learn how similar its processes, programs, and resources are to commonly accepted ones.

2. An institution's self-study process leads to a thorough examination by faculty and administration of every aspect of the institution, leading to self-discovery and often to significant change.

3. Recommendations from an accrediting body can provide an institution's leadership considerable leverage to change a given practice.

4. Because of the collegial nature of accreditation, it is capable of providing consultative guidance to institutions.

WHAT CAN THE BALDRIGE EDUCATION PILOT AND TRADITIONAL ACCREDITATION LEARN FROM EACH OTHER?

We believe accreditation, in its role of stimulating improvement, can learn a great deal from the Baldrige:

Use of Data

Any casual reading of the Baldrige Core Values and Criteria reveals that a Baldrige assessment is data driven. Accreditation generally encourages the use of data for planning and assessment, hoping that data will be integrated into ongoing management and be reflected in self-studies. Nevertheless, the guidelines for self-study and on-site visits do not constrain a college or university to link its approaches and their deployment to results through data as do the Baldrige Criteria. For example, accreditors might ask institutions to report percentages of: (1) recruits who enroll, (2) first-time freshmen who graduate in six years, and (3) graduates placed in work or graduate/professional schools six months after graduation. By so doing, institutional leaders would begin to see the lateral linkages. While an entire educational experience cannot be represented by data, accreditation might insist on more use of such data to increase faculty's and administrators' understanding of their institutions.

The Horizontal View

Colleges and universities are, as a rule, rigidly bound by vertical, hierarchical functions, e.g., academic affairs, business affairs, student affairs. Academics carefully police the boundaries between disciplines, schools, and departments. It is difficult to imagine that universities will remove their administrative and student services walls, and even more difficult to imagine its disciplinary boundaries dissolving. To the extent that conventional, academic thinking assumes "the higher and less permeable the academic walls—the better the institution," it is more difficult to achieve cooperation that provides students a seamless educational experience. Deming might gruffly ask, "Who's trying to get it all to work together for the student's benefit?"

Deming might gruffly ask, "Who's trying to get it all to work together for the student's benefit?"

Accreditors might begin to ask questions intended to lead faculty and administrators to think horizontally about their institutions. For example, accreditors might ask how students flow through the institution. If institutions were to track students as they are recruited, admitted, advised, placed in classes, assessed, graduated, and placed in jobs or further education, they would learn a great deal about themselves. In doing this tracking, an institution would begin to understand its admission-retention-placement as a cross-functional process. Persons working in such a process could come to see how their work fits into an interconnected system as it is mapped and measured. The maps (extensive flowcharts) and measures allow those responsible for the process to see how students actually move through the institution. Service blueprints or flowcharts constitute the road map. When the existing process is mapped, the "white spaces" where there are no linkages between components of the process become starkly apparent. "White spaces" appear where two functions, perhaps admissions and housing, do not provide a simple hand-off of students from one to the other. In such cases, the process is not "seamless."

How many of us in higher education really understand or even know our recruitment/matriculation yields, our year-to-year retention rates, our graduation rates, and our placement rates? A *Wall Street Journal* article (April 5, 1995) asserts that many institutions do not even accurately know the average ACT score of their entering freshmen. Others have found discrepancies in what institutions report to bond rating agencies and what they report to rating organizations such as the *U.S. News and World Report*. How many of us know our losses at each point and their primary causes? How many of us understand how the typical student journeys through our curricula? We may know the formal sequence of courses we *expect* students to follow to complete a major, but what is the sequence of courses students actually *do* follow?

A Baldrige evaluation inevitably causes an organization to look at itself horizontally. An organization has not really begun its journey to becoming a learning organization until persons within it begin to see it as a series of inter-linking processes comprising a system aimed at adding value to its customers and stakeholders. As early as page 4 of *Out of the Crisis*, Deming provides a simple lateral diagram of an organization. Adapted to higher education, it might be seen as follows:

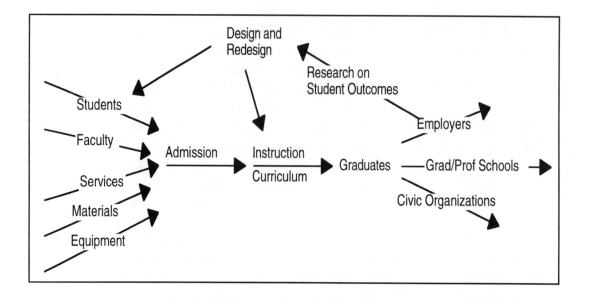

Accreditation has begun to transform the way colleges and universities see themselves when it asks them to consider results or outcomes. Yet a focus on results alone does little to promote learning about how to improve processes if there is no accompanying shift in our organizational paradigm. Again, we're back to the Baldrige sequence: Approach > Deployment > Results. It requires a lateral, flow-through view of the system. Accreditation could lead colleges and universities to understand themselves better by asking that they identify the primary systems or processes that link various functional units. As suggested above, faculty and administrators rarely have a clear picture of how students actually flow through their institutions.

Self-Study and Review Process

Because accreditation basically functions to assure at least minimal compliance with common standards, self-studies and visiting teams must deal with those standards. Most self-study manuals are written to deal with faculty in one section, curriculum in another, administration in still another. For example, the SACS Commission on Colleges' *Criteria for Accreditation* (1994) has six sections:

1. Institutional Commitment and Responsibilities
   in the Accreditation Process
2. Institutional Purpose
3. Institutional Effectiveness
4. Educational Program
5. Educational Support Services
6. Administrative Processes

Institutional Effectiveness, while still having a "tacked on" sense, is now a significant part of a SACS evaluation. All SACS evaluation teams have one person who takes responsibility for Institutional Purpose and Institutional Effectiveness. The other team members investigating compliance with standards on curriculum, libraries, faculty, finances, etc., cooperate with the individual responsible for Institutional Effectiveness by reporting what their areas are doing to evaluate effectiveness. Every area must assess how well it works, even an office responsible for institutional effectiveness such as the Institutional Research Office. Yet these sections of the self-study and the visiting committee reports can still be written (and sometimes are written) as stand-alone sections.

In contrast, the Baldrige Education Pilot Criteria Framework, with its driver, system, goals, and measures of progress constitute an integrated system of quality. The Baldrige writers chose to lay out their Criteria as a horizontal system focused on student and school performance results and student and stakeholder satisfaction. In contrast, the SACS Criteria suggest an orderly checking of compliance with standards. In general, accreditors have not intended for their Criteria to assess an institution as a quality system orchestrated to facilitate student learning, or even to express gradations of achievement, effectiveness, or success.

Most colleges and universities see their primary mission as "teaching students" or "doing research," thus defining themselves in terms of activities. The Baldrige assumes that organizations exist as systems designed to accomplish certain ends. Consequently, the Baldrige assumes those ends can be most effectively and efficiently accomplished when institutions organize as lateral systems composed of processes related in such a way as to contribute the greatest value toward the intended results.

The Baldrige assumes that organizations exist as systems designed to accomplish certain ends.

Case Study Training

The Baldrige office trains examiners by the case study approach. The aim is to develop consistency among examiners by training through intensive evaluation and scoring exercises, small group discussions, and comparison of evaluations with those of senior examiners. While case study training is costly to develop and implement, it can be highly effective in creating consistency among examiners. Accreditation might find the use of case studies very helpful in training members of visiting committees. By reviewing their case study homework, senior accreditation evaluators could provide feedback to new or potential team members. Such a system would also ensure that only accreditors willing to devote significant time to the process would participate.

The Baldrige, on the other hand, can learn something from the traditional accreditation system:

The Complexity of Assessment in Education

The accreditation system can help the Baldrige recognize the complexity of educational assessment. Many of the most significant goals in education are less tangible and not as easily measured as business goals. In addition, many important learning results do not occur solely by simple, linear "treatments" or processes. For example, a stamping press shapes automobile fenders so that all of them are virtually identical. The shape of the fender correlates highly with the behavior of the press. We know such a relationship does not exist between a student's understanding and the teacher's behavior.

Actually, the Baldrige framework for assessing educational processes does not imply that educational goals are so trivial as "customer satisfaction," particularly if one uses the phrase to describe merely the students' responses measured at the conclusion of an individual course. Here it is perhaps useful to distinguish among process (delivery of course materials), content (selection of learning objectives and the means by which those are pursued), and learning or intellectual growth (not a simple linear process). The Baldrige framework encourages using various evaluations of these dimensions of the educational experience.

To get an idea of the complexity of assessment in higher education, we might look at one basic aspect of the Baldrige, the measurement of "customer satisfaction." In higher education the relationship is not simple. Who is *the* customer? Do we mean the student? Certainly, the student is a major customer, but not the only one. In order to be satisfied, a student may desire a particular grade or a degree; yet those are not the "products" our colleges and universities offer. They offer an education—intellectual development, expansion of values, ability to evaluate and discriminate, increased communication skills, general knowledge in basic disciplines, and specific and complete knowledge in at least one field. In most cases, the student is not even the one who pays for the "product." It would be a mistake, then, to think that "student satisfaction" must drive higher education. That is only part of the formula.

Perhaps parents are the customers. To some extent, they are. Parents often pay the bill and must be "satisfied" with what their son or daughter receives in return. Still other specific stakeholder groups could be identified. In a broader sense, however, the customer is the American public. Higher education must produce leaders and prepare students to become articulate, productive, involved citizens who can think, reason, make judgments, and appreciate quality and integrity in every aspect of life.

It should be noted that the Baldrige system of evaluation is more subtle and sophisticated than might appear at first glance. Its use of certain business terminology might lead to the belief that it employs a simplistic view of quality and customer relations, when in reality the Baldrige framework for education encourages the assessor to go beyond visible figures and to consider integration of purpose, process, results, and improvement cycles. Nevertheless, the accreditation system of evaluation, with its years of experience in dealing with the complexities and subtleties of educational evaluation, can contribute to the Baldrige program's understanding of these realities.

The Limitations of Numbers

The Baldrige might also learn from accreditation's long struggle with such measurement issues as the limitations of numbers in educational evaluation. Numbers cannot readily represent such significant values as a broadened vision of the world, perceptiveness about human nature, recognition and appreciation of quality, ability to enjoy good music and art and literature, appreciation for both similarities and differences in people, ability to make decisions based on logical thinking, or mature evaluation of one's ideas and abilities. Perhaps this recognition has caused colleges and universities to focus on their resources. Such a focus assumes that good human and institutional resources necessarily yield good results.

Patience

Compared to business, education changes slowly. The experience of the Commission on Colleges of SACS illustrates how difficult and time consuming change is for colleges and universities. It has taken at least ten years to move from an introduction of the institutional effectiveness concept to legislating it, enforcing it, and seeing substantial movement toward it. While some may prefer more rapid change, a conservative approach helps to preserve a stable system and avoid trivial responses to passing fads.

On the other hand, acceptance of the Baldrige method may come more readily, simply because of the voluntary nature of the Baldrige. Colleges and universities must be accredited, but they do not have to undertake a Baldrige assessment. No college or university funding or student aid depends on its Baldrige rating. There is less pressure to change something everyone is not required to do. This voluntary factor should allow the Baldrige to retain its procedures with integrity, with little dilution. Baldrige leadership should use this advantage to maintain a rigorously systematic approach to assessing educational quality. And by remaining voluntary, the Baldrige will likely speed its acceptance and even the internalization of its processes.

Lack of Trade Secrets in Higher Education

Higher education functions collegially. Colleges and universities, unlike businesses, do not have patentable processes. Consequently, the intense procedures employed to protect trade secrets in the handling of the Baldrige applications and examiners' evaluations are not as necessary in higher education, and will likely be seen as extreme. The principles and procedures of confidentiality as practiced by accreditors have been worked out over time and better suit higher education. We suggest that the Baldrige leadership review accrediting policies and procedures on confidentiality.

The Importance of Choosing Evaluators Carefully

Accreditation has learned, as Deming did in Japan, that you can't penetrate the system unless you get to the leaders. We suggest starting with presidents. Baldrige-based evaluation, appropriately presented, should appeal to presidents. Presidents, along with students, feel the hurt (or the "heat") when the parts of their institutions do not work together. The lateral, flow-through paradigm inherent in a systems-view—a view that can help faculty and staff understand the need to work together—will appeal to presidents. Therefore, we suggest that the Baldrige office seek opportunities to educate presidents in the Baldrige. Furthermore, they could be recruited as examiners, just as senior executives have been recruited for the Baldrige Award process for businesses, since they may have greater influence among their local or national colleagues than others who flock to the quality flag in higher education.

Accreditation has learned, as Deming did in Japan, that you can't penetrate the system unless you get to the leaders.

HOW CAN THE BALDRIGE INFLUENCE ACCREDITATION IN THE FUTURE?

More Extensive Use of Data, Especially in Evaluation of Outcomes

Since outcomes assessment is relatively new in accreditation, accreditation can learn from the Baldrige, whose entire system assumes a tight linkage among approach, deployment, and results. Colleges and universities can become more competent in determining how successfully they accomplish their educational goals if they learn to collect, organize, and interpret data more effectively. Accreditors could lead colleges and universities to more effective use of numbers if they adopt and adapt some of the Baldrige approach.

Horizontal Perspective

We suggest that accreditors explore ways to guide self-studies that would lead institutions to identify and assess major cross-functional systems or processes. For the SACS Commission on Colleges, this could be done by seeing its criteria arranged as follows:

Driver	System	Goal
Institutional Purpose >	Ed. Program > Ed. Support Services > Adm. Services > Human Resources>	Institutional Effectiveness
Approach/Deployment		*Results*

This way of looking at the SACS criteria leads one to see that Purpose drives Educational Program, Support Services, and Administrative Services. They, in turn, should yield results for Institutional Effectiveness.

Benchmarking

Accrediting associations are strategically placed to stimulate and facilitate benchmarking. They already collect data by which institutions can make comparisons against averages. Beyond this, each one could be an excellent source, for example, for a department in one institution attempting to compare its instructional approaches with another similar department in another institution.

Recognition

Working with the American Society for Quality Control, the Baldrige recognizes and showcases institutions that win each year. In like manner, accrediting associations might find ways to recognize institutions that have conducted exemplary self studies and/or made dramatic quality improvements. Such recognition might be better than trying to give institutions quality scores or grades. If grades were given, institutions would feel forced to go for the highest grade. In that case, the score rather than the actual improvement might become the object. Identifying institutions that have conducted and have made significant improvements through their self-studies could inform other institutions of best-practices in self-studies.

CONCLUSION

We believe that the Baldrige represents a comprehensive and effective way to assess an organization's quality, and that accreditation can learn from it. At the same time, the Baldrige should continue to be sensitive to the complexities of higher education and should guard against pushing technocratic language and techniques on the academy. We commend the Baldrige leadership for its thoughtful pilot approach to applying the Baldrige to education.

We do not think that higher education will—or should—discard its emphasis on *inputs*. But it can and should incorporate the Baldrige concept that approach, deployment, and results are tightly linked. This incorporation only strengthens the relationship among inputs, resources, credentials and educational results—the intent of accreditation's adoption of institutional effectiveness.

Simply put, we believe the Baldrige methodology can be extremely useful in helping institutions of higher learning achieve their educational goals.

REFERENCES

Commission on Colleges of the Southern Association of Colleges and Schools. 1994. *Criteria for Accreditation.* Decatur, GA: CCSACS

Deming, W. E. 1982. *Out of the Crisis.* Cambridge: MIT Press.

Edgerton, R. 1990. *Change* (September/October): 4-5.

Hutchings, P. and T. Marchese. 1990. Watching Assessment: Questions, Stories, Prospects. *Change* (September/October): 12-38.

Keenan, W. Making the Grade. 1994. *Sales and Marketing Management* (March): 66-73.

Seymour, D. 1994. The Baldrige Cometh. *Change* (January/February): 16-27.

13
The View from the Top: Accountability and Improvement

Jon A. Hittman

Historically, the American system for the delivery of higher education has been universally recognized as excellent. Yet, despite this unparalleled success, *An American Imperative* (1993)—a report of the Wingspread Group on higher education—begins with these words: "a disturbing and dangerous mismatch exists between what American Society needs from higher education and what it is receiving" (1). The "mismatch" stems from America's significant shift from an industrial economy, dependent on an abundance of laborers to fill low-skill jobs for a relatively high wage, to an economy that is knowledge-based and requires high levels of productivity and a skilled workforce. Many of those who are labeled as "low skill" job applicants are college graduates.

The Wingspread Group Report suggests that there is a pervasive sense of dissatisfaction with the performance of higher education resulting in a quest for increased accountability for higher education. This trend toward greater accountability began as early as 1970. *The Outputs of Higher Education* (1970)—a report summarizing the proceedings of a seminar sponsored by the Western Interstate Commission for Higher Education, the American Council on Education, and the Center for Research and Development in Higher Education at the University of California, Berkeley—began, "We (higher education) are going to have to prove that we deserve the dollars spent on education and justify our asking for each additional dollar" (Lawrence, Wethersby, and Patterson 1970, 1). The trend toward increased levels of accountability for higher education continues and is gathering momentum (Ewell, Finney, and Lenth 1990).

The fundamental question to be addressed by this chapter is whether or not modern state governing or coordinating boards (GCBs) can meet their immediate need to demonstrate accountability to the public using the framework of the Malcolm Baldrige National Quality Award Criteria. This chapter will (1) briefly examine the traditional role of state higher education governing or coordinating boards in assuring and assessing the progress of institutions toward meeting the needs of society, (2) discuss some of the factors that have caused the apparent "mismatch" between societal needs and what higher education is delivering, (3) discuss the movement toward a system of performance indicators (PI) used by GCBs to assess the effectiveness of institutions of higher education, and (4) based on one through three above, review the appropriateness of the Malcolm Baldrige National Quality Award Criteria as a framework for promoting, assuring, and assessing quality in higher education.

THE TRADITIONAL ROLE: QUALITY ASSURANCE

GCBs, accrediting agencies, and the U.S. Department of Education join to form a triad with loosely defined, inter-related, and frequently overlapping regulatory and quality assurance/assessment functions and authority. At the vanguard of this triad is the GCB because, generally speaking, eligibility for accreditation (national, regional, or professional) and access to federal programs and funding are predicted upon prior state approval.

The general purpose of GCBs is to provide leadership and coordination to institutions and their governing boards, and to ensure excellence in education for the state's youth through the efficient and effective utilization and concentration of resources (*Texas School Law Bulletin* 1990). In order to fulfill this statutory charge, GCBs have established standards to assure the delivery of quality programs in institutions of higher education. These standards must be met before an institution may begin an authorized degree granting program or receive state financial support for any program. In a sense, then, GCBs are the gatekeepers to degree conferral authority, access to state funding for public higher education institutions, and eligibility for accreditation (national, regional, or professional).

Traditionally, quality in higher education has been defined in terms of quality assurance demonstrated through institutional compliance with established standards. These standards require the institution to have a statement of purpose, and to demonstrate evidence of planning compatible with the published purpose (e.g., institutional effectiveness plan, curriculum development plan, faculty development plan) and availability of adequate resources to execute the plans (e.g., qualified faculty, capital, library holdings, equipment). In short, the institution must demonstrate the minimum capacity—in terms of plans and resources—to deliver a quality education *before* the state agency will endorse the institution by providing state funding or degree conferral authority.

Consistent with these established policies, GCBs have based quality assessment efforts upon three major points: (1) assessing or measuring quality by requiring that plans be established and implemented, (2) determining whether the institution has maintained and allocated appropriate resources, and (3) improving performances in these areas when standards are not met. These established minimum standards have been used to assess whether or not the institution has maintained the capacity to deliver effective quality education programs to students.

These policies were established to address the overriding societal concerns of access, in an age when the number of people demanding education is increasing at an exploding rate, fueled by financial prosperity and watershed events such as Sputnik, the civil rights movement, and the attainment of college age by the "baby boom" generation. Quality assurance procedures that emerged during this era focused on acquisition and appropriate utilization of resources, a logical approach in an environment where accommodating access and growth were of paramount importance. Ewell and Jones (1994) describe the era of the late sixties as a time when "states were struggling to fund unprecedented growth in higher education" (23).

This traditional quality assurance mechanism assumed that if appropriate resources were present, whatever occurred inside the "black box" of higher education would produce an excellent result. GCBs have altered their requirements through the years, but until very recently the concept of access and adequacy of resources has been at the core of the approval and quality assurance processes.

HIGH PERFORMING COLLEGES

FACTORS CAUSING THE "MISMATCH"

In the decades after WWII, American higher education was the envy of the world. It was at the pinnacle of a system founded on access, nurtured by a proud populace and a supportive government. Recently, this pride and support have eroded because "our universities are criticized for costing too much, spending carelessly, teaching poorly, planning myopically, and, when questioned, acting defensively" (Griffiths 1993, 90). The limitations inherent in traditional quality assurance methods explain why GCBs have been unable to prevent this erosion of pride and support. First, traditional methods of quality assurance set conformance to minimum standards as their goal, thus encouraging a static approach to quality. This strategy implicitly creates a condition in which it is difficult, if no impossible, to obtain information from the analysis of cases in which prevailing standards have been met. Within the classroom itself the common practice of "grading on a curve" assumes that some rate of poor outcomes is acceptable. In addition, should quality assurance standards be set too low, these programs will not be perceived as contributing to quality education; conversely, should the standards be set unrealistically high, they are likely to alienate or frustrate the providers.

Second, the classic definition of quality assurance is too narrow to accommodate the needs of the modern provider of higher education. In addition to meeting the needs of students, institutions of higher education are increasingly being called on to meet the needs of other individuals and groups such as employers, students' families, taxpayers, and legislators. Generally speaking, the needs of these additional stakeholders are not adequately addressed by traditional quality assurance procedures.

A third limitation of the traditional approach is that it tends to concentrate on faculty performance and to de-emphasize the contributions of non-faculty components and other organizational processes. Administrators, admissions representatives, psychometric personnel, student service professionals, and placement staff have an impact upon the success of the student. Other non-personnel components— such as equipment, institutional financial stability, physical surroundings, and socioeconomic environment—also influence student outcomes and the overall quality of the program.

A fourth limitation of the classic approach is that it tends to emphasize certain aspects of the instructor's pedagogical preparation or performance. Academic credentials and/or research projects are highly valued. Other aspects of an instructor's performance also have a bearing on the quality of education delivered. One important—but unassessed—trait related to quality instruction is the teacher's ability to concentrate the resources of an organization on the individual needs of the students.

THE MOVEMENT TOWARD PERFORMANCE INDICATORS

There has been a swift and remarkable shift in the environment that confronts modern higher education. The preeminent national challenge is no longer to win the Cold War. The current challenge is to attain a "decent national living in an increasingly competitive global economy" (Edgerton 1993, 65). America has improved its overall productivity; however, this is primarily due to increasing the number of people in the workforce (women entering the workforce) and increasing the number of hours worked for the average worker (Magaziner 1990). Today, more Americans work, and are working longer hours than ever before. Therefore, future gains in productivity will have to come from improved use of technology and by working smarter, not longer. Society expects higher education to play an important role in developing that workforce.

Today, entitlement programs, health care, and education find themselves in direct competition for dwindling levels of public funding.

Competition for markets and resources has not been limited to Fortune 500 companies jostling for competitive advantage in the global marketplace. Social service agencies, including higher education, compete increasingly for funding allocated by state agencies and legislatures. During the prosperous expansion period of the sixties and seventies, all social programs grew and were funded—at least in part—by the federal or state government's tax dollars. Today, entitlement programs, health care, and education find themselves in direct competition for dwindling levels of public funding.

While the total dollar amount received by public institutions of higher education from state sources has increased, the percent of current fund revenue emanating from this source has decreased. This has caused an escalation of tuition costs for students. The increase in cost has triggered a demand for increased accountability on the part of consumers, both individual students and state governments.

There has also been a significant change in the demographics of the student body. The traditional eighteen to twenty-one year old student is in the majority on most campuses, but there has been a sizable increase in the enrollment of older, or "non-traditional" students. In addition, there has been an increase in the number of female and minority students enrolled. These students bring a variety of special requirements to the portals of the university.

Basic research has historically been an important function of higher education and it remains so today. However, applied research is currently more valuable to American businesses who are struggling to remain globally competitive in an era of reduced corporate research and development budgets. The Federal Government policy regarding indirect cost reimbursement and the financial lure of entering into partnerships with the private sector has encouraged academic research that is closer to industrial (i.e., practical) application. The pressures on institutions of higher education to emphasize the university's research component is considerable. Consequently, "our institutions rely on a professoriate which is both expected and rewarded to spend most of its time conducting basic or applied research" (Pappas 1993, 120). At the same time, an exasperated public is calling for a generation of educated young men and women who possess the basic knowledge, analytical skills, and understanding of institutional behavior which promote productive participation in economic activities and democratic process (Weber 1993). Societal need suggests a renewed emphasis on undergraduate education to achieve a better balance with the research element of higher education's mission.

The convergence of these forces has created an environment where societal leaders are beginning to ask about the benefits received from the funds invested in higher education. In response to this, institutions of higher education have invested significant resources in demonstrating their effectiveness through institution-wide strategic planning efforts, compliance with state mandated student outcomes assessment initiatives, and voluntary academic program review. Yet, in spite of these efforts to convey value and effectiveness to the general public, Borden and Banta (1994) report that there is ever increasing pressure on institutions to demonstrate accountability. The primary sources of pressure are state governing and coordinating boards who are themselves responding to the call for increased accountability for higher education from legislators, taxpayers, students, parents, and business.

The question of whether or not there is an adequate balance between benefits derived from resources invested (return on investment) has manifested itself in the concept of performance-based funding. The conceptual thrust of performance-based funding is that state financial support should, at least in part, be based upon demonstrated performance on pre-identified crucial indicators—for example, course completion rates, total degrees awarded, and graduate placement rates (Richardson 1994). The emergence of performance indicators shifts the focus of quality assurance methodology from resources (input) to results (output). Ewell and Jones (1994) describe these indicators as policy-relevant statistics that are used to support overall policy planning and monitoring.

This results-oriented assessment has been attempted or is currently functioning in at least ten states. The effectiveness of performance-based funding has yet to be definitively determined. In Tennessee, for example, performance-based funding has been in place for several years and appears to be accepted. There, up to five percent of annual allocation is now awarded on an institution's ability to demonstrate performance in five weighted areas (Cave, Hanney, and Kogan 1991). In Texas, on the other hand, the legislative proposal to adopt performance-based funding failed to materialize. According to Epper (1994), the effort failed because the proposal would have reallocated funds to politically powerful institutions from those with less political strength, legislators disliked the complexity and volume of budgeting documents necessary for performance-based funding, the original proposal called for incentive (add-on) funding, and some performance indicators (e.g., degree production) appeared to many to be anti-quality measurements because they are equated with "diploma mills."

In *Charting Higher Education Accountability*, Ewell and Jones (1994) proffer several cogent reasons why it would be beneficial for GCBs to adopt a system utilizing performance indicators. First, it can simplify the evaluation of the state's return-on-investment in the enterprise of higher education by providing a mechanism that uses indicators to evaluate efficiently the performance of higher education against the state's objectives for higher education. Second, well-constructed indicators can serve as a powerful, efficient, and unambiguous decision making tool to guide the flow of state dollars toward areas where they can be most effective. Third, the indicator system can summarize the results of institutional assessment efforts and can stimulate the implementation of recognized good practices in under-graduate education (Ewell and Jones 1994). Fourth, performance indicators have the potential to enhance state and institution level goal development by making outcomes more visible and concrete. Fifth, they can mobilize concerted action within the higher education community and galvanize support for higher education among the public at large. Finally, they can facilitate development of a set of state policies directed toward continued improvement.

The employment of performance indicators has merit; nonetheless, they are not a panacea because systems of crucial indicators are generally indirect. Policy makers can determine which institutions have high retention rates and low per pupil expenditures, and what kinds of resources are being invested. However, the indicators alone will not provide a single, reliable index of higher education quality. In the short term, they tend to encourage goal displacement, particularly if the stakes associated with poor performance are high. This means that if the ramifications of short-term poor performance are severe, then institutions may act to maximize the numeric values of indicators without really changing practice or performance. They can also focus attention on the activity of information gathering rather than on organizational behavior change. Or, as Ewell and Jones (1994) suggest, "initiating common statewide basic skills testing may require significant new institutional investment without eliminating the need for institutions to maintain their own duplicative, local assessment systems" (9).

SUMMARY OF THE TRADITIONAL ROLES

Initially, GCBs were formed to ensure that the quality and integrity of higher education was protected by requiring that the resources committed by the state were effectively and efficiently utilized. Maintaining high standards in an environment of rapid growth and broadened access to higher education for all citizens was the overriding concern driving the behavior of GCBs. Against a backdrop of prosperity and growth driven by societal and international events, the GCBs appropriately focused on quality assurance, establishing standards to assure that institutions had adequate resources and plans to perform the function of education. During this time, high tuition rates came to be equated with high quality.

As the robust economies of the fifties and sixties fade into the more problematic economy of the nineties, societal priorities have shifted toward accountability in the form of outcomes.

As the robust economies of the fifties and sixties fade into the more problematic economy of the nineties, societal priorities have shifted toward accountability in the form of outcomes. Institutions are held accountable for favorable outcomes and are expected to achieve them without diminishing the existing requirement of equitable and adequate access to higher education. Some GCBs have responded by developing performance indicators upon which performance funding for institutions is based. This shift does not affect the need for adequate resources to be available before education is delivered. It adds the dimension of outcomes to the quality equation. Institutions must not only have the resources available and have plans to deploy those resources, but must demonstrate that favorable outcomes were derived from the application of those resources.

The traditional input-focused approach emphasizing resources and the demonstrated capacity to deliver quality education has been found to be deficient in meeting modern societal expectations of higher education. The more recent output-centered approach, characterized by the utilization of performance indicators, has been implemented in some states with mixed results. Goal displacement, complexity of tracking, and disagreement over what measures indicate quality are thorny issues that the output-centered (performance indicators) approach to quality has not yet adequately addressed. Employed independently and individually, the shortcomings of input (traditional) and output (performance indicator) methodologies have been documented. This suggests that combining the two in a comprehensive systems approach linking input-process-output and emphasizing data-driven continuous self-examination and improvement may have merit as a means to ensure quality in the future.

According to Russell Edgerton (1993), president of the American Association for Higher Education, the challenge for GCBs and institutions will be to refine and improve the classic functions of higher education—teaching, research, and service—and do it for less cost. The fundamental question we need to return to, then, is whether or not the Malcolm Baldrige National Quality Award (MBNQA) Criteria can be used by GCBs as a catalyst to spur institutions of higher education to better meet the requirements of their ultimate customer—the American society.

THE BALDRIGE AS A FRAMEWORK FOR PROMOTING AND ASSESSING QUALITY IN HIGHER EDUCATION

The MBNQA Criteria have been designed to improve the overall performance of organizations by emphasizing a comprehensive systems approach to managing people and processes. This approach emphasizes continuous improvement in the delivery of service and provides a mechanism for responding to and satisfying stakeholders. The Education Pilot Criteria guide institutions toward improved overall organizational performance results. The Criteria combine to form a comprehensive, non-prescriptive, interrelated (input-process-results) diagnostic system.

The core issue is whether or not the MBNQA Criteria provide GCBs with a more dynamic, comprehensive, non-prescriptive, and flexible process for determining accountability. I'd like to respond to that issue by asking and answering a series of related questions.

Is There a Precedent for Transfer of Business Concepts to Higher Education?

The MBNQA Criteria were designed to encourage American businesses to be more competitive in the global marketplace. The process emerged from the business sector and reflects the fundamental management skills found in total quality management. Therefore, the first question that must be addressed in trying to determine whether GCBs could apply the MBNQA Criteria to higher education is whether or not there exists any precedent for the application of business management to education.

There is extensive evidence of transfer of business principles to higher education. In *Total Quality Management in Higher Education*, Sherr and Lozier (1991) provide such examples as multiple levels of management and a formal chain of command, the implementation of multiple checks and approvals for expenditure, competitive bidding, and the institution of elaborate planning functions. From these and other examples it is clear that there is a precedence for transferal of GCB sanctioned business practices to the university.

The notion of customer satisfaction permeates the fabric of American business. At the micro level, individual customers are aware of their power as customers and, as a result, "quality" has become the expectation rather than the exception. Individuals expect quality treatment in all venues, including higher education. Grocery stores and department stores promise that if there are more than three customers in a check-out line they will immediately open another cash register. Students exposed to this type of service at Walmart don't like to stand in long lines at the state university to register. Customers who can receive instant information regarding their credit card balances do not want to wait weeks for response on financial aid decisions form the admissions office. Customers who are accustomed to being entertained even during infomercials do not like having education delivered in a sage-on-the-stage format where hundreds of students listen to a lecturer. The expectations for the delivery of higher education have risen in part because businesses have fundamentally changed the way they view consumers (customers). At the macro level, society—the ultimate customer of higher education—has clearly communicated that its expectations have not been met. Given the state of "enlightenment" enjoyed by consumers, it seems prudent for higher education to emulate the private sector, whenever feasible, in its interactions with students and other stakeholders.

The expectations for the delivery of higher education have risen in part because businesses have fundamentally changed the way they view consumers (customers).

The MBNQA framework arose out of the manufacturing industry, and some educators reject it for that reason. However, it is important to note that there has been transference from the private sector to education in the past and the MBNQA Criteria can be a vehicle for bridging the chasm between higher education and the private sector. Also, like it or not, higher education is currently in competition for funding with other social service agencies and entitlements. This, in addition to the move toward performance-based funding, makes comparisons to the practices in the private sector inevitable.

Do the MBNQA Criteria Address the Traditional Quality Assurance Standards Required by the Public and GCBs?

Category 3.0, "Strategic and Operational Planning," directly addresses the traditional quality assurance requirement. This category requires that the institution describe how its strategic direction is determined and how the strategies developed address student needs, external factors (environment and regulatory), internal factors (involvement of all of the institution's functional units), and improvement of student and overall institutional performance.

In order to score well in this category, an institution would (1) inventory its current resources (inputs), (2) conduct an environmental scan (within and outside the organization), (3) develop a strategic direction based upon the environmental scan, (4) translate the results of the environmental scan into identified critical success factors, (5) design an operational plan to perform successfully on the critical success factors, and (6) implement a process by which both the results and the planning function itself are evaluated.

The MBNQA Criteria are not designed as a set of static standards that must be met for approval of degree programs or for access to public funding. However, the Criteria are fundamentally compatible with traditional quality assurance (resources and planning) methods. In order to be accepted by the higher education community, the MBNQA Criteria must—and do—address the traditional requirements and standards of quality assurance. The Criteria are comprehensive and do attend to the input side of the quality equation.

Do the MBNQA Criteria Address the Emerging Accountability Requirements (outputs identified by performance indicators) Expected by the General Public and the GCBs?

One of the key characteristics of the MBNQA Criteria is that they are comprehensive. They address all internal and external requirements (outputs). Category 6.0, "School Performance Results," specifically and thoroughly addresses outcomes. It is in this category that trend data results are reported in such areas as student performance, school climate improvement, research, scholarship, service, and school business performance. Of the seven categories, this category accounts for 230 of the 1000 possible points in the award scoring system. Trend data are also reported in 7.5 (Student and Stockholder Satisfaction Results) and 7.6 (Student and Stockholder Comparison). Items 7.5 and 7.6 account for another 90 points in the Baldrige scoring system.

The data selection process is predicated upon determining which data elements (indicators) are critical to the success of the institution.

Which data to capture, how the data are to be analyzed, and how the reliability of the data is assured, is addressed in Category 2.0 (Information and Analysis). The data selection process is predicated upon determining which data elements (indicators) are critical to the success of the institution. This methodology is essentially consistent with the movement toward the utilization of performance indicators. The MBNQA Criteria and performance indicators derive significance from their ability to link outcomes with purposes and processes. The relationship between data selection (Category 2.0) and trend reporting (Category 6.0 and Items 7.5 and 7.6) illustrates the interrelatedness of the MBNQA Criteria.

Results or outcomes are integral components of the MBNQA Criteria. The number and relative weighting of the categories addressing results amply illustrates their importance in the Criteria.

Do the MBNQA Criteria Address the Emerging Challenge to Refine, Balance, and Improve Teaching, Research, and Service and Do It for Less Cost?

Attention to the teaching and learning function permeates the MBNQA Criteria. From Category 1.0—"How does senior leadership maintain a climate conducive to teaching and learning?"—to Category 7.0, "How information is used throughout the school to improve satisfaction and active learning"—virtually every category addresses some aspect of the teaching and learning process.

Education process management is directly addressed in Items 5.1 (education design), 5.2 (education delivery), and 5.3 (education support service design and delivery). The results associated with the education design are reported in Items 6.1 (student performance results) and 6.2 (school education climate improvement results).

The research and service functions of higher education are addressed in Item 5.4 (Research, Scholarship and Service). This Item asks the institution to describe "how it contributes to knowledge creation, knowledge transfer, and services via programs and activities to key communities." The results of these efforts are reported in Item 6.3 (Research, Scholarship, and Service Results). This item gives the institution the opportunity to report current levels and trends in key indicators of the institution's contributions to knowledge creation, transfer, and service. The Item also encourages the inclusion of comparative data, or benchmarking. Item 1.3 (Public Responsibility and Citizenship) addresses the service function by adding for a description of how the institution includes public responsibilities in its performance evaluation.

The MBNQA Criteria are comprehensive in that they address all the core functions of higher education. In addition, the Criteria allow the institutions the flexibility to identify key stakeholders and develop processes and functions to meet the needs of those stakeholders.

Do the MBNQA Criteria Address the Sense of Urgency to Demonstrate Accountability Experienced by GCBs?

The MBNQA Criteria do encourage institutions to report, compare, and assess current levels of performance concerning the key indicators identified. However, the Criteria emphasize learning cycles, meaning that the institution improves by deployment of a Plan-Do-Check-Act cycle (Shewhart 1986). In many cases, institutional performance is reported on an annual basis and therefore trend data may take years to accumulate. While this is problematic to an impatient public clamoring for immediate results, a systems approach to quality assurance suggests that cause and effect are not necessarily close in time or space. Peter Senge, in *The Fifth Discipline* (1990), states that unless a systems approach is adopted, certain obvious and expedient interventions may cause a short-term improvement but generate unexpected and disastrous long-term effects. He further suggests that learning to see underlying structures rather than events, and thinking in terms of processes of change rather than snapshots, are beneficial in creating meaningful long-term effects. As stated earlier, the MBNQA Criteria do not function as a hurdle to leap over, but as a framework for continued improvement.

Legislators clamoring for a single rating derived through simple calculations by which the performance of institutions may be rated, may not be satisfied with the long-term trend assessment approach of the MBNQA Criteria. However, commitment to a longer time horizon may provide more effective solutions to issues faced by GCBs and mitigate the effects of goal displacement.

CONCLUSION

Both the traditional inputs-focused model and the outputs methodology of performance indicators have merit and are logical, rational approaches to quality assurance. Yet, each is limited and neither has provided GCBs with a satisfactory quality assurance tool. The comprehensive systems approach of the MBNQA Criteria melds the strength of resource acquisition and planning of the traditional approach with the strength of monitoring outcomes of the performance indicator approach, and adds the dimensions of process development and continuous improvement. The MBNQA Criteria are a structured non-prescriptive framework designed to direct institutions to apply resources prudently, align their processes, and monitor progress (continuous improvement) toward the achievement of recognized, agreed upon (local and state), and desired outcomes.

Since some institutions of higher education will be applying for the MBNQA, it is possible that GCBs could use these institutions as volunteers to pilot test the efficacy of the Criteria as a mechanism for quality assurance. The pilot institutions could receive a waiver from the traditional quality assurance methods to eliminate the barrier of double reporting. Performance results and stockholder satisfaction could be assessed after an appropriate period of time to determine whether the MBNQA Criteria merit use in a broader arena.

GCBs are charged with the responsibility of assuring the delivery of quality education. The mismatch between societal expectations and the performance of higher education has caused GCBs to seek alternative methods of quality assurance. Since the MBNQA is credited, at least in part, for the resurgence in confidence in American products and services, it is logical to believe that appropriate application of these Criteria may have a positive effect upon higher education's performance.

REFERENCES

Borden, V., and T. Banta. 1994. Data, Indicators, and the National Center for Higher Education Management Systems. New Directions for Institutional Research, no. 82 (summer): 95-106. San Francisco: Jossey-Bass.

Cave, M., S. Hanney, and M. Kogan. 1991. *The Use of Performance Indicators in Higher Education*. London: Jessica Kingsley Publishers.

Edgerton, R. 1993. Contributed Essay. In *An American Imperative: Report of the Wingspread Group on Higher Education*, 64-67. Racine, WI: Johnson Foundation.

Epper, R. 1994. Focus on the Budget: Rethinking Current Practice. Joint publication of SHEEO and Education Commission of the States.

Ewell, P. and D. Jones. 1994. Data, Indicators, and the National Center for Higher Education Management Systems. New Directions for Institutional Research, no. 82 (summer): 23-36.

———. 1994. Pointing the Way: Indicators as Policy Tools in Higher Education. In *Charting Higher Education Accountability*, 6-16. Denver: Education Commission of the States.

Ewell, P., J. Finney, and C. Lenth. 1990. Filling in the Mosaic: The Emerging Pattern of State Based Assessment. *AAHE Bulletin* (April): 1-3.

Griffiths, P. 1993. Contributed Essay. In *An American Imperative: Report of the Wingspread Group on Higher Education*, 90-92. Racine, WI: Johnson Foundation.

Lawrence, B., G. Wethersby, and V.W. Patterson. 1970. *The Outputs of Higher Education: Their Identification, Measurement, and Evaluation*. Boulder, CO: WICHE.

Magaziner, I. 1990. Report of the Commission on the Skills of the American Workforce. In *America's Choice: High Skills or Low Wages*. Washington D.C.: National Center on Education and the Economy.

Pappas, A. 1993. Contributed Essay. In *An American Imperative: Report of the Wingspread Group on Higher Education*, 119-21. Racine, WI: Johnson Foundation.

Richardson, R. 1994. Effectiveness in Undergraduate Education: An Analysis of State Quality Indicators. In *Charting Higher Education Accountability*, 131-46. Denver: Education Commission of the States.

Senge, P. 1990. *The Fifth Discipline*. New York: Doubleday.

Sherr, L, and G. Lozier. 1991. Total Quality Management in Education. In *Total Quality Management in Higher Education,* edited by L.A. Sherr and D.J. Teeter. New Directions for Institutional Research, no. 71. San Francisco: Jossey-Bass.

Shewhart, W. 1986. *Statistical M ethod from the Viewpoint of Quality Control*. New York: Dover Publications.

Texas School Law Bulletin. 1990. Austin: West Publishing Co.

Weber, A. 1993. Contributed Essay. In *An American Imperative: Report of the Wingspread Group on Higher Education*, 159-62. Racine, WI: Johnson Foundation.

14
The Baldrige and the Board

Eugene R. Smoley, Jr.

John Davidson looked forward with anticipation to his first meeting of Johnson University's Board of Trustees. He had kept in close touch with his alma mater during the twelve years since his graduation, first as a sales representative and then district manager of the Babbage Company. When he started his own company five years ago, his University alumni contacts helped him to build the business. As a future businessman of influence in the state, it was not a surprise when the governor asked him to accept an appointment to the Board.

At the meeting, the university president, Dr. Singcliff, briefed the Board on a new initiative that he and his senior staff were undertaking. They had decided to apply for the Malcolm Baldrige National Quality Award. John listened intently, particularly because of his own work with quality improvement in the corporate world. The discussion brought home to him the complexity of the new task he had undertaken as a University trustee.

Although the scenario is fictitious, the problem it poses is real: What is a board's role in considering the Baldrige Award at its university? And what opportunity does the Baldrige offer the board as it performs its responsibilities? This chapter discusses six critical issues that an effective board and its executive officer should address:

- At the core, what is the board's role overall; how can we add value?

- What are the critical issues facing our university?
- How can our institution address these issues?
- How can continuous quality improvement be of help?
- Where does the Baldrige National Quality Award fit in this improvement effort?
- What is a board's role in a Baldrige initiative?

WHAT SHOULD BOARDS DO?

If you want to consider your Board's role with the Baldrige, you should first be clear about the Board's role overall. Most boards do not steer their own strategic course; they are drawn to a range of issues that emerge because of partisan or political interest, customary practice, or the need for urgent attention. Yet, the fundamental purpose of a university board is to ensure institutional direction that preserves and enhances the university in the future. How is that accomplished?

The answer is surprisingly straightforward: the board must engage in conversations about value and quality—conversations within the institution, with key stakeholders, and with the marketplace. "If a board is not adding value, what good is it?" asks Association of Governing Boards' Vice President, Barbara Taylor (1995).

Why boards? Boards are entrusted with preserving and furthering the purposes and values of the institutions they represent. They must protect the continuity, stability, and integrity of their institutions (Nason 1982). Within this charge a board must be sure the institution is fulfilling its mission, expending its funds wisely, and pursuing actions which enhance its quality and character (Taylor 1987).

Why conversation? Conversation captures the essence of the board's role. Although ultimately responsible—both ethically and legally—for the institution, the operational decisions that influence value and quality in the institution will be made by full-time administration, faculty, and staff who provide leadership to the university in its many facets (Taylor 1987). The leadership role of the board—whose membership is volunteer, part-time, and often physically remote from campus—is to raise questions, assess differences in points of view, suggest directions, set expectations, and monitor results.

Finally, why institutions, stakeholders, and marketplace? Value and quality are defined by standards and market. The conservators of the cultural and academic values of our society, in the context of universities, have traditionally been the professors, the experts, those who possess the deepest knowledge and experience of particular subjects. Increasingly, however, value has been defined by the "market," by those who purchase the services provided. If boards are to add value, they must understand the views of those who guard the standards, those who purchase the services provided, and those who stand to benefit both from the preservation of standards and the provision of higher quality and more cost-effective services. Since viewpoints will differ, the board must determine what courses of action add value. It is the resolution of fundamental differences in viewpoint into institutional action through which the board's contribution may most directly represent value added to the institution.

Increasingly, however, value has been defined by the "market," by those who purchase the services provided.

Fundamental Differences

There are three fundamental differences in viewpoint, the resolution of which generates added value :

- Who does the board (and the institution) serve?
- What is the balance between cost and quality?
- What are the priorities that maximize the public good?

Who does the board serve? The board must both preserve and extend those principles and standards that are basic to the university, and ensure that the programs and services reflecting those standards are serving the clients or customers of the university. But these objectives may conflict when the needs of various constituents are in conflict. Funds for scholarship to improve diversity may alternatively be used to improve the chemistry program. The state's interest in lowering taxpayer burden may be at odds with providing smaller classes for undergraduates in the core subjects.

The board members themselves may reflect these conflicting needs. An individual board member may perceive his or her role as representing particular constituent interests, in conflict with those of another board member. This is even legitimized by those who argue that a board of trustees should function according to a legislative model, where trade-offs and compromise provide accommodation of disparate viewpoints. This is in contrast to a corporate governance model, where the board tries to reach consensus on issues based on each member's consideration of what is in the overall best interest of the organization and its constituents.

The second question—What is the balance between cost and quality?—implies a trade-off among conflicting values. Universities, by their actions, often confuse quality and value. Howard Bowen has articulated the "revenue theory of costs" in which colleges and universities raise all the money they can and spend it all on valued activities (Breneman 1993). In fact, value represents the balance between quality and cost, and adding value means determining the point at which increased quality is not worth the cost required. Boards must ensure a focus on value.

Finally, there is the question of priorities. The third area of fundamental differences in viewpoint is in choosing among programs and services, fashioning a mix of those that maximize the public good. Boards must be sure that universities assess the relative contribution of programs, that they discontinue those of lower priority, and that these decisions are in keeping with the essential principles and standards of the institution.

Addressing the Issues

There are two fundamental steps that boards can take: (1) they can build their ability to work as a board, and (2) they can focus on the key activities that can add value to the institution. If you want to improve as a board, you should assess how you behave and agree on ways to improve. The most useful framework for doing this is found in a book entitled *The Effective Board of Trustees* (Chait et al. 1991). In their framework, there are six competencies of an effective board:

• **Contextual**—The board understands and takes into account the culture and norms of the organization it governs.

• **Educational**—The board takes the necessary steps to ensure that trustees are well informed about the institution, the profession, and the board's roles, responsibilities, and performance.

• **Interpersonal**—The board nurtures the development of trustees as a group, attends to the board's collective welfare, and fosters a sense of cohesiveness.

• **Analytical**—The board recognizes complexities and subtleties in the issues it faces and draws upon multiple perspectives to dissect complex problems and to synthesize appropriate responses.

• **Political**—The board accepts as one of its primary responsibilities the need to develop and maintain healthy relationships among key constituencies.

• **Strategic**—The board helps envision and shape institutional direction and helps ensure a strategic approach to the organization's future.

The board can then use a continuing process to focus on its own improvement. Such a process requires attention to the key issues that demand board action, as well as a desire to improve the board's effectiveness as a working unit. It fosters deeper levels of communication, shared views, sharpened understanding, and committed action (Savage 1994).

The assumption underlying this framework and process is that board members must take time to discuss the values underlying their views about the university and its programs and services, its present and future, its costs and revenues. And they must affirm their collective responsibility to add value to the institution through their individual trusteeship. It is through this framework and process that individual trustees with different perspectives develop the consensus necessary to give their trusteeship enduring character and value.

If boards can concentrate on a few essential activities, they enhance their chances of adding value to the institutions they serve. The following activities are the key ones:

If boards can concentrate on a few essential activities, they enhance their chances of adding value to the institutions they serve.

• **Choosing a Chief Executive:** There is strong consensus that the most important activity of a board is to choose a president. Embedded in this simple action are many sub-activities: constituents are involved in the process, the qualifications of a new chief executive are specified to correspond with future strategic plans for the institution, and the contractual arrangements set the stage for the support, feedback, incentives, and security that will enhance effective leadership.

• **Engaging in Strategic Activities:** Whatever the specific working relationship between the board, the president, and other university constituents, the board should participate in the strategic decisions that create future programs and services, distribution of resources, and enhancement of revenues.

• **Gathering and Reviewing Information:** The board must be informed. The nature of this information, the forthright disclosure of data, and the formulation of these data to illuminate key value and quality-related issues is central to the board's ability to engage in strategic activities and add value to the organization. Two types of information are particularly important: first, a set of strategic indicators that form a basis for monitoring the health of the institution; and second, the results of dialogues with constituents.

• **Conversing with Constituents:** The board must understand the value of programs and services to constituents of the university, including direct recipients of services, those who pay for the services, and those who gain indirect benefits from these services.

• **Monitoring Results:** The capacity of a board to talk about value and quality depends upon the type of information available and the form in which it is transmitted to the board. The information, both data and constituent dialogue, provides the means that trustees can use in filtering or screening significant institutional actions. As a board functions collectively, it acts as one in applying the filter to institutional activities. The feedback from this filtering becomes the expectation, or framework for action, that the board applies to university leadership.

WHAT ARE THE CRITICAL ISSUES FACING UNIVERSITIES TODAY?

Although there will be variations among individual universities and across types of institutions, the general message is clear: this is a time of crises for higher education, and business as usual is not the order of the day. The critical issues facing universities are those that boards and their presidents must address. Whatever items (such as the Baldrige Award) are on the board agenda must be viewed in the context of these issues.

The primary "driver" of these issues is cost. Were there sufficient revenues to continue higher education as it currently functions with incremental improvement, the crisis would diminish. Within this context there are at least five external forces and three characteristics of

HIGH PERFORMING COLLEGES

universities that shape the critical issues of the day. It is not the purpose here to provide a comprehensive description of these issues, but an outline of these eight elements will help frame our "Baldrige and the Board" discussion.

External Forces

Financial Support. The next decade will be different from previous ones. Financial support for higher education will be less, and this diminished support will be on a continuing basis. This is based on analyses of major revenue sources: state and federal governments will have less discretionary income to devote to higher education, individual students and families will not have discretionary money for significantly increased tuition, and private philanthropy will not expand to make up the difference (Breneman 1993; Guskin 1994).

Demand For Service. This takes two forms: first, the increasing tendency for students and their parents to judge universities based on their perception of the educational services provided; second, the inclination for policy makers and public agencies to use these same market forces to determine what is in the public interest (Pew 1994).

Eroding Confidence. The public strongly expresses its concern about the increasing cost of higher education and the negative impact this has on accessibility. Leaders of state and federal government convey the view that higher education has failed to foster economic development, serve under-represented populations, and produce economically productive workers. Their negative view intensifies by what they perceive as a self-centered, non-service-oriented attitude by those who staff the universities (Pew 1994).

Demand For Accountability. The eroding confidence, the escalating cost and diminished revenues, and concern about jobs and careers come together in a concern expressed by employers, government, parents, and students: Are we getting a good return on our investment in higher education, and how do we know (Guskin 1993; Pew 1994)?

Technology. The new electronic technologies raise questions about the way students will learn and teachers will teach. There is the potential for radical change in the delivery of educational services with cost reduction and increased student learning, but with a departure from the traditional classroom structure (Guskin 1993; Pew 1994; McGuinness and Ewell 1994).

University Characteristics

Shared Governance Is In Trouble. Where can change leadership come from? Faculty are reluctant to confront the external forces they face; and no wonder, since any change represents a basic disruption of their priorities and the structure of their work lives. Yet, faculty have central authority in areas related to curriculum and instructional services. This leads to a conservative perspective in the face of a mandate for fundamental change. Other participants in shared governance are also problematic. Trustees, particularly in public institutions and especially in large systems, are increasingly detached from campus life and less able to influence governance decisions. Presidents must focus on finding a course of action that moves through the often narrow negotiated window of consensus (Kerr 1994; Guskin 1994).

Mission Is Diffuse And Unfocused. Universities find it difficult to answer the question of what they will, and more importantly, what they will not, do. University values have emphasized the individual faculty member and his or her central position in determining priorities. Thus, many university missions are to an important degree, a fragmented collage of individual priorities' (Guskin 1994; Pew 1993).

Action Toward Efficiency And Productivity Is Difficult. Higher education is people-intensive. Significant improvements in efficiency or productivity require fundamental changes in the way work is done, and thus in the number of faculty and staff and their responsibilities. In this radical view, it is the people who need to change (Smoley 1990; Guskin 1994; Pew 1993).

Universities find it difficult to answer the question of what they will, and more importantly, what they will not, do.

HOW CAN THE UNIVERSITY ADDRESS THESE ISSUES?

It's clear that whatever universities do to confront these issues, they must address fundamental change—and such change will be difficult. There are three fundamental courses of action: (1) change what the university does, (2) change how it does what it does, and (3) change the fundamental cultural values that drive the decisions about what is done and how it is done. In any action, the university must consider the process by which decisions are made—who is consulted, and who is empowered to make the decision.

The Study Group on Restructuring, commissioned by the Pew Higher Education Research Program (Pew 1993), suggests six categories of action: enhance and diversify revenues, impose budget discipline, reshape the institution, develop incentives for educational quality and productivity, reengineer work, and change the culture to instill quality management principles. These actions focus on how to change what is done, with the exception of reshaping the institution which focuses on prioritizing programs.

McGuinness and Ewell (1994) suggest three ways of improving productivity and quality: change within the current academic structure, transformation of core processes, and learning productivity. David Breneman, noted economist and dean of the University of Virginia's College of Education, suggests four possible actions: doing less with less, doing the same with less, changing the educational delivery system, or sharpening and differentiating the mission (Breneman 1993).

The suggested actions reflect the difficulty of fundamental change. Little attention is directed to changing cultural values; some—but limited—attention is paid to focusing and directing the mission by refining program emphasis. Most attention is focused on change in the organization of work, and most of this is on incremental changes that can be accomplishcd gradually without major institutional disruption. Much attention is directed to administrative change, less to change within the instructional program and organization of faculty work.

How the university addresses these issues can be central or peripheral. Consideration of mission, culture, and transformational change, and a focus on academic issues are indicators of how fundamental (and difficult) possible actions may be.

WHERE DOES CONTINUOUS QUALITY IMPROVEMENT FIT?

Perhaps Marchese (1993) said it best in his lead article in *Change*: "Total Quality [or continuous quality improvement, CQI] is complicated, important, difficult to implement, and far from figured out" (13). The pursuit of total quality is a continuous journey, not a program; at best, it may help, but won't get universities where they need to go. The good news is that its basic ideas provide a framework for addressing, at least partially, the critical issues facing higher education today.

Marchese suggests six basic ideas of CQI:

• *Customer Focus*—Quality is what the customer says it is. Key questions are who is the customer, what does he or she believe, and how do we resolve conflicts among customers' preferences? These questions imply that work should be defined by customers' wants.

• *Continuous Improvement*—We need to focus on the processes by which work gets done; how well do they deliver value—that is, quality service at a reasonable price—to the customer? Process improvement can result in better service or more efficient use of resources.

• *Management By Fact*—The quality and efficiency of performance should be judged based on data systematically collected and analyzed—data about the processes, the customers, and the interconnections among processes and customer satisfaction.

• *Benchmarking*—The design of work processes should be based on a systematic search for and comparison with best practices in other organizations.

• *People*—People are the greatest resource an organization has. We should invest in them through training, coaching, support, and an accountability process that sets standards and gives feedback. We should view the work process as a continual learning and improvement opportunity for employees and for the organization; we should form groups of people to enhance this learning.

• *Structures*—Work should be organized around the needs of customers and the best opportunities to deliver services to them.

There is a seventh idea, embedded in Marchese's discussion:

• *Culture*—Work should be driven by our intrinsic desire to do our best. We should experience the powerful rewards of working together—a sense of contribution, of belonging, of possibilities for the future.

These key ideas, arrayed against the significant issues facing higher education, suggest the value of a total quality management perspective. For example, total quality directly addresses the demand for service and eroding confidence facing higher education. The challenge is to improve systemically those services that significantly affect customer satisfaction. Moreover, the increased customer satisfaction, cost savings, improved processes, and better information may contribute to the confidence and support of government decision-makers.

Establishing and acting on performance data leads to a better basis for decisions and improved work processes. Using employees who understand processes, and letting them make data-based improvement decisions about these processes, has the potential of improving the quality of work processes and reducing costs. It also leads to a heightened sense of ownership and commitment to the university and to the employee's work.

While the benefits are many, continuous quality improvement has significant limitations, both those that are a part of its definition as a program or way of operating, and those that occur through the complexity of implementation. CQI is focused on how work can be accomplished such that it meets the customer requirements and is of high quality while limiting cost. It does not raise or answer the more fundamental questions of mission or program focus. So if a university questions which schools or colleges should be funded and which should not, CQI does not provide the answer. Strategic priorities must be determined differently, although informed by customer information that may be more readily available through closer customer relationship.

So if a university questions which schools or colleges should be funded and which should not, CQI does not provide the answer.

Even within its operational scope, CQI tends to focus on discrete individual processes, not on the broader systems that represent integrated networks of these processes. Because of this specific operational focus, CQI tends to be used on administrative, rather than instructional, processes.

Finally, because those involved in CQI processes are those closest to the work, there is the conservatism of those most affected by change. The suggestions tend to be incremental rather than broadly restructuring in nature.

The second limitation highlights the fact that a CQI initiative is complex and ambitious. It takes tremendous time and energy on the part of many different people, including top leadership where support is critical to success. It puts into play high expectations for results from employees involved, expectations that are not always easy to realize. It is open to easy distortion and oversimplification. Many initiatives count the number of teams and participants and the amount of CQI training without producing results (Brigham 1993).

The conclusion of this brief outline is that CQI can be a worthwhile endeavor, but it is certainly not the cure. It should be undertaken with careful study and planning and linkage with the strategic directions of the university.

WHERE DOES THE BALDRIGE FIT INTO CONTINUOUS IMPROVEMENT?

As Johnson and Seymour have described in an earlier chapter in this volume, the Baldrige Award is designed as an audit instrument and as an incentive for recognition of achievement. In an audit capacity, it promotes an understanding of the requirements for quality excellence and the criteria for achieving this excellence. It also promotes awareness of quality as an important element in effective functioning. It promotes the sharing of information about successful quality strategies and the benefits derived from implementation of these strategies.

As a member of a board of trustees, there are four questions you should answer as you consider the possibility of your university embarking on a Baldrige self-assessment:

• Do we plan to pursue the award or simply to use the framework independently?
• Does the Baldrige contribute to our quest for institutional quality and value?
• Do we have the leadership and the deeper support of the institutional culture to mount a strong CQI effort?
• Do the benefits outweigh the costs?

In order to help answer these questions, a series of interviews were conducted with both continuous improvement experts and higher education practitioners. Their responses helped inform the following discussion.

The first question again is an issue of scope: Do we plan to pursue the award or simply to use the framework independently? The framework is viewed as providing a comprehensive and sophisticated approach to continuous quality improvement. At its essence it is a thought process. According to Chuck Johnson (1995), Principal of Towers

Perrin, an international management consulting firm providing services in quality improvement, "It is the spirit of the criteria that is most important." Using the criteria as a goal gives the institution a way of thinking about improvement, whether or not specific criteria are fully met or not.

Pursuing the award itself has additional advantages. It can lead to recognition and publicity that may help the university in the marketplace for students or for additional funding. It may serve as validation for credibility with government and corporate leaders. It may provide motivation to focus staff energy on fulfilling the Baldrige Criteria. However, there are those who urge caution in accepting the challenge of pursuing the award. According to John Brighton (1995)—one of the key leaders of continuous quality improvement at Penn State where he serves as provost—it's a helpful framework, but time consuming and hard to coordinate in a large, decentralized setting. Jim Shaffer (1995), co-leader of Towers Perrin's Quality Center for Excellence agrees: "Baldrige is a useful template, but the cost of compliance with the terms of the award diverts energy from the real need to continue to make improvement in a fast moving environment. It's possible to win quality awards without substantially improving quality. Companies are focused on winning customers, not awards."

There is also the danger of damaging morale if the university or college does not succeed in its application or does not do as well as expected. Linda Thor (1995), president of Rio Salado Community College and the author of the earlier chapter on the Leadership Criterion (1.0), reports that even though her institution won the state mini-Baldrige award, the feedback report was initially devastating to the college CQI steering team. It was difficult for them to handle the perceived criticism ("areas for improvement") until they could step back and recognize the value to be gained from the external evaluation.

A second question: Does the Baldrige contribute to our quest for institutional quality and value? For most, the answer is an enthusiastic, positive response. The Baldrige sensitizes the university to quality improvement; it focuses the attention of the organization on operational effectiveness; it provides a standard for operational improvement; it fosters communication within the institution and between the university and other organizations. It teaches problem solving tools, provides training, and brings people together in teams to focus on improvement. It provides a common vocabulary, develops better information, provides motivation for improvement, and focuses attention on the customer. It has the potential to move the university a significant distance within the quality improvement framework.

The caution is that the distance isn't far enough or fast enough. Sean Rush (1995), former Coopers and Lybrand consultant to higher education, says that "the problem with TQM is it focuses on numbers of teams and numbers of people involved. There is typically a lot of activity—thinking about how to improve—but there is a lack of accountability and measurement; TQM tends to be incremental, evolutionary and multi-year." But—Rush adds—higher education needs more radical change. There is a need to get to basic structure and culture.

Bill Troutt, president of Belmont University, is a leading practitioner of continuous quality improvement. He quotes Harvard management expert Rosabeth Moss Kanter's statement about "bold strokes and long marches." According to Troutt (1995), continuous quality improvement focuses more on long marches than on bold strokes. Tim Gilmour (1995)—until recently, responsible for CQI at Georgia Institute of Technology and now the chief academic offices at Northwest Missouri State University—says there's a need to get deeper, to foster cultural change. There's a strongly rooted resistance to fundamental change that is difficult to overcome. Unless basic values can be modified, the energy required to continue the change effort is difficult to sustain.

Unless basic values can be modified, the energy required to continue the change effort is difficult to sustain.

There is a third question worth asking: Do we have the leadership and the deeper support of the institutional culture to mount a strong CQI effort? An institution must be ready to undertake the Baldrige process. Top leadership is essential. As Rush (1995) says, "it's where the rubber hits the sky." It is essential that there be institutional leadership at the presidential and executive staff levels. AAHE's publication, *25 Snapshots of A Movement* (1994), further illustrates this point. Case after case highlights the president and his or her cabinet as a critical factor in success.

As John Brighton (1995) points out, universities are cautious. CQI represents incremental change. An improvement initiative helps staff understand and participate in the changes needed. The president needs to be public and supportive of CQI. There is a need to decide whether to apply CQI everywhere or selectively. The president is in the middle. He must be supportive of CQI and collaborative with faculty, serving or she an academic colleague. Thus, the strength of presidential leadership is shaped by the readiness of faculty and staff to consider such an initiative. There is a traditional skepticism, particularly about ideas coming from the private sector.

A final question might be, do the benefits outweigh the costs? The board must be conscious of this balance as proposals unfold. It will likely not be a question of *whether* change should be pursued through quality improvement, but *how* to pursue change and quality improvement at this institution at this point in time. A board must examine the benefits and costs of administrative initiatives and weigh them in balance. A Baldrige initiative is essentially an administrative initiative. The board's issues are whether it serves the institution well—utilizing human resources effectively and with the promise of institutional improvements.

WHAT IS THE BOARD'S ROLE IN A BALDRIGE INITIATIVE?

If the university undertakes the Baldrige review process, does the Board have a role to play, what is that role, and how can the president assist as the Board works to support the Baldrige process?

The Board Supporting Baldrige

As with any major university initiative, the Board has two important roles. The first is to provide a filter or screen through which the institution can assess the quality and value of the initiative. The second is to provide support for top leadership.

In providing a filter or screen, the Board should give balance and insight. Undertaking the Baldrige offers significant opportunities but also real institutional risk. It's an opportunity for the board to exercise its responsibility for conversation about value and quality.

The initiation of a Baldrige self-assessment is one point of Board involvement. In some instances, it is an individual member of the Board who suggests the possibility of CQI for the institution and the use of the Baldrige. Here the Board can encourage the administration to consider the opportunities while avoiding the danger of setting unrealistic expectations. The Baldrige framework is complex, comprehensive, and sophisticated; it's hard for the novice to use. It requires significant time and energy. It requires preparation and building commitment. It requires balance with other university efforts. A case in point is a college in the East where a board member strongly suggested that the college implement a Baldrige-type approach. The college spent a year trying to use a sophisticated instrument. The year ended in failure and frustration. The college would have been better served to reject the board member's suggestion or to move more cautiously.

At the point of initiation and once the Baldrige process is underway, the Board should review its progress with a critical eye. In the spirit of conversation, the Board should ask the tough questions. What are the costs and benefits of the initiative? To what extent is energy consumed in the process—in team meetings to review specific operational issues, for example? To what extent are results realized? Are the results which will emerge from the Baldrige process likely to support the university's mission, strategic direction, service quality, and cost reduction?

The Board should watch for the pitfalls. Is the Baldrige effort focused too much on meeting the formal Criteria and not enough on the real university improvements required? Is the time required viewed as an add-on to the usual work of the university? Are employee participants discouraged by lack of results? Is the president sufficiently involved? Does the planning process involve faculty and staff? How will the university know it's improving? What information is systematically collected, organized, and shared to provide accountability?

The second role that the Board must reflect upon is providing support for top leadership. There is clear consensus that the president must have a strong and visible commitment to any quality initiative if it is to be successful and must exercise leadership in developing broad-based commitment to and consensus around the Baldrige process. The Board has an important role to play in the support of this leadership. It must be clear to the university community that the Board understands and supports the initiative's concept and anticipated results. That support is never more critical than in situations where controversial administrative decisions are made. That support is deliberate in organizing, with the president, board activities that reinforce the work toward quality improvement.

One university president reports that for the past five years, in one way or another, CQI has been a part of every board meeting. Often a team will report directly to the trustees—their thoughts, data, and results. He uses a clerk from the cashiers unit, who spoke directly to the trustees about how the collection of information about one of the sub-processes had resulted in better service to students, as an example. The cashier was proud of the results, and the positive trustee response contributed to the positive spirit around improvement, its importance and its recognition.

By contrast, at one major university in the south, a quality initiative developed with joint faculty and administrative leadership was brought to the board, and the board added caveats, changing the proposal. This unilateral action created a schism between faculty and board; the fragile faculty trust was damaged and the positive working relationship necessary for significant progress will be difficult to rebuild.

The Baldrige Improving the Board

The involvement of universities in continuous quality improvement and a Baldrige process provides an remarkable opportunity for the Board itself to improve its own operations, and this is in fact happening at many campuses where CQI and Baldrige efforts are being undertaken.

How does it help? Baldrige provides a language and framework that not only allows staff to talk about value and quality issues, but extends that conversation to the Board. Since the Board has this kind of conversation as a major responsibility, it facilitates the Board's exercise of its responsibility. Because board attention is often diverted to financial and physical plant decision-making and operational crises, the undertaking of a Baldrige self-assessment adds an urgency to Board discussions of value and quality in central areas of instructional and support services.

Baldrige provides a language and framework that not only allows staff to talk about value and quality issues, but extends that conversation to the Board.

The Baldrige is driven by the kinds of information Boards need if they are to hold their institutions accountable, not only for fiscal integrity but for enhancing service quality. This information includes the indicators of the efficiency and quality of work processes and systems, the core of the Baldrige. Administrative service improvement must be evident in indicators of improved customer satisfaction and reduced costs. At the core, the information must address faculty work. What purposes are being served? How do you know you are successful? How does the structure and focus of work contribute to these purposes? How are the issues of academic productivity being addressed by the faculty?

While it helps clarify the information the board needs to track service improvement and permit it to review institutional progress, Baldrige information is not necessarily addressing strategic questions of institutional direction and focus. That is, the information will help the Board determine how well the university is performing, but other discussions and information puts this in the context of the university's major purposes and changing direction, and the need for selected services to support those directions and purposes.

The Baldrige also helps the Board as the Board works to build institutional credibility in the community. Conversations about quality conducted often and in public, the quality indicators of service improvement, and the symbolic significance of undertaking a Baldrige initiative help to communicate to the business, political, and alumni communities the seriousness with which the university is undertaking quality improvement. This can help as legislatures consider public funding; it can help as businesses and alumni consider giving to the university; it can attract students and their parents to the university.

Finally, discussion of the Baldrige and continuous quality improvement often leads to an internal look at the board itself and the processes by which it does its work. Boards, like academic departments and administrative units, have a more difficult time looking at themselves analytically than at others. But discussion of the Baldrige often leads to consideration of the effectiveness of Board functioning in a more fundamental way than the typical operational concerns about agenda and information. Are we as a board spending time on the right topics? Do we allow enough time for substantive discussions of quality and value? Do we engage the right people in conversations on these topics?

The Board and President: Working As A Team

The picture of a board/president team emerges when you talk with individuals whose universities have taken continuous quality improvement seriously. In many instances, these are the institutions pursuing the application of the Baldrige framework.

The Pennsylvania State University is one of the contributors to this publication. It is an example of a large, complex university moving deliberately, and with an emphasis on systematic consultation. As Provost and Executive Vice President, John Brighton was responsible for initiation of the effort and continues to oversee it for the university. Louise Sandmeyer has the administrative responsibility for quality improvement. The president participates in the University Council on Continuous Quality Improvement and maintains a balanced perspective to support the collaborative nature of the work. The board of trustees receives reports of progress made by the quality teams each year. Last year, the Council reviewed the university policies and practices that might inhibit progress toward quality improvement. When substantive reports are made to the Board in areas such as graduate programs and recruitment processes, the person responsible will often indicate the role that CQI has played in their work. The thirty-two Board members vary in their degree of knowledge and support for CQI. Brighton and Sandmeyer believe the pursuit of quality helps the relationship between the Board and executive staff. Some Board members are executives of companies involved with quality efforts. A development officer in one academic college reports that a positive impression is provided when corporations are told that Penn State is pursuing CQI.

Another illustration of the president and Board working as a team is Belmont University (also a contributor to this volume). Belmont is governed by the Tennessee Baptist Convention and the Board members must be Tennessee Baptists. There are thirty-nine Board members with six additional ex-officio members. The former chairman of the board is a strong advocate of CQI, but it was the president, Bill Troutt, who first initiated it six years ago. For the past five years, in one way or another, CQI has been a part of every Board meeting. The activity and spirit around continuous improvement has led to more candor in the working relationship with the Board. The tools used with continuous improvement teams have been useful in designing board meetings and planning retreats. Through Board meetings using small groups and reflection about difficult issues, the consciousness of the Board has been raised—thinking about the work of the university, its vision, and its service to customers. Troutt and his Board chair meet every week. The agendas of Board meetings are developed at this time. Administrators, and then Board members themselves, serve as facilitators of the small group sessions during Board meetings. The Board is viewed as a part of the overall system by which the university delivers higher education services. This is a part of Troutt's (1995) view that top leadership must create the environment within which CQI can flourish. He has tried to move to a set of conversations among Board members and staff on important issues. He believes this leads Board members to a willingness to invest time and energy in the university, which leads to commitment to the values of the institution, which leads to assistance in enhancing resource support.

Finally, Rio Salado Community College is one of ten colleges in the Maricopa Community College District, governed by a five member board. Each member is elected for a six year term. Linda Thor, Rio Salado's, president introduced CQI at her institution in March of 1991—six months after she arrived there. At the end of her first year, Rio Salado had a North Central accreditation review. The college received praise for TQM, teamwork, collaborative decision making, open communication, and a clear understanding of mission. This attracted the attention of the district Chancellor who thought TQM should be explored district-wide. He established a commission to review the idea. Thor chaired the commission which recommended that the district proceed with TQM. The district-wide initiative is governed by an executive council called Quantum Quality. The council has two of the five governing board members on it.

The Board has received TQM training and has also studied John Carver's model of board governance. As a consequence of these two influences, the board has changed the way it operates. In the past, it held two meetings per month; one was a business meeting and one a work/study meeting. Now, the Board has shortened its business meeting through a consent agenda which allows one motion for routine items, giving the Board more time for substantive issues. The second meeting has now become "Strategic Conversations." At this meeting the Board engages in conversation with its constituents. The Board does not direct the conversation, but rather participates from the audience with guidance from the selected facilitator. There are ground rules—all voices have an equal right to be heard. There are small group discussions, issues are listed, and results are reported back to the district. Examples of topics include:

- How well do we assess and meet the needs of the community?
- What should our relationship be with our K-12 system?
- Are we a learning organization?

Through this process, the Board has developed statements of vision, mission, strategic goals, and shared values.

NEXT STEPS FOR JOHNSON UNIVERSITY

As John Davidson reflected on the Johnson University board's discussion of the Baldrige initiative, he organized his thoughts and the steps he believed the Board should take, both for ensuring the effective progress of the University and building Board effectiveness. He made a note to set up a meeting with Dr. Singcliff to review the Board's meeting so that he could contribute to planning the next steps for Board involvement.

Two weeks later, he and Dr. Singcliff met for lunch. Davidson got right to the point. "First and foremost," he said, "the Johnson Board must provide added value. It must focus on value and quality, engage in conversation with its constituents about value, and sort out the conflicts that arise because of value differences. Second, the Board must build the capacity to function as a unit in this value enhancement effort and must deliberately focus on important functions, conserving the Board's limited time where it can have the greatest impact."

Singcliff listened with focused attention. "I was actually thinking of taking the Board members on a retreat so we could further probe the quality initiative," he said. Davidson replied that was exactly the sort of action he thought would be invaluable.

He added that, in his view, there was an urgency to taking action, particularly because of the extraordinary challenges to Johnson as well as many other universities today, both from outside and within the institution. Diminished financial resources, demand for service and accountability, eroding confidence, and the difficulty in establishing an effective decision-making process that focuses on limited purposes and improved productivity, increases the urgency of the Board's contribution to institutional improvement.

Davidson added that he was convinced that all universities were going to have to change, and the quantum changes that may be required—the refocusing of mission, the restructuring of services, and greater accountability for results—would be exceptionally difficult. He asserted that the Johnson Board would have to work closely with Dr. Singcliff to stimulate and support his initiatives for change and that a retreat could strengthen the Board's resolve in providing this support.

Davidson added that, within the context of current mission and structure, he believed change may be urgently needed to improve the quality and efficiency of current services provided. Continuous quality improvement, he thought, could provide a methodology for accomplishing this change and the Malcolm Baldrige Award framework suggested by Dr. Singcliff could provide a sophisticated and useful framework for accomplishing quality improvement.

Davidson then shared with Dr. Singcliff a list of questions he thought the Board might discuss at a retreat in response to the prospect of a Baldrige self-assessment:

• Is it right for this institution at this point in time? How can it be modified to represent a constructive initiative? What are possible suggestions for improvement in its implementation?

• How can we support the president in his leadership of this initiative?

• What conclusions can we reach about its effectiveness and what information do we need to support assessment of the initiative? Is service quality improved? Are costs reduced?

• How can we improve our own capacity to work toward quality improvement? What is the relationship between the Baldrige initiative and the Board's central concerns for institutional strategy and direction? How can we work with the president and constituents toward more effectively addressing the critical issues facing the university?

Dr. Singcliff agreed these questions represented a good start in planning the retreat. As they parted, Singcliff and Davidson agreed that they would suggest a concept of the Board as a filter for administrative decision-making, the support structure for the president's leadership, and the governing force—in collaboration with the president—toward enhancing institutional value.

REFERENCES

American Association for Higher Education. 1994. *25 Snapshots of A Movement: Profiles of Campuses Implementing CQI.* Washington, DC: AAHE.

Breneman, D. W. 1993. Higher Education: On a Collision Course with New Realities. *AGB Occasional Paper Series*, no. 22, reprinted in *American Student Assistance*, December.

Brigham, S. E. 1993. TQM: Lessons We Can Learn from Industry. *Change* (May/June): 42-48.

Brighton, J. 1995. Telephone conversation with the author, 12 January.

Chait, R. P., T. P. Holland, and B. E. Taylor. 1991. *The Effective Board of Trustees.* New York: Macmillan.

Gilmour, T. 1995. Telephone conversation with the author, 16 January.

Guskin, A. E. 1994. Reducing Student Costs and Enhancing Student Learning: The University Challenge of the 1990s. *Change* (July/August): 23-29.

Johnson, C.E. 1995. Telephone conversation with the author, 16 January.

Kerr, C. 1994. *Troubled Times For American Higher Education: The 1990s And Beyond.* Albany, NY: State University of New York Press.

Marchese, T. 1993. TQM: A Time For Ideas. *Change* (May/June): 10-13.

McGuinness, A. C., Jr., and P. T. Ewell. 1994. Improving Productivity and Quality in Higher Education. *AGB Priorities* 2 (fall).

Nason, J. W. 1982. *The Nature of Trusteeship: The Role and Responsibilities of College and University Boards.* Washington, DC: Association of Governing Boards of Universities and Colleges.

Pew Higher Education Roundtable. 1993. A Call to Meeting. *Policy Perspectives* 4, no. 4 (February): section A.

Pew Higher Education Roundtable. 1994. To Dance with Change. *Policy Perspectives* 5, no. 3(April): section A.

Rush, S. 1995. Telephone conversation with the author, 9 January.

Sandmeyer, L. 1995. Telephone conversation with the author, 9 January.

Savage, T. J. 1994. *Seven Steps to a More Effective Board.* Rockville, MD: Cheswick Center.

Shaffer, J. C. 1995. Telephone conversation with the author, 9 January.

Smoley, E. R., Jr. 1990. *Tough Choices: A Guide to Administrative Cost Management in Colleges and Universities.* Washington, DC: U.S. Department of Education.

Taylor, B. E. 1987. *Working Effectively with Trustees: Building Cooperative Campus Leadership.* ASHE-ERIC Higher Education Report No. 2. Washington, DC: Association for the Study of Higher Education.

Taylor, B. E. 1995. Telephone conversation with the author, 5 January.

Thor, L. 1995. Telephone conversation with the author, 9 January.

Troutt, B. 1995. Telephone conversation with the author, 10 January.

Appendix

This section is an adaptation of the Malcolm Baldrige National Quality Award's 1995 Education Pilot Criteria. It provides background information about the Education Criteria as well as its purposes and goals. The core values and concepts are described in detail while key education themes are also enumerated. The Education Criteria Framework—a visual schema—is presented. Finally, the Criteria themselves are outlined along with their accompanying Items or areas to address. Other aspects of the Education Pilot Criteria, specifically those that relate to conducting a self-assessment and using the scoring system, are described in the appendix of *Volume II—Case and Practice*.

INTRODUCTION
Background

The Malcolm Baldrige National Quality Award (Baldrige Award) was established in 1987 through legislation (P.L. 100-107). The purposes of the Baldrige Award are threefold:

• to promote awareness of the importance of quality improvement to the national economy;
• to recognize organizations which have made substantial improvements in products, services, and overall competitive performance; and
• to foster sharing of best practices information among U.S. organizations.

Baldrige Award Program Strategy

The Baldrige Award Program strategy consists of two parts: (1) conceptual and (2) institutional. The conceptual part of the strategy involves the creation of consensus criteria which project clear values, set high standards, focus on key requirements for organizational excellence, and create means for assessing progress relative to these requirements. The institutional part of the strategy involves use of the Criteria as a basis for consistent communications within and among organizations of all types. Such communications stimulate broad involvement and co-

operation, and afford a meaningful and consistent basis for sharing information. An important part of the communications is the sharing of information by Baldrige Award recipients.

Through the Baldrige Award, rigorous criteria were created to evaluate applicants for the Award. The Baldrige Award Criteria, based upon a set of core values and concepts, focus on key requirements for organizational excellence. These requirements are incorporated in a seven-part Criteria framework. Accompanying this framework is a set of Scoring Guidelines which permit evaluation of performance relative to the detailed Criteria. The evaluation leads to a feedback report—a summary of strengths and areas for improvement. All Baldrige Award applicants receive a feedback report.

The Baldrige Award Criteria and scoring guidelines have led to a number of key developments:

• creation of a means for self-assessment;
• replication of the Award system by hundreds of organizations, including states, cities, companies, and not-for-profit organizations; and
• creation of training programs.

Throughout the life of the Baldrige Award Program, the principal uses of the Criteria have been for such other purposes. To date, more than one million copies of the Criteria have been disseminated, and a like number of copies have been duplicated by others. This compares with a total of 546 applicants for the Baldrige Award.

Since the Baldrige Award was established in 1987, there have been 22 Award recipients (1988-1994) in three categories—manufacturing, service, and small business. Award recipients have demonstrated a wide range of improvements and achievements, including product and service quality, productivity growth, customer satisfaction, reduced operating costs, and improved responsiveness. Also, Award recipients are among the nation's leaders in investment in developing the skills of the work force.

Working Toward an Education Category

Since the inception of the Baldrige Award in 1987, some educators have been involved in the Program through their service on the Award's Board of Examiners. In addition, the Award recipients have sought to involve educators and educational organizations, locally and nationally. Also, some state and local award programs already include education categories. In conjunction with these Award developments, many educators have launched quality improvement efforts. National initiatives such as Goals 2000 reflect a growing national consensus to strengthen education. As a result of these and related developments, interest has grown in establishing a Baldrige Award category for education. In 1993, a decision was reached to launch pilot activities in 1994 and 1995 to address the many issues that arise in extending eligibility to education. In 1994, preliminary activities were conducted, primarily to involve more educators,

test training programs, and seek comment on the Criteria. For 1995, the second phase of these activities will be undertaken to evaluate all elements of an Award eligibility category.

DESCRIPTION OF THE EDUCATION CRITERIA

Education Criteria Purposes

The Education Criteria are the basis for evaluating the improvement practices of education organizations and for giving feedback to Education Program participants. In addition, these Criteria have four other purposes:

• to help improve college or university performance practices by making available an integrated, results-oriented set of key performance requirements;
• to facilitate communications and sharing of best practices information within and among institutions of all types based upon a common understanding of key performance requirements;
• to foster development of partnerships involving educational institutions, businesses, human service agencies, and other organizations; and
• to serve as a working tool for improving college or university performance, planning, training, and institutional assessment.

Education Criteria Goals

The Criteria are designed to help institutions improve their educational services through focusing on dual, results-oriented goals:

• delivery of ever-improving educational value to students, contributing to their overall development and well-being; and
• improvement of overall institutional effectiveness, use of resources, and capabilities.

Core Values and Concepts

The Education Criteria are built upon a set of core values and concepts, the foundation for developing and integrating all requirements. These core values and concepts are:

Learning-Centered Education

Learning-centered education places the focus on learning and the real needs of learners. Such needs derive from the requirements of the marketplace and the responsibilities of citizenship. Changes in technology and in the national and world economies are creating increasing demands on employees to become knowledgeable workers and problem solvers, keeping pace with the rapid changes in the marketplace. Most analysts conclude that institutions of all types need to focus more on students' active learning and on the development of problem-solving skills.

Colleges and universities exist primarily to develop the fullest potential of all students, affording them opportunities to pursue various avenues to success. A learning-centered institution needs to fully understand and translate marketplace and citizenship requirements into appropriate curricula. Education delivery needs to be built around learning effectiveness. Teaching effectiveness needs to be defined in terms of learning effectiveness.

Key characteristics of learning-centered education are:

• High developmental expectations and standards for all students.
• Understanding that students may learn in different ways and at different rates. Also, that student learning rates and styles may differ over time, and may vary depending upon subject matter. Learning may be influenced by support, guidance, and climate factors, including factors that contribute to or impede learning. Thus, the learning-centered institution needs to maintain a constant search for alternative approaches to enhance learning. The institution also needs to develop and utilize actionable information on individual students that bears upon their learning.
• Providing a major emphasis on active learning. This may require the use of a wide range of techniques, materials, and experiences to engage student interest. Techniques, materials, and experiences may be drawn from external sources such as businesses, community services, or social service organizations.
• Regularly and extensively using formative assessment as a key strategy to measure learning early in the learning process and to tailor learning experiences to individual needs.
• Periodically using summative assessment to measure progress against key, relevant external standards and norms regarding what students should know and be able to do.
• Assisting students to use self-assessment to chart progress and to clarify goals and gaps.
• Focusing on key transitions such as school-to-college, college-to-college, and college-to-work.

Leadership

An institution's senior administrators and leadership team play a crucial role in the development of a student-focused, learning-oriented climate. This requires the creation of clear and visible directions and high expectations. Senior administrators need to lead and take part in the development of strategies, systems, and methods for achieving excellence. Such strategies, systems, and methods should be built upon a foundation of continuous improvement in the way the institution operates. This requires the commitment and development of all faculty and staff. Senior administrators need to ensure that institutional policies reinforce the learning and improvement climate and encourage initiative and self-directed responsibility throughout the college or university.

In addition to their important role within the institution, senior administrators have other avenues for strengthening education. Reinforcing the learning environment in the institution might require building community support and aligning community and business leaders and community services with this aim.

Continuous Improvement and Organizational Learning

Achieving ever-higher levels of institutional performance requires a well-executed approach to continuous improvement. A well-executed continuous improvement process has several important characteristics:

(1) it has clear goals regarding what to improve;
(2) it is fact-based, incorporating measures and/or indicators;
(3) it is systematic, including cycles of planning, execution, and evaluation; and
(4) it focuses primarily on key processes as the route to better results.

The approach to improvement needs to be embedded in the way the college or university operates. Embedded means:

(1) improvement is a regular part of the daily work of all faculty, staff, and students;
(2) improvement processes seek to eliminate problems at their source; and
(3) improvement is driven by opportunities to do better, as well as by problems that need to be corrected.

Opportunities for improvement come from many sources, including:

(1) faculty and staff ideas;
(2) successful practices of other organizations; and
(3) educational and learning research findings.

The approach to continuous improvement should seek to engage students as full participants in and contributors to improvement processes. A major opportunity exists to build active student learning around goal setting, assessment, and improvement. In addition to creating an improvement-oriented climate, this approach could help identify the best approaches to learning on an individual basis, and to build upon demonstrated improvement to strengthen student confidence and commitment to learning.

Faculty and Staff Participation and Development

An institution's success in improving performance depends critically upon the capabilities, skills, and motivation of its faculty and staff. Faculty and staff success depends upon having meaningful opportunities to develop and practice new knowledge and skills. Colleges and universities need to invest in the development of faculty and staff through ongoing education, training, and opportunities for continuing growth.

For faculty, development means building not only discipline knowledge, but also knowledge of student learning styles and of assessment methods. Faculty participation may include contributing to institutional policies and working in teams to develop and execute programs and curricula. Increasingly, participation is becoming more student-focused and multi-disciplinary. College and university leaders need to work to eliminate disincentives for groups and individuals to sustain these important, learning-focused professional development activities.

For staff, development might include classroom and on-the-job training, job rotation, and pay for demonstrated skills. Increasingly, training, education, development, and work organizations need to be tailored to a more diverse work force and to more flexible, high performance work practices.

Partnership Development
Colleges and universities should seek to build internal and external partnerships to better accomplish their overall goals.

Internal partnerships might include those that promote cooperation among faculty and staff groups such as unions, departments, and work units. Agreements might be created involving employee development, cross-training, or new work organizations such as high performance work teams. Internal partnerships might also involve creating network relationships among institutional units to improve flexibility and responsiveness.

External partnerships might include those with other colleges and universities, schools, businesses, business associations, community and social service organizations, and suppliers—all stakeholders and potential contributors.

Partnerships should seek to develop longer-term objectives, thereby creating a basis for mutual investments. Partners should address objectives of the partnership, key requirements for success, means of regular communication, approaches to evaluating progress, and means for adapting to changing conditions.

Design Quality and Prevention
Education improvement needs to place very strong emphasis on effective design of educational programs, curricula, and learning environments. The overall design should include clear learning objectives, taking into account the individual needs of students. Design must also include effective means for gauging student progress. A central quality-related requirement of effective design is the inclusion of an assessment strategy. Such strategy needs to emphasize the acquisition of formative information—information that indicates early on whether or not learning is taking place—to minimize problems that might arise if learning barriers are not promptly identified.

Management by Fact
An effective education management system based upon cause-effect thinking needs to be built upon measurement, information, data, and analysis. Measurements must derive from and support the institution's mission and strategy and address all key requirements. A strong focus on student learning requires a

comprehensive and integrated fact-based system—one that includes input data, environmental data, and performance data. Analysis refers to extracting larger meaning from data to support evaluation and decision making through the institution. Such analysis might entail using data to reveal information—such as trends, projections, and cause and effect—that might not be evident without analysis. The effective use of measurement and analysis to support student learning and institutional performance improvement requires a strong focus on information system design. This might entail organizing data systems to provide key information to support design of improvement strategies. Examples include organization of data by cohorts, longitudinal information, and comparative information.

Long-Range View of the Future
Pursuit of education improvement requires a strong future orientation and a willingness to make long-term commitments to students and to all stakeholders—communities, employers, faculty, and staff. Planning needs to anticipate many types of changes, including changes in education requirements, instructional approaches, resource availability, technology, and demographics. A major longer-term investment associated with institutional improvement is the investment in creating and sustaining an assessment system focused on learning. This entails faculty education and training in assessment methods. It also entails institutional leadership becoming familiar with research findings and practical applications of assessment methods and learning style information.

Public Responsibility and Citizenship
A college or university's leadership should stress the importance of the institution serving as a role model in its operations. This means protecting public health, safety, and the environment, and engaging in ethical business practices and non-discrimination in all that it does. Planning related to public health, safety, and the environment should anticipate adverse impacts that might arise in facilities management, laboratory operations, and transportation. Ethical business practices need to take into account proper use of public and private funds. Non-discrimination should take into account factors such as student admissions, hiring practices, and treatment of all students and stakeholders. Inclusion of public responsibility areas with an institution's performance system means meeting all local, state, and federal laws and regulatory requirements. It also means treating these and related requirements as areas for continuous improvement "beyond mere compliance." This requires that appropriate measures of progress be created and used in managing performance.

Institutional citizenship refers to leadership and support—within reasonable limits of its resources—of publicly important purposes, including the above-mentioned areas of responsibility. Such purposes might include environmental excellence, community service, and sharing quality-related information. Leadership as an organizational citizen might include influencing other organizations, private and public, to partner for these purposes.

Fast Response
An increasingly important measure of institutional effectiveness is faster and more flex-

ible response to the needs of customers—students and stakeholders—of the institution. Many organizations are learning that explicit focus on and measurement of response times helps to drive the simplification of work organizations and work processes. There are other important benefits derived from this focus: response time improvements often drive simultaneous improvements in organization, quality, and productivity. The world's greatest organizations are learning to make simultaneous improvements in quality, productivity, and response time, while strengthening their customer focus.

Results Orientation
A college or university performance system should focus on results—reflecting and balancing the needs and interests of students and all stakeholders. To meet the sometimes conflicting and changing aims that balance implies, institutional strategy needs to explicitly address all student and stakeholder requirements to ensure that actions and plans meet the differing needs and avoid adverse impact on students and/or stakeholders. The use of a balanced composite of performance indicators offers an effective means to communicate requirements, monitor actual performance, and marshal broadly-based support for improving results.

From the point of view of overall institutional performance and improvement, two areas of performance are particularly important: student performance, and the effectiveness and efficiency of the institution's use of resources.

Education Criteria Framework
The core values and concepts are embodied in seven Categories, as follows:

1.0 Leadership

2.0 Information and Analysis

3.0 Strategic and Operational Planning

4.0 Human Resource Development and Management

5.0 Educational and Business Process Management

6.0 Institutional Performance Results

7.0 Student Focus and Student and Stakeholder Satisfaction

The framework connecting and integrating the categories is given in figure 1. The framework has four basic elements:

Driver—Senior leadership sets direction, creates shared values, goals, and systems, and guides the pursuit of student and institutional performance improvement.

System—A set of well-defined and well-designed processes for improving the institution's performance.

Measures of Progress—Provide a results-oriented basis for channeling activities to deliver ever-improving student and institutional performance.

Goal—The basic aims of the system are to deliver ever-improving educational services, leading to success and satisfaction.

INTEGRATION OF KEY EDUCATION THEMES

The adaptation of the Baldrige Award Criteria to education requires an explanation of how several important educational concepts are addressed throughout the Education Criteria. A discussion of these concepts and how they are addressed follows:

Concept of Excellence

The concept of excellence built into the Criteria is that of demonstrated "value-added" performance. Such performance has two manifestations:

(1) year-to-year improvement in key measures and indicators of overall performance; and
(2) demonstrated value-added leadership in overall performance relative to comparable institutions or appropriate benchmarks.

The value-added concept of excellence is selected because:

(1) it places the major focus on teaching and learning strategies;
(2) it poses similar types of challenges for all colleges and universities regardless of resources or incoming students' preparation and abilities;
(3) it is most likely to stimulate learning-related research and to offer a means for disseminating the results of such research; and
(4) it offers the potential to create an expanding body of knowledge of successful teaching and learning practices in the widest range of institutions.

The focus on value-added contributions by the institution does not presuppose manufac-turing-oriented, mechanistic, or additive models of student development. Nor does the use of a value-added concept imply that a college or university's management system should include documented "procedures" or attempt to define "conformity" or "compliance." Rather, the value-added concept in the Education Criteria means that the institution should view itself as a key development influence (though not the only influence), and that the institution should seek to understand and optimize its influencing factors, guided by an effective assessment strategy, as described below.

Central and crucial to the success of the excellence concept in the Education Criteria is a well-conceived and well-executed assessment strategy. The characteristics of such a strategy should include the following:

• Clear ties between what is assessed and the institution's mission objectives. This means not only what students know, but also what they are able to do.
• A main focus on improvement—of student performance, faculty capabilities, and institutional program performance.
• Assessment as embedded and ongoing. This means that assessment needs to be curriculum-based, and criterion-referenced, aimed at fostering improved understanding of learning goals and overall performance requirements.
• Clear guidelines regarding how assessment results will be used and how they will not be used.
• An ongoing approach for evaluating the assessment system to improve the connection between assessment and student success. Success factors should be developed based on external requirements derived

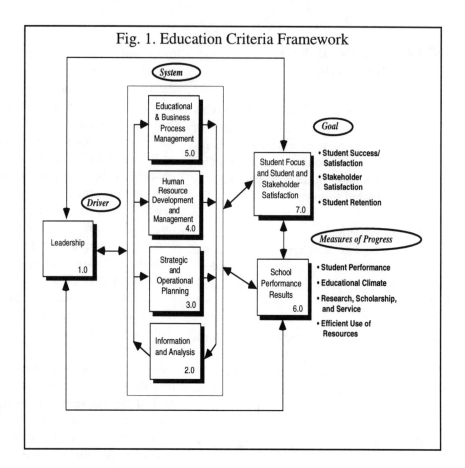

Fig. 1. Education Criteria Framework

from the marketplace, other institutions, and so on.

Mission Specificity

Although education organizations share common aims, individual institutional missions, roles, and programs vary greatly. Use of a single set of criteria to cover all requirements of all organizations means that these requirements need to be interpreted in terms of specific institutional missions. That is, specific requirements and critical success factors differ from institution to institution. For this reason, effective use of the Criteria depends upon operationalizing mission requirements consistently across the seven cat-

egories of the Criteria framework. In particular, the Strategic and Operational Planning Category (3.0) needs to address all key mission requirements, setting the stage for the interpretation of all the other requirements. Similarly, results reported in the Institution Performance Results Category (6.0) need to reflect results that are consistent with the college or university's mission objectives.

The Education Criteria are most explicit in the area of student learning, as this requirement is common to all educational organizations, regardless of their larger missions. Despite this commonality, the focus of student learning and development depends upon the institutional mission. For example, results

HIGH PERFORMING COLLEGES

reported by trade schools, engineering schools, and music schools would be expected to differ and reflect the institutions' programs. Nevertheless, all three types of institutions or units would be expected to show year-to-year improvements in their educational results to demonstrate the effectiveness of their performance improvement results.

The point values for the Items in the Education Criteria represent an initial attempt to provide a basis for approximate early-stage scoring of institutions. In later stages of the evaluation, particularly at the judging stage, point values are less important than the overall pattern of strengths and weaknesses. This means that a pattern of strengths in critical mission areas and weaknesses in non-critical mission areas would receive much higher evaluation than the reverse, regardless of initial scoring. The main role of initial scoring is to identify those participants with sufficient merit to warrant further, more detailed review. Margins of safety are built into the review process to minimize the likelihood of early elimination of applications which demonstrate good progress in performance improvement.

Customers

The Baldrige Award Criteria use the generic term "customers" to reflect the users of products or services. Although marketplace success depends heavily upon user preference, setting organization requirements needs to consider other stakeholders as well. Successful operation of an organization may depend upon satisfying environmental, legal, and other requirements. Thus, meaningful criteria need to incorporate all relevant requirements that organizations must meet to be successful.

Colleges and universities also must respond to a variety of requirements, all of which need to be incorporated into the Education Criteria. The adaptation of the Baldrige Award Criteria to education poses alternative approaches for defining key requirements. The approach selected for the Education Criteria seeks to distinguish between students and stakeholders for purposes of clarity and emphasis. Stakeholders include parents, employers, other institutions, communities, and so on. To further clarify the requirements related to students, the requirements for current students are separated from those of future students. Requirements for current students are more current concrete, specific, and immediate; determining requirements for future students is part of the institution's planning, and needs to take into account changing student populations and changing requirements future students must be able to meet. A major challenge colleges and universities face is "bridging" between current student needs and the needs of future students. This requires an effective learning/change strategy.

Primary Focus on Teaching and Learning

Although the Criteria framework is intended to address all institutional requirements, including research and service, primary emphasis is placed upon teaching and learning. This is done for three main reasons:

1. Teaching and learning are the universal goals of the more than 3,400 colleges and universities in this country. Thus, sharing of teaching and learning strategies and methods would have the greatest impact on our educational system.

2. Those who encourage the creation of a Baldrige Award Category for education cite improvement in teaching and learning as their primary or only rationale for such an award.

3. Research is the primary mission of only a small percentage of college and universities. Peer review systems exist to evaluate research. Funding organizations and businesses provide avenues to channel the directions of much research. Numerous excellent forums and media already exist for sharing research results. Much of the research performed in our colleges and universities involve students as part of the students' overall education. Thus, the educational value of research is incorporated in the Education Criteria as part of teaching and learning. Other important aspects of research—faculty development and student and faculty recruitment—are also addressed in the Criteria.

Systems Concept

The systems concept is reflected in the integrated structure of the Criteria. The structure consists of the seven categories with Category Items listed beneath the Category titles. The integrated structure of the Criteria consists of the numerous direct linkages between the Categories and Items. Such linkages are intended to ensure alignment and integration of the overall requirements. The Criteria stress cause-effect thinking and a process orientation. The intent is to accumulate a body of knowledge to help the institution learn and improve from that learning. One of the main elements in the systems approach is the set of measures and/or indicators used. Such measures and indicators link key processes to key results.

Business Operations

Most colleges and universities carry out a wide variety of activities which directly and indirectly support and/or impact the overall institutional mission and operation, but which are not themselves primarily educational. Examples include food services, facilities management, security, and purchasing. Such activities are addressed in the Education Criteria as "business operations." In general, there are two types of requirements such business operations need to address in an integrated way: (1) requirements of key customers such as students, faculty, staff, and administration; and (2) effective and efficient use of resources. The Education Criteria imply that each business operation should address both types of requirements.

Some institutions might use their business operations as educational experiences and/or means of financial support for students. Such institutions would then be expected to include information regarding these practices in their responses to the Education Criteria.

Employees

The Baldrige Award Criteria use the generic term "employees" for those on the organization's payroll responsible for all aspects of product and service development and delivery. Practices related to the development and utilization of employees are referred to as human resource practices. These Criteria place great emphasis upon employees as a primary strategic resource whose interests, satisfaction, and development are keys to an organization's success.

These same themes are central to success in education and are thus emphasized in the Education Criteria, beginning with the Core

Values and Concepts described earlier. Institutional employees are labeled under three headings: administration, faculty, and staff. The reason for this delineation derives from the main purpose of the Education Criteria— to focus better on critical issues such as leadership, education, and development of all employees. For example, senior administrators, together with other institutional leadership, need to create a leadership system to build and sustain an improvement effort. The strong focus on teaching and learning in the Education Criteria places great emphasis on instructional and assessment practices—important components of faculty development. By singling out faculty, such development requirements can be addressed more explicitly than would be possible if all employee groups' development needs were addressed in more generic language. Staff in the Education Criteria refers to all other employees— those with non-instructional roles. Staff responsibilities vary widely, particularly with regard to contact with faculty and students. The Education Criteria anticipate that all staff are integrated into the institution's mission and management system. This implies a strong mission orientation and customer focus. Staff development needs to reflect these requirements as well as individual development.

Suppliers

The increasing emphasis on design quality, problem prevention, and cost reeducation has led leading businesses to reach back into the supply chain to ensure that incoming parts, materials, and services meet high standards. In many cases, such businesses have undertaken focused efforts to improve supplier performance. Such efforts include joint planning, customer-supplier teams, training, and other partnering arrangements. The Baldrige Award Criteria include an Item (5.4) entitled Management of Supplier Performance, which addresses the important issues associated with supplier performance.

Colleges and universities face similar requirements in their business operations, as they also purchase supplies and services to support institutional programs and operations. Thus, there should be opportunities for institutions to realize improvements in effectiveness and cost through improved management of supplier performance. Such opportunities are addressed in Item 5.6, Business Operations Management, of the Education Criteria. Effective management of supplier performance by the institution entails an analysis of all purchased materials and services to determine critical information such as expenditures, number of suppliers, impact on education, and supplier performance. This analysis should provide key information to create a supplier improvement effort. The purpose should be to improve performance and to lower overall costs.

The underlying concepts in supplier management also relate to incoming students and new faculty. For students, these issues are addressed in Item 5.5., Enrollment Management. For new faculty, these issues are addressed in Item 4.1 Human Resource Planning and Evaluation. In both cases, the concept of working with and development of "suppliers" closely parallels supplier development efforts of leading businesses.

KEY CHARACTERISTICS OF THE EDUCATION CRITERIA

The Criteria are directed toward improved overall institutional performance results.

The Criteria focus principally on five key areas of institutional performance.

Improvements in these five results areas contribute to overall institutional performance. The use of a composite of indicators helps to ensure that strategies are balanced—that they do not trade off among important stakeholders or objectives. The composite of indicators also helps to ensure that institutional strategies bridge short-term and long-term goals.

The Criteria are nonprescriptive.

The Criteria are a set of 28 basic, inter-related, results-oriented requirements. However, the Criteria imply wide latitude in how requirements are met. Accordingly, the Criteria do not prescribe:

• specific tools, techniques, technologies, systems, or starting points;
• that a college or university should or should not have a quality or a planning department or unit; or
• how the institution itself should be organized.

The Criteria do emphasize that these and other factors be regularly evaluated as part of the institution's improvement processes. The factors listed are important and are very likely to change as needs and strategies evolve. The Criteria are nonprescriptive because:

1. The focus is on results, not on procedures, tools, or institutions. Colleges and universities are encouraged to develop and demonstrate creative, adaptive, and flexible approaches for meeting basic requirements. Non-prescriptive requirements are intended to foster incremental and major ("breakthrough") improvement.

2. Selection of tools, techniques, systems, and organizations usually depends upon many factors such as institution size and type, the institution's stage of development, and faculty/staff capabilities.

3. Focus on common requirements within a college or university, rather than on specific procedures, fosters better understanding, communication, and sharing, while supporting creativity in approaches.

The Criteria are comprehensive.

The Criteria address all internal and external requirements of the institution, including those related to fulfilling its public responsibilities. Accordingly, all processes of all institutional units are tied to these requirements. New or changing strategies may be readily adapted within the same set of Criteria requirements.

The Criteria include interrelated (process—results) learning cycles.

There is dynamic linkage among the Criteria requirements. Learning (and action based upon that learning) takes place via feedback among the process and results elements. The learning cycles have four, clearly defined stages:

1. planning, including design of processes, selection of indicators, and deployment of requirements;

2. execution of plans;
3. assessment of progress, taking into account internal and external (results) indicators; and
4. revision of plans based upon assessment findings.

The Criteria emphasize alignment.

The Criteria call for improvement (learning) cycles in all parts of the institution. To ensure that these cycles carried out in different part of the institution support one another, overall aims needs to be consistent or aligned. Alignment in the Criteria is achieved via connecting and reinforcing measures, derived from overall college or university requirements. These measures tie directly to educational value and to operational performance. The use of measures thus channels different activities in agreed-upon directions. Use of measures often avoids the need for detailed procedures or centralization of decision making or process management. Measures thus provide a communications tool and a basis for deploying consistent student and operational performance requirements. Such alignment ensures consistency of purpose while at the same time supporting speed, innovation, and decentralized decision making.

The Criteria are part of a diagnostic system.

The Criteria and the Scoring Guidelines (described in the appendix of *Volume II— Case and Practice*) make up a two-part diagnostic (assessment) system. The Criteria are a set of 28 basic, results-oriented requirements. The Scoring Guidelines spell out the assessment dimensions—Approach, Deployment, and Results—and the key factors used in assessment relative to each dimension.

An assessment thus provides a profile of strengths and areas of improvement relative to the 28 requirements. In this way, the assessment directs attention to actions that contribute to the results composite described above.

1995 EDUCATION CRITERIA ITEM LISTING

Point Values

1.0 Leadership   **90**
    1.1 Senior Adminstration Leadership   40
    1.2 Leadership System and Organization   30
    1.3 Public Responsibility and Citizenship   20

2.0 Information and Analysis   **75**
    2.1 Management of Information and Data   25
    2.2 Comparisons and Benchmarking   15
    2.3 Analysis and Use of Institutional-Level Data   35

3.0 Strategic and Operational Planning   **75**
    3.1 Strategy Development   45
    3.2 Strategy Deployment   30

4.0 Human Resource Development and Management   **150**
    4.1 Human Resource Planning and Evaluation   30
    4.2 Faculty and Staff Work Systems   30
    4.3 Faculty and Staff Development   50
    4.4 Faculty and Staff Well-Being and Satisfaction   40

5.0 Educational and Business Process Management   **150**
    5.1 Education Design   40
    5.2 Education Delivery   25
    5.3 Education Support Service Design and Delivery   25
    5.4 Research, Scholarship, and Service   20
    5.5 Enrollment Management   20
    5.6 Business Operations Management   20

6.0 Institutional Performance Results   **230**
    6.1 Student Performance Results   100
    6.2 Education Climate Improvement Results   50
    6.3 Research, Scholarship, and Service Results   40
    6.4 Business Performance Results   40

7.0 Student Focus and Student and Stakeholder Satisfaction   **230**
    7.1 Current Student Needs and Expectations   40
    7.2 Future Student Needs and Expectations   30
    7.3 Stakeholder Relationship Management   40
    7.4 Student & Stakeholder Satisfaction Determination 30
    7.5 Student and Stakeholder Satisfaction Results   50
    7.6 Student and Stakeholder Satisfaction Comparison 40

TOTAL POINTS   **1000**

1995 EDUCATION CRITERIA

1.0 Leadership (*90 pts.*)

The **Leadership** Category examines senior administrators' personal leadership and involvement in creating and sustaining a student focus, clear goals, high expectations, and a leadership system that promotes performance excellence. Also examined is how these objectives and expectations are integrated into the institution's management system.

1.1 Senior Administration Leadership (*40 pts.*)

Describe senior administrators' leadership and personal involvement in setting directions and in developing and maintaining a leadership system and a climate fostering excellence.

A   D   R

A=alignment
D=deployment
R=results

AREAS TO ADDRESS

a. how senior administrators provide effective leadership and direction in improving the institution's performance and capabilities. Describe how senior administrators: (1) create and reinforce high expectations throughout the institution; (2) set directions and performance excellence goals and measures through strategic planning; (3) maintain a climate conducive to teaching and learning, including safety and equity; and (4) review student-related and overall institutional performance and trends.

b. how senior administrator evaluate and improve the effectiveness of the institution's leadership system, organization, and policies to purse performance improvement goals. Describe: (1) how this evaluation addresses the effects of institutional practices and policies on student, faculty, and staff performance, learning environment, and student learning; and (2) how this evaluation addresses senior administrators' knowledge and use of continuous improvement cycles in performance improvement.

1.2 Leadership System and Organization (*30 pts.*)

Describe how the institution's student focus and performance expectations are integrated into the institution's leadership system, organization, and policies.

A   D   R

AREAS TO ADDRESS

a. how the institution's leadership system, management, organization, and policies focus on student and overall institutional performance improvement objectives. Describe: (1) how these objectives are incorporated into institutional practices; and (2) how the institution maintains focus and cooperation among units or departments to pursue these objectives.

b. how the institution effectively communicates and regularly reinforces its expectations and directions throughout the college or university community. Describe policies and practices that reflect the expectations and directions.

c. how overall institutional and individual unit performance are reviewed and how the reviews are used to improve performance. Describe: (1) the types, frequency, and content of reviews and who conducts them; (2) how the results of reviews are used to improve performance; and (3) how reviews are used to strengthen awareness and use of learning-oriented assessment in all education programs.

1.3 Public Responsibility and Citizenship *(20 pts.)*

Describe how the institution includes its responsibilities to the public in its performance improvement practices. Describe also how the institution leads and contributes as an organizational citizen in its key communities.

AREAS TO ADDRESS

a. how the institution includes its public responsibilities in its performance evaluation and improvement efforts. Describe: (1) the risks and regulatory and other legal requirements addressed in planning and in setting operational requirements and targets; (2) how the institution looks ahead to anticipate public concerns associated with its operations; and (3) how the institution promotes legal and ethical conduct in its operation.

b. how the institution serves as a role model in areas of public interest and concern.

2.0 Information and Analysis (*75 pts.*)

The **Information and Analysis** Category examines the management and effectiveness of use of data and information to support overall mission-related performance excellence.

2.1 Management of Information and Data (*25 pts.*)

Describe the institution's selection and management of information and data used for planning, management, and evaluation of overall college or university performance improvement.

AREAS TO ADDRESS

a. how information and data needed to drive improvement of education and business operational performance are selected and managed. Describe: (1) the rationale for the main types of information and data used to drive and to track educational progress; (2) the rationale for the main types of information and data used to drive and to track business operational performance; and (3) how needs such as reliability, rapid access, rapid update, and privacy are addressed.

b. how the institution evaluates and improves the selection, analysis, and integration of information and data, aligning them with the institution's priorities. Describe how the evaluation considers: (1) scope of information and data; (2) analysis and use of information and data to support overall performance improvement; and (3) feedback from users of information and data.

2.2 Comparisons and Benchmarking (*15 pts.*)

Describe the institution's processes for selecting and using comparative information and data to support overall college or university performance improvement.

AREAS TO ADDRESS

a. how comparisons and benchmarking information and data are selected and used to help drive improvement of overall institutional performance. Describe: (1) how needs and priorities are determined; (2) criteria for seeking appropriate information and data—from within and outside the academic community; (3) how the benchmarking information and data are used within the institution to improve understanding of processes and process performance; and (4) how the information and data are used to set improvement targets and/or encourage breakthrough approaches.

---

b. how the institution evaluates and improves its overall process for selecting and using comparisons and benchmarking information and data to improve planning and overall college or university performance.

2.3 Analysis and Use of Institutional-Level Data (*35 pts.*)

Describe how data related to educational progress and business operational performance are analyzed to support institutional-level review, action, and planning.

AREAS TO ADDRESS

a. how information and data from all parts of the institution are integrated and analyzed to support education-related reviews, decisions, and planning. Describe how analysis is used to gain understanding of: (1) student and student group performance; (2) institutional program performance; and (3) comparative performance of students, student groups, and institutional programs.

b. how information and data from all parts of the institution are integrated and analyzed to support business operations-related reviews, decisions, and planning. Describe how analysis is used to gain understanding of: (1) college or university business operational performance; and (2) college or university business operational performance relative to appropriately selected organizations.

3.0 Strategic and Operational Planning (*75 pts.*)

The **Strategic and Operational Planning** Category examines how the institution sets strategic directions and how it determines key plan requirements. Also examined is how the plan requirements are translated into an effective performance management system, with a primary focus on student performance.

3.1. Strategy Development *(45 pts.)*

Describe how the institution's strategic planning process and how this process determines and addresses kept student and overall college or university performance. Describe also how this process focuses on student and overall institutional performance improvement and includes an effective basis for the implementation of plans and the evaluation of progress relative to plans.

3.2 Strategy Deployment *(30 pts.)*

Summarize the institution's critical **success** factors and how they are deployed. Show how the institution' s performance projects into the future.

4.0 Human Resource Development and Management *(150 pts.)*

The **Human Resource Development and Management** Category examines how faculty and staff development are aligned with the institution's performance objectives. Also examined are the institution's efforts to build and maintain a climate conducive to performance excellence, full participation, and personal and organizational growth.

4.1 Human Resources Planning and Evaluation *(30 pts.)*

Describe how the institution's human resource planning and evaluation are aligned with the institution's overall performance improvement plans and address the development and well being of faculty and staff.

AREAS TO ADDRESS

a. how the institution translates overall performance requirements from planning (Category 3.0) to specific human resource plans. Summarize key plans in the following areas: (1) faculty and staff preparation and development; (2) faculty and staff recruitment; (3) promotion, compensation, and benefits; and (4) expectations of faculty and academic units. For (1) through (4), distinguish between the short term and the longer term, and segment by employee category and types, as appropriate.

b. how the institution evaluates and improves its human resource planning and the alignment of human resource plans with overall plans. Include how faculty- and staff-related data and institution performance data are analyzed and used: (1) to evaluate the development and well-being of all categories and types of faculty and staff; (2) to evaluate the linkage of human resource practices with key performance results; and (3) to ensure that reliable and complete human resource information is available for planning.

4.2 Faculty and Staff Work Systems *(30 pts.)*

Describe how the institution's faculty and staff position responsibilities promote a student focus, cross-functional cooperation, and high performance. Describe also how evaluation, compensation, promotion, and recognition reinforce these objectives.

HIGH PERFORMING COLLEGES

AREAS TO ADDRESS

a. how faculty responsibilities promote a focus on student performance improvement. Describe how the responsibilities: (1) ensure effective communications and cooperation across functions or units that need to work together to meet student and college and university educational requirements; and (2) are reinforced by the institution's approach to evaluation, compensation, promotion, and recognition.

b. how the institution's work and job design promote high staff performance. Describe how work and job design: (1) create opportunities for initiative and self-directed responsibility; (2) foster flexibility and rapid response to changing requirements; (3) ensure effective communications and cooperation across functions or units that need to work together to meet student and or business operational requirements; and (4) are reinforced by the institution's approach to evaluation, compensation, promotion, and recognition.

4.3 Faculty and Staff Development *(50 pts.)*

Describe how the institution's faculty and staff development advance college or university plans and contributes to faculty and staff performance improvement, development, and advancement.

AREAS TO ADDRESS

a how the institution encourages and enables faculty to meet institution and personal objectives. Describe how each of the following is addressed: (1) orientation of new faculty regarding key institution plans and expectations; (2) workshops, classes, and training programs for all faculty addressing key performance requirements and performance assessment methods; and (3) how the institution evaluates the effectiveness of faculty development efforts.

b. how the institution's staff education and training are designed, delivered, reinforced, and evaluated. Include: (1) how employees and supervisors work together in determining specific education and training needs and designing education and training; (2) how education and training are delivered; (3) how knowledge and skills are reinforced through on-the job application; and (4) how education and training are evaluated and improved to achieve institutional and personal objectives.

4.4 Faculty and Staff Well-Being and Satisfaction *(40 pts.)*

A D R

Describe how the institution maintains a work environment and a work climate conducive to the well-being and satisfaction of faculty and staff and focused on the institution's performance objectives.

AREAS TO ADDRESS

a. how the institution maintains a safe and healthful work environment. Describe: (1) how faculty and staff well-being factors such as health, safety, and ergonomics are included in improvement activities; and (2) for each factor relevant and important to the institution's work environment, principal performance improvement requirements, measures and /or indicators, and targets. Note significant differences based upon differences in work environments or special requirements among faculty and staff categories or units.

b. what services, facilities, activities, and opportunities the institution makes available to faculty and staff to support their overall well-being and satisfaction and/or enhance their work experience and development potential.

c. how the institution determines faculty and staff satisfaction, well-being, and motivation. Include a brief description of methods, frequency, the specific factors used in this determination, and how the information is used to improve satisfaction, well-being, and motivation. Note any important differences in methods or factors used for different categories or types of employees, as appropriate.

5.0 Educational and Business Process Management *(150pts.)*

The **Educational and Business Process Management** Category examines the key aspects of process management, including learning-focused education design, education delivery, institutional services, and business operations. The Category examines how key processes are designed, effectively managed, and improved to achieve higher performance.

5.1 Education Design *(40 pts.)*

Describe how new and/or modified educational programs and offerings are designed and introduced.

AREAS TO ADDRESS

a. how educational programs and offerings are designed. Describe how the institution ensures that: (1) all programs and offerings address student needs and meet high standards; (2) sequencing and offering linkages are appropriately considered; (3) a measurement plan is in place; and (4) faculty are properly prepared.

b. how design takes into account educational programs and offering delivery. Describe how the institution ensures that all educational programs and offerings: (l) focus on active learning, anticipating and preparing for individual differences in student learning rates and styles; (2) make effective use of formative and summative assessment; (3) have adequate faculty-student contact, and (4) include appropriate formative and summative feedback mechanisms.

c. how the institution evaluates and improves its design of educational programs and offerings. Describe: (1) the factors and information used in the evaluation; and (2) the frequency and content of evaluations and who conducts the evaluation.

5.2 Education Delivery *(25 pts.)*

Describe how the institution ensures that delivery of educational programs and offerings meets the design requirements.

AREAS TO ADDRESS

a. how the institution ensures that ongoing educational programs and offerings meet the design requirements addressed in Item 5.1. Describe: (1) what observations, measures, and/or indicators are used to provide timely information to help students and faculty.

b. how educational programs and offerings are evaluated and improved. Describe how each of the following is used or considered: (1) information from students and stakeholders; (2) benchmarking best practices in education and other fields; (3) use of assessment results; (4) peer evaluation; (5) research on learning, assessment, and faculty presentation; (6) information from employers and governing bodies: and (7) use of technology.

5.3 Education Support Service Design and Delivery *(25 pts.)*

Describe how the institution's education support services are designed and managed to meet the needs of students and key stakeholders.

AREAS TO ADDRESS

a. how key education support services are selected and designed. Include: (1) how key requirements for each service are set, taking into account the needs of students and faculty; (2) how the key requirements are translated into effective operational requirements, including appropriate observations and/or measurements; and (3) how the institution ensures that education support services are performing effectively.

b. how the education support services are evaluated and improved. Describe how each of the following is used or considered: (1) feedback from students and faculty; (2) benchmarking; (3) peer evaluation; and (4) data from observation and measurements.

5.4 Research, Scholarship, and Service *(20 pts.)*

Describe how the institution contributes to knowledge creation, knowledge transfer, and service via programs and activities. Describe also the benefits of these programs and activities to key communities and to the institution's mission objectives.

AREAS TO ADDRESS

a. how the institution contributes to knowledge creation and knowledge transfer to external communities. Describe: (1) key goals, target communities, and key measures and/or indicators of benefits; and (2) how the institution actively seeks to ensure the effective transfer of knowledge to key communities.

b. how research, scholarship, and service contribute to student learning, faculty development, and other key institutional mission objectives.

c. how research, scholarship, and service activities are evaluated and improved. Describe how each of the following is used or considered: (1) feedback from participants and beneficiaries; (2) peer evaluation; (3) data from observations and measurements; and (4) benchmarking information.

5.5. Enrollment Management *(20 pts.)*

Describe how the institution manages its recruitment, admissions, and/or entry processes to ensure effective transitions for incoming students. Describe also the institution's actions and plans to improve the preparation of potential students.

AREAS TO ADDRESS

a. how the institution communicates key requirements to feeder schools or colleges, families, and prospective students to ensure proper choice and effective transition. Describe how the following are addressed: (1) equity; (2) orientation, placement, and other services; and (3) feedback to feeder schools or colleges.

b. how the institution evaluates and improves its management of interactions with feeder schools or colleges, prospective students, and families. Describe current actions and plans: (1) to assist feeder schools and colleges and families to make proper choices and to prepare students for entry; and (2) to improve selection and admissions processes based upon feedback from feeder schools or colleges, students, and families.

5.6 Business Operations and Management *(20 pts.)*

Describe how the institution's key business operations are managed so that current requirements are met and operational performance is continuously improved.

AREAS TO ADDRESS

a. how the institution ensures effective management of its key business operations. For each key business operation, describe: (1) how customers are defined; (2) how key customer requirements are determined; (3) how measures and/or indicators and goals are set; and (4) how performance is monitored. For key purchasing activities, briefly describe how requirements are communicated to suppliers and how the institution determines whether or not its requirements are met by suppliers.

> b. how business operations are evaluated and improved to achieve better performance, including cost, productivity, and cycle time. Describe how each of the following is used or considered: (1) feedback from customers of the processes; (2) benchmarking processes, performance, and cost; and (3) process analysis/redesign. For key purchasing activities, briefly describe the supplier improvement process.

6.0 Institution Performance Results *(230 pts.)*

The **Institution Performance Results** Category examines student performance and improvement, improvement in the institution's education climate and institutional services, and improvement in performance of business operations. Also examined are performance levels relative to comparable institutions and/or appropriately selected organizations.

6.1 Student Performance Results *(100 pts.)*

Summarize results of improvement in student performance using key measures and/or indicators of such performance.

AREAS TO ADDRESS

a. current levels and trends in key measures and/or indicators of student performance.

b. for the results presented in 6.1a, demonstrate that there has been improvement in student performance.

c. for the results in 6.1a, show how student performance and performance trends compare with comparable institutions and/or comparable student populations.

6.2 Institution Education Climate Improvement Results (50 pts.)

Summarize results of improvement in the institution's education climate using key measures and/or indicators of this climate.

AREAS TO ADDRESS

a. current levels and trends in key measures and/or indicators of institutional education climate. Graphs and tables should include appropriate comparative data, when available.

6.3 Research, Scholarship, and Service Results *(40 pts.)*

Summarize results of improvement in the institution's contribution to knowledge creation, knowledge transfer, and service.

AREAS TO ADDRESS

a. current levels and trends in key measures and/or indicators of the institution's contribution to knowledge creation, knowledge transfer, and service. Graphs and tables should include appropriate comparative and benchmark data.

6.4 Business Performance Results *(40 pts.)*

Summarize results of improvement efforts using key measures and/or indicators of business operational and financial performance.

AREAS TO ADDRESS

a. current levels and trends in key measures and/or indicators of business operational and financial performance. Graphs and tables should include appropriate comparative and benchmark data.

7.0 Student Focus and Student and Stakeholder Satisfaction *(230 pts.)*

The **Student Focus and Student and Stakeholder Satisfaction** Category examines how the institution determines student and stakeholder needs and expectations. Also examined are levels and trends in key measures of student and stakeholder satisfaction and satisfaction relative to comparable institutions and/or appropriately selected institutions.

7.1 Current Student Needs and Expectations *(40 pts.)*

Describe how the institution develops and maintains awareness of the needs and expectations of current students and seeks to create an overall climate conducive to active learning, well being, and satisfaction for all students.

AREAS TO ADDRESS

a. how the institution develops and maintains awareness of key general and special needs and expectations of current students. Describe: (1) how student needs and expectations are determined, aggregated, and analyzed to ensure the availability and preparation of appropriate offerings, facilities, and services; and (2) how this information is deployed to all appropriate institutional units.

b. how the institution monitors student utilization of offerings, facilities, and services to determine their influence upon satisfaction and active learning. Include how information on student segments and/or individual students is developed for purposes of engaging students in active learning.

c. how the institution evaluates and improves its processes for determining current student needs and expectations. Describe: (1) how this process utilizes information from students, faculty, staff, and other stakeholders; and (2) how this information is used throughout the institution to improve satisfaction and active learning.

7.2 Future Student Needs and Expectations *(30 pts.)*

Describe how the institution determines needs and expectations of future students and maintains awareness of the key factors affecting these needs and expectations.

AREAS TO ADDRESS

a. how the institution determines and anticipates changing needs and expectations for future students. Summarize: (1) demographic factors and trends that may bear upon enrollments and needs; (2) changing requirements and expectations its graduates will face; (3) changing needs and expectations resulting from national, state, or local requirements; and (4) educational alternatives available to its pool of future students. For each of these four factors, briefly describe the basis for the conclusions.

b. how the institution analyzes the information from 7.2a to develop actionable data and information for planning.

c. how the institution evaluates and improves its processes for determining emerging needs and expectations. Describe: (1) how the institution's own trend data are used to support the determination; and (2) how reports of national, state, educational, and research organizations are used.

7.3 Stakeholder Relationship Management *(40 pts.)*

A   D   R

Describe how the institution provides effective linkages to key stakeholders to support and enhance the institution's mission-related services and to meet stakeholder needs and expectations.

AREAS TO ADDRESS

a. how the institution creates clear bases for relationships with key stakeholders. For each stakeholder, describe: (1) key objectives of the relationship; (2) key needs of the stakeholder and how these needs are determined and kept current; and (3) key needs of the institution and how these needs are communicated to the stakeholder.

b. how the institution maintains effective stakeholder relationships. Describe: (1) how regular and special access needs are addressed; (2) how the institution follows up on its interactions with key stakeholders to determine satisfaction, progress in meeting objectives, and to resolve problems; (3) key measures and/or indicators the institution uses to monitor the effectiveness and progress of its key relationships; and (4) how the institution develops partnerships with key stakeholders to pursue common purposes.

c. how the institution evaluates and improves its relationships with key stakeholders. Describe how the evaluation/improvement process operates, including the key information and data and how they are used.

7.4 Student and Stakeholder Satisfaction Determination *(30 pts.)*

A   D   R

Describe how the institution determines student and stakeholder satisfaction and their satisfaction relative to comparable institutions.

AREAS TO ADDRESS

a. how the institution determines the satisfaction of current and past students. Include: (1) a brief description of processes and measurement scales used; frequency of determination; and how objectivity and validity are ensured. Indicate significant differences, if any, in processes and measurement scales for different student groups; (2) how satisfaction measurements capture key information on factors that bear upon students' motivation and active learning; and (3) how student satisfaction relative to comparable institutions is determined.

---

b. how the institution determines the satisfaction of key stakeholders. Include: (l) a brief description of processes and measurement scales used; frequency of determination; and how objectivity and validity are ensured. Indicate significant differences, if any, in processes and measurement scales for different stakeholder needs; and (3) how stakeholder satisfaction relative to comparable institutions is determined.

c. how the institution evaluates and improves its overall processes and measurement scales for determining students and stakeholder satisfaction. Include how dissatisfaction indicators such as gains and losses of students and complaints are used in the evaluation/ improvement process. Describe also how the evaluation takes into account the effectiveness of the use of satisfaction information and data throughout the institution.

7.5 Student and Stakeholder Satisfaction Results *(50 pts.)*

Summarize the institution's student and stakeholder satisfaction and dissatisfaction results using key measures and/or indicators of performance.

AREAS TO ADDRESS

a. current levels and trends in key measures and/or indicators of satisfaction and dissatisfaction of current and past students.

b. current levels and trends in key measures and/or indicators of satisfaction and dissatisfaction of key stakeholders.

7.6 Student and Stakeholder Satisfaction Comparison *(40 pts.)*

Compare the institution's satisfaction results with those of comparable institutions.

AREAS TO ADDRESS

a. current levels and trends in key measures and/or indicators of student satisfaction relative to comparable institutions.

b. current levels and trends in key measures and/or indicators of stakeholder satisfaction to comparable institutions.

John R. Barker, Institutional Research Associate at the University of Mississippi Medical Center in Jackson, Mississippi, is an advisor to several institutional committees, a research consultant for numerous projects, and a vocal proponent of evidence-based management of academic health centers. He is an evaluator for the Malcolm Baldrige National Quality Award Education Pilot and was a member of the inaugural class of evaluators in the Tennessee Quality Award program. Barker currently serves as principal program evaluator of the Mississippi Health Sciences Information Network project funded by the National Library of Medicine.

Valerie Broughton is Director of Institutional Research and Associate Vice Chancellor for Academic Administration at the University of Minnesota–Duluth, and previously has held positions at Wichita State University and the Iowa Board of Regents Office. She has been active in the Association for Institutional Research for more than ten years, serving on its executive committee and chairing the Higher Education Data Policy Committee. In addition to papers in her field of education research and evaluation, she has written chapters and articles on the application of quality management principles to the academic setting.

Thomas E. Corts, President of Samford University in Birmingham, Alabama, has completed terms as chair of the Commission on Colleges of the Southern Association and as president of the American Association of Presidents of Independent Colleges and Universities, and currently serves as President-elect of the Southern Association of Colleges and Schools. He has contributed articles to many professional journals and has won numerous honors, including the Outstanding Educator Award in Alabama, Citizen of the Year Award, and the National Council of Accreditation for Teacher Education's Most Supportive President Award.

Linda Deneen is Director of Information Services at the University of Minnesota–Duluth where she is responsible for both academic and administrative computing, telecommunications and networking, and audiovisual services. Prior to her directorship, she served as a faculty member and department head in computer science at the University. She has also been a faculty member in mathematics, statistics, and computer science at Beloit College, and has been active in Educom and CAUSE, professional associations for information technology professionals in higher education.

Satinder K. Dhiman is Assistant Professor in the School of Business and Management at Woodbury University in Burbank, California, where he was honored as Faculty Member of the Year in 1995. His professional experience includes faculty positions at Glendale Community College and at DAV College in India. Dhiman's research and teaching interests span a broad area—from accounting and finance to the application of quality principles to higher education. He also has a number of publications dealing specifically with academic leaders' ability to create cultural transformations at their institutions.

Ronald F. Dow is Associate Dean for Planning and Administrative Services at Pennsylvania State University Libraries. Previously, he has been a first vice president and director of libraries at Shearson Lehman Brothers and American Express. Dow has written more than twenty-five journal articles, monographs, and book chapters. Dow has been a frequent speaker on topics related to library innovation, human resource development, and total quality management. He is currently working on his dissertation in pursuit of a Ph.D. in higher education.

John P. (Jack) Evans, Professor and former Dean of the Kenan-Flagler Business School at The University of North Carolina at Chapel Hill, served first as an examiner then as a senior examiner, and currently serves as a judge for the Malcolm Baldrige National Quality Award. In addition, he serves as a judge for the North Carolina Quality Leadership Award. He is a past-president of the American Assembly of Collegiate Schools of Business (AACSB) and was the chair of the AACSB task force that redesigned the accreditation process for business schools.

John W. Harris is Assistant to the Provost for Quality Assessment and Orlean Bullard Beeson Professor of Education at Samford University. Prior to his current positions, Harris taught at David Lipscomb University, Florida State University, University of North Carolina at Greensboro, University of Georgia, and Tennessee State University. Co-author of *Assessment in Education* and co-editor of *Quality Quest in the Academic Process*, he is also an evaluator for the Malcolm Baldrige National Quality Award Education Pilot.

Mary Ann Heverly has been the Director of Institutional Research at Delaware County Community College since 1983. With the advent of quality management at the College in 1987, she has reorganized institutional research services to respond to the changing needs of the college's personnel for training in the collection and use of data. She is a member of the publications board of the Association of Institutional Research (AIR), President of the National Council for Research and Planning (NCRP), and has published extensively in the field of institutional research.

Susan G. Hillenmeyer is Vice President for Quality and Professional Development at Belmont University in Nashville, Tennessee, where she works directly with the president in leading Belmont's quality improvement effort. Much of her study and many of her publications deal with adult learning and quality improvement in higher education. She is an active consultant and public speaker for both businesses and universities. Her efforts center around quality systems, team building, and productivity as they relate to education and service industries. In 1993, Hillenmeyer became a Malcolm Baldrige National Quality Award examiner and currently serves as a senior evaluator for the Education Pilot Program. She also serves on the board of directors for the Tennessee Quality Award.

Jon A. Hittman, President of IDEACO—an education and management consulting firm located in St. Louis, Missouri—is a senior evaluator for the Malcolm Baldrige National Quality Award. His professional experience includes serving as director of the ITT Technical Institute in Austin, Texas, as quality coordinator for the Texas Higher Education Coordinating Board, and as a member of the Austin Quality Council's Education Committee. He has also served as a member of numerous accreditation site visit teams and has authored several articles on the topic of quality and education.

Marian L. Houser, Visiting Instructor in the Speech Communication program at Miami University, currently supervises graduate teaching assistants in the Department of Communication while pursuing her research interests on the relationship between classroom performance, immediacy, relevance, and affinity-seeking behavior. Houser has been recognized by the Department of Communication with her nomination for the Graduate Student Teaching Award and receipt of the Outstanding Student in the Department of Communication Award from faculty and staff. She is an active member of the Speech Communication Association.

Reid Johnson is Director of Institutional Effectiveness, Planning and Assessment at Francis Marion University in Florence, South Carolina. Since 1985, Johnson has devoted his attention to higher education, particularly assessing student progress as a primary indicator of college and university effectiveness. During that time he has published numerous articles, book chapters, newsletters, and monographs on the subject, as well as serving as Professor in psychology at Winthrop University and Director of the fifty-member South Carolina Higher Education Assessment Network. He is an evaluator for the Malcolm Baldrige National Quality Award Education Pilot Program.

Elisabeth A. Luther is Human Resources Manager for R. G. Ray Corporation. Prior to joining the Ray Corporation, she was the director of human resources at Alverno College, served as a member of the Quality Council, and taught in workshops on continuous quality improvement. She has also worked as an employment and benefits supervisor at Nestle Corporation where she was involved in quality training and was certified as a Master Facilitator in such areas as Quality Action Teams and Continuous Daily Improvement.

William McEachern is Dean and Associate Professor in the School of Business at Alverno College in Milwaukee, Wisconsin. Before coming to Alverno, McEachern worked in public accounting in Canada and the United States. At Alverno, his teaching interests include accounting, finance, and small business management. He has also been active in the design and implementation of student performance assessments. In addition to serving on Alverno's Quality Council, he is a member of the Milwaukee Section of the American Society for Quality Control and the Milwaukee First in Quality Committee.

Kathleen A. O'Brien, currently Academic Dean at Alverno College in Milwaukee, Wisconsin, established the Business and Management Division at Alverno in 1976 and chaired it until 1991, when she became academic dean. She has written numerous articles and book chapters on the relationship of performance assessment and continuous quality improvement. In addition, O'Brien has served as a consultant to colleges and universities on ability-based education and assessment, both throughout the U.S., the United Kingdom, and the Netherlands.

James T. Rogers is Chief Executive Officer of the Commission on Colleges of the Southern Association of Colleges and Schools. Rogers was named to his present position after a fifteen year career as president of Brenau College in Gainesville, Georgia. Prior to his Brenau presidency, Rogers held various teaching and administrative positions at Pensacola Junior College and Armstrong State College in Savannah. He is currently the co-chair of the National Policy Board on Higher Education Institutional Accreditation, the entity working to redesign the structure for reviewing and certifying accrediting bodies.

Daniel Seymour, President of Q-Systems, a quality management consulting firm located in Palm Springs, California, has held teaching and administrative positions at the College of William and Mary and the University of Rhode Island. He has been a visiting scholar at UCLA and the Claremont Graduate School. The author of fourteen books—including the American Council on Education's *On Q: Causing Quality in Higher Education* (1992) and *Once Upon a Campus: Lessons for Improving Quality and Productivity in Higher Education* (1995)—Seymour is also a senior evaluator for the Malcolm Baldrige National Quality Award's Education Pilot.

Gary M. Shulman is Professor and Communication Department Chair at Miami University. He has been the recipient of the prestigious annual Speech Communication Association Golden Anniversary Publication Award, the Central States Communication Association Outstanding Teacher Award, and a Lilly Foundation Post-Doctoral Fellowship. His research interests include the use of quality improvement principles in educational organizations, assessment, preparing for and coping with organizational change, and the value of promoting organizational learning. He is an active member of the International Communication Association, the Academy of Management, and the American Association for Higher Education.

Eugene R. Smoley, Jr. is President of The Cheswick Center, a research and education trust established to assist in the improvement of nonprofit governance. He is also Associate Professor of Educational Leadership at the University of Delaware. Smoley has been a vice president of Towers Perrin, an international human resources consulting firm, and has worked with the U.S. Department of Education in studying techniques for reducing costs in colleges and universities. His current consulting and research projects emphasize various aspects of governance, organizational analysis, human resource management, and strategic planning.

Gloriana St. Clair, Associate Dean and Head of Information Access Services at the University Libraries of the Pennsylvania State University, is also Editor of *College & Research Libraries*, the refereed journal of the Association of College and Research Libraries. She has authored many scholarly articles and editorials herself, including several on the subject of quality, and has served as an examiner for the Pennsylvania Quality Leadership Award. Prior to her current position, St. Clair was an administrator at both the Oregon State University and Texas A & M University libraries.

Susanna B. Staas is Quality Coordinator and Assistant to the President of Delaware County Community College. Her primary responsibility is to assist administrators and faculty members in applying quality management principles to their work. Staas also serves as an Evaluator for the Malcolm Baldrige National Quality Award's Education Pilot. She has made many presentations on the subject of quality in education at national conferences, and consults on the subject through Delaware County Community College's Center for Quality and Productivity.

Linda M. Thor is President of Rio Salado Community College, one of the Maricopa Community Colleges in Phoenix, Arizona. The author of *Total Quality Management in Community Colleges,* she serves on the Arizona Governor's Advisory Council on Quality and is President-elect of the Continuous Quality Improvement Network for Community and Technical Colleges. Thor also serves on the board of the Greater Phoenix Economic Council, the board of the Council for Adult and Experiential Learning, the AACC Commission on Academic and Student Development, the ACE Commission on Leadership Development, and is President of the Arizona Community College Presidents' Council.

equity theory 218–221, 223, 224, 225, 241
and Category 7.0 223
assumptions 221

F

faculty and staff participation 150, 307
faculty development 169, 178, 179
fast response 83, 150, 246, 309
Federal Express 28, 34, 35, 36, 38
feedback 54, 63, 70
reports 63, 70
force field diagram 101, 102

G

Globe Metallurgical Inc. 29
goal setting 155, 156, 307
stretch goals 204, 206
Gore, Al 38
governing or coordinating boards 263, 268, 280, 281
activities 283–284
desired competencies of 282–283
purpose 263
traditional roles 263–264, 269–270
working with president 297–299
Governor's Award for Quality 122
winners 122
GTE 32, 38, 57

H

human resources
management compared to CQI 171
objectives 170
theory 170–171
hypothetical investment reports 34–35

I

IBM 33, 36, 44, 48, 132
information management 126, 127, 138
systems 126, 127
information sharing 47–53
institutional effectiveness 72

K

key processes 186, 197

L

language
translating from business 136, 141, 145, 157, 164, 166
leadership xiii, 107
and hypocrisy 97
as driver of the system 90, 98
attributes 110
defined 108
effective 108, 109
focused on quality 97
post-heroic 109
role of 74, 112, 115, 116, 280
styles 97, 109–110
learning-centered education 149, 150, 162
long-range view 150, 309
loosely coupled systems 89, 90

M

Malcolm Baldrige National Quality Award (MBNQA) 304–318
and accountability 65
as an assessment instrument 54, 64, 66, 68, 69, 70, 244, 263
as an award for achievement 55–56, 70
as an educational program 54, 311–314
Criteria 54, 56, 61, 62, 63, 68, 69
1.0 Leadership 108, 112, 113, 119–120, 274
2.0 Information and Analysis xiii, 108, 125, 133, 135, 139, 274
3.0 Strategic and Operational Planning xiii, 108, 273
4.0 Human Resource Development and Management xiii, 177
5.0 Educational and Business Process Management xiii, 186
6.0 School Performance Results xiii, 151, 273
7.0 Student Focus–Student/Stakeholder Satisfaction xiii, 151, 274

criticisms of 55
defined 23, 24
Education Pilot Criteria 56, 141, 146, 164, 304–318
framework 61, 66
origins 26, 245
program strategy 72
  pitfalls to avoid 155–157
scoring guidelines 37
values 58
winners of 32, 57
management by objectives 194
management-by-fact 94, 308
Metanoic organization 110, 111
Metropolitan Life 44
Miami University 218, 225–239, 241, 338, 340
mission 169, 170, 175, 176, 179, 180, 181, 182
Motorola 28, 34, 35, 36, 47, 48, 50, 117

N

Northwest Missouri State University 209, 292

O

operating systems 129, 130
organizational adaptation 74, 77
organizational boundaries
  contraction 79, 80
  expansion 79
organizational development 74, 77, 78
organizational identity 80–82, 83
organizational structure 75

P

paradigm(s) 18, 22, 23, 24, 65, 112, 186
  defined xii
partnership development 308
Pennsylvania State University 145, 158, 159, 163, 297
performance
  defined xii
  measures xiii, xiv

performance measures 148
plan-do-check-act cycle (P-D-C-A) 129, 275
process
  defined 195
process management
  and higher education 189–194
  barriers to 191–192
  characteristics 189
  defined 187–189
  history 187
  supporting infrastructure 190–193
processes 245
production model 210
professional bureaucracy 19–22, 24
professional organizations
  Academic Quality Consortium ix, x, xi, xv
  American Association of Higher Education (AAHE) ix, xi, xv, 169, 270, 292
  American Council on Education (ACE) 63
  American Society for Quality Control 260
  Association of Governing Boards 280
  NACUBO 232, 236
   NACUBO/Coopers & Lybrand Benchmarking Project 237, 238
  Southern Association of Colleges and Schools 249
program review 83, 84
public citizen 117
Public Law 100-107 26, 28, 38, 55, 62
public responsibility 309

Q

quality
  as a descriptive term 24
  customer-driven 21
  defined 84
  in the 21st century 38
  in the academy 21, 60, 61, 100, 101
  transcendent notion of 22
quality assurance 22, 263, 264
  limitations 265–266

R

reflective practices 24
results 245, 310
results orientation 150, 162
Rio Salado Community College 118, 120,
        121, 122, 123, 298
Ritz-Carlton 31, 44, 46, 52

S

scholarship of discovery 169
scoring guidelines 37, 91
    approach 91, 108, 247
    deployment 91, 108, 247
    emphasis on results 37
    results 91, 108
self reports 30, 30–31
servant leader 110
Smith, Adam 187
social comparison theories 219, 220, 221,
        225
    assumptions 221
Solectron 34, 35, 36
stakeholders 147, 165
strategic planning 145–146
    defined 146
    in educational institutions 146
strategy deployment 152–154
strategy development 150–151
students
    recommendations 134
    tracking of 252
surveys 137
SWOT analysis 145, 147, 158
    defined 147
systems thinking 92, 314
    defined 90

T

talent development 87
Tennessee Quality Achievement Awards 212
Texas Instruments 32, 36, 39
Theory Y 109

Total Quality Management
    as a holistic philosophy 183
training 173, 256

U

unit of analysis 80, 88–92, 93
University of Minnesota–Duluth 125, 132,
        142, 143

V

value-added model 193, 194, 311
Vanderbilt University 213
visible figures 247, 257
Vision 2000 140
vision statement 147

W

Wainwright Industries 32, 38
Wallace Company 28, 29, 38
Westinghouse 36, 47, 48
Wingspread Group Report 262

X

Xerox 30, 32, 34, 36, 45, 47, 48, 49, 50